Being Me Being You

Being Me Being You

Adam Smith and Empathy

SAMUEL FLEISCHACKER

The University of Chicago Press
Chicago and London

The University of Chicago Press, Chicago 60637
The University of Chicago Press, Ltd., London
© 2019 by The University of Chicago
All rights reserved. No part of this book may be used or reproduced in any manner
whatsoever without written permission, except in the case of brief quotations in
critical articles and reviews. For more information, contact the University of
Chicago Press, 1427 E. 60th St., Chicago, IL 60637.
Published 2019
Printed in the United States of America

28 27 26 25 24 23 22 21 20 19   1 2 3 4 5

ISBN-13: 978-0-226-66175-9 (cloth)
ISBN-13: 978-0-226-66189-6 (paper)
ISBN-13: 978-0-226-66192-6 (e-book)
DOI: https://doi.org/10.7208/chicago/9780226661926.001.0001

Library of Congress Cataloging-in-Publication Data

Names: Fleischacker, Samuel, author.
Title: Being me being you : Adam Smith and empathy / Samuel Fleischacker.
Description: Chicago : The University of Chicago Press, 2019. |
    Includes bibliographical references and index.
Identifiers: LCCN 2019018464 | ISBN 9780226661759 (cloth : alk. paper) |
    ISBN 9780226661896 (pbk. : alk. paper) | ISBN 9780226661926 (e-book)
Subjects: LCSH: Smith, Adam, 1723–1790. | Empathy.
Classification: LCC B1545.Z7 F54 2019 | DDC 152.4/1—dc23
LC record available at https://lccn.loc.gov/2019018464

♾ This paper meets the requirements of ANSI/NISO Z39.48-1992 (Permanence of Paper).

In all people I see myself, none more and not one a barley-
    corn less,
And the good or bad I say of myself I say of them.
                    WALT WHITMAN, "Song of Myself"

Contents

Preface ix
List of Abbreviations xiii

1 Varieties of Empathy 1
2 Smithian Empathy 23
3 Updating Smith 49
4 Empathy and Culture 77
5 Empathy and Affectional Ties 89
6 Utilitarianism and the Limits of Empathy 102
7 Empathy and the Limits of Utilitarianism (I) 116
8 Empathy and the Limits of Utilitarianism (II) 128
9 Empathy and Demonization 149

Acknowledgments 167
Notes 169
Bibliography 201
Index 209

Preface

Talk of empathy seems to be everywhere these days. Psychologists, primatologists, political scientists, promoters of Eastern religions—everyone seems to have something to say on empathy. Why write another book on the subject?

Three reasons: First, the vast literature on empathy has yet to distinguish clearly among the different meanings of that term. Second, there has yet to be any good response to the powerful critiques of empathy recently put out by writers like the philosopher Jesse Prinz and the psychologist Paul Bloom; those who praise empathy and those who criticize it also seem to be talking past each other. Third, these problems are linked, and the eighteenth-century thinker Adam Smith's understanding of empathy can, I think, help us address both of them. I'll try in this preface to summarize how I propose to do that.

Human beings share feelings with one another and, out of those shared feelings, care for one another. Neither our shared feelings nor our concern for others need run deep, however, and sometimes they lead us in the wrong direction, morally speaking: they direct us to fellow members of our local groups, rather than to humanity as a whole, and thereby contribute to prejudice and ethnocentrism. Why put any moral weight on this capacity for shared feelings—on empathy?

Well, to begin with, we empathize in many different ways, some of which are more morally valuable than others. I devote the first chapter of this book to laying out the wide range of meanings that the word "empathy" can bear, and to suggesting that confusion among these things helps explain why some writers are so enthusiastic about empathy while others regard it as misleading and dangerous. I also argue that Smith's version of empathy has advantages that other versions of that idea lack. I end by indicating in outline what these advantages are. The rest of the book will fill in that outline.

Chapter 2 explores Smithian empathy in detail. For Smith, empathy has cognitive content. As against his friend Hume, who had seen it as a sort of contagion, spreading automatically from one human being to another, Smith thought that it requires us to enter in imagination into the circumstances of others. We thereby gain insight into what it is like to occupy their perspective. In fact, it turns out, this understanding of others' perspectives is essential to learning what it is to have a perspective at all: to recognizing even that we ourselves have a perspective. And these linked phenomena—empathy, on the one hand, and the having of a perspective, on the other—are uniquely human accomplishments. They indeed help define what it is to *be* human.

Empathy, perspective, humanity: the idea that these things are linked, and that they give us a crucial way of understanding who we are, is at the core of my book. I develop these links, using Smith, and argue that the conception of humanity we get from them compares favorably to the austere emphasis on rationality in Kantian thought, as well as to the more blindly emotional picture of human nature in Hume. Smith's empathetic and perspectival picture of humanity is one we also find in the richly psychological novels that became popular in the nineteenth century. And it makes room for individuality even while stressing our shared imaginative and emotional capacities. This fits well with our contemporary need to strike a balance between personal or cultural difference and some sort of universally shared humanity.

But one might question whether Smith, writing two hundred years ago, really can speak to our contemporary concerns. In chapter 3, I bring Smithian empathy into conversation with contemporary empirical research and moral theory. I take up a somewhat disparate array of topics in this chapter, beginning with the relationship of Smith's work to theories in cognitive psychology and the philosophy of mind, and moving from there to empirical work on novel reading and empathy, psychotherapy and empathy, the nexus between empathy and altruism, and the question of whether animals have empathy. Some contemporary findings reinforce Smith's views; others give us reason to modify Smithian empathy in certain ways. I conclude with a look at how Smith's account of empathy can illuminate, and be illuminated by, work in contemporary moral theory on care and on epistemic justice.

Chapter 4 asks whether Smithian empathy can adequately account for cultural difference. For all the room that Smith makes for human difference, many social scientists will see Smith as too universalist for their taste. Why suppose that we can enter into the circumstances of any and every other human being? The very capacity for universal empathy that Smith presupposes is likely to be rejected by those who favor hermeneutic approaches to social science—for whom understanding other cultures takes more than imagining

PREFACE xi

ourselves, thickly acculturated as we are, into the shoes of someone with a different upbringing. I grant something to the objection made by believers in strong cultural difference, but argue that it exaggerates the gap between Smith's and other ways of understanding that difference. Johann Gottfried von Herder is often thought to have helped found the hermeneutic approach, and I stage a disputation between Smithian and Herderian empathy. Smith (unsurprisingly) comes off well.

In addition to the challenge of culture, there is the danger that empathy, even of the Smithian variety, will entrench our biases in favor of our friends and close kin. Chapter 5 takes up this possibility. On Smith's view, we are unlikely to become cosmopolitans, caring equally for anybody and everybody. He describes and defends, instead, our tendency to form "circles of sympathy." I elaborate his defense of these limits on our empathy, arguing that it is true, as he says, that the local quality of our affections leads us to care most for those we can most effectively help, and that this point nicely explains many of our social bonds. I also suggest that the partiality of empathy has some moral advantages. Our biases can be used against themselves: we are better placed to nudge our friends and family away from their prejudices than we are to urge such moral transformation on strangers. Would-be cosmopolitans, I propose, can use our local affections to further the goals of cosmopolitanism—employing the trust we can call on, in groups to which we are loyal, to push those groups toward a greater concern for humanity as a whole.

The subject of bias remains relevant in chapter 6, which begins an extended response to the critiques of empathy launched recently by Jesse Prinz and Paul Bloom. Prinz and Bloom stress the partiality of our empathetic caring, pointing out in addition that it can lead us to desire harsh revenge on behalf of the people we care for, and that it can overwhelm our rational capacities in circumstances where cool calculation is essential to finding fair or effective solutions to a problem.

Chapters 6 through 8 respond to these concerns. Chapter 6 argues that our empathetic emotions are no more biased toward our near and dear than are our other moral emotions. Bloom and Prinz maintain, oddly, that indignation and guilt have a more cosmopolitan cast than empathy; I argue that this is incorrect. I also point out that Smith's "impartial spectator" device can do a lot to help correct for our biases.

Chapters 7 and 8 take up Bloom's and Prinz's praise for cool rationality over a reliance on empathy, something they share with other contemporary theorists of the moral emotions, like Joshua Greene and Jonathan Haidt. At bottom, this praise reflects a view on which we do best to be guided by a utilitarian calculus in our individual moral actions and in public policy—to seek simply to minimize harm and maximize happiness for our fellow human beings. I review some of the flaws of utilitarianism, stressing in particular its inability to spell out, in a plausible yet substantive manner, what counts as "harm" and "happiness." Smithian empathy, because it enables us to enter other people's perspectives, is able precisely to give us a deeper understanding of what harms them or makes them happy. Empathy can thus do crucial moral work for us that the utilitarian calculus cannot. This is its deepest moral function. It cannot alone provide us with an adequate moral or political view, but it plays an irreplaceable role in providing the starting points for such views.

I go on to recommend a political view that combines empathy with a respect for rules of justice and a realistic understanding of what makes for effective social and political institutions. I also show how this approach meshes with both Smith's moral philosophy in the *Theory of Moral Sentiments* and his approach to public policy in the *Wealth of Nations*. For Smith, our moral emotions and our reason work intimately together; he rejects the sharp dichotomy between them that drives critiques of empathy like Bloom's. This integrated approach to morality is both more suited to the way we actually make moral judgments and, I contend, more humane than a reliance on reason alone. Suitably combined with a respect for justice and efficiency, an empathetic approach to our moral and political problems is vastly preferable to a utilitarian one.

I close, in chapter 9, with a discussion of demonization. If Smithian empathy is central to our humanity, then closing off empathy to others, and seeing them as closed to empathy, is a way of dehumanizing them. That is precisely what enabled people to regard Jews as diabolical in former years, and to see Muslims that way today. But a tendency toward demonization crops up even among people who see themselves as committed to a cosmopolitan concern for all humanity. Critics of capitalism and colonialism not infrequently portray the targets of their critique as inhumanly devoid of empathy, and even those who balk at this portrayal tend to employ a demonic picture of racists and Nazis. Antidemonization requires us to seek an empathetic understanding even of racists and Nazis: to attempt to attribute their motivations, as much as possible, to tendencies we can also see in ourselves. This does not require us to *accept* their views, of course. On the contrary, it gives us powerful tools for criticizing them, and for ensuring that we never become like them.

In pursuing many of these topics, I go beyond Smith's own writings. But thinking with a philosopher, and not just about him, is a tribute to the continuing value of his work. And as regards empathy, it should come as no surprise that we can learn something by thinking with Smith. He was, after all—along with his friend David Hume—one of the first thinkers to offer a theory of empathy. It's a rich theory, and there remains much of value in it yet to be mined.

Abbreviations

The works listed here are cited by abbreviation and page number (as well as by part, section, and chapter, in the case of Smith's books). If I cite a text repeatedly in the same paragraph, I use its abbreviation the first time, but just give a page number in subsequent citations.

AEB Paul Bloom, *Against Empathy*. London: Bodley Head, 2016.

AEP Jesse Prinz, "Against Empathy." *Southern Journal of Philosophy* 49 (2011).

LJ Adam Smith, *Lectures on Jurisprudence*, ed. R. L. Meek, D. D. Raphael, and P. G. Stein. Oxford, UK: Oxford University Press, 1978. Unpublished in the author's lifetime.

RWR Immanuel Kant, *Religion within the Boundaries of Mere Reason*, ed. A. Wood and G. Giovanni. Cambridge: Cambridge University Press, 1998.

T David Hume, *Treatise of Human Nature*, second edition, ed. L. A. Selby-Bigge and P. H. Nidditch. Oxford, UK: Clarendon Press, 1978. First published in 1738.

TMS Adam Smith, *Theory of Moral Sentiments*, ed. D. D. Raphael and A. L. Macfie. Oxford, UK: Oxford University Press, 1976. First published in 1759.

WN Adam Smith, *An Inquiry into the Nature and Causes of the Wealth of Nations*, ed. R. H. Campbell, A. S. Skinner, and W. B. Todd. Oxford, UK: Oxford University Press, 1976. First published in 1776.

1

Varieties of Empathy

1. We're torn, today, over what to think about empathy. On the one hand, everyone talks about the need for it; there seems to be a new book on it every week; and we hold it up as the key to bridging divides between hostile groups. On the other hand, we say, "You can't know what it's like to be me," and we insist on the importance of perspective and difference. Some psychologists— Paul Bloom, prominently, in a recent book called *Against Empathy*—add that empathy reinforces our divisions into closed, xenophobic tribes, and directs us to help only individuals we see or whose stories we know, rather than doing things that would benefit larger numbers of people.

So which is it? Is empathy an irreplaceable moral instrument, essential to our caring about all our fellow human beings? Or is it a way of ignoring our differences, reinforcing our ethnocentrism, and distracting ourselves from fair and effective moral action? Part of the answer depends on empirical evidence, of the sort that a psychologist or sociologist might provide. But part of the answer depends on what we *mean* by empathy and how it connects to what we mean by, and value in, humanity and cosmopolitanism—as well as what we mean by, and value in, difference and perspective. Investigations into what we mean and what we value—into the nature of our concepts and the role they play in our ethical as well as our descriptive projects—is, however, the work of philosophy rather than of science. So the answers to our questions about empathy depend on philosophical as well as empirical concerns. The point of this book is to explore these philosophical concerns.

As the subtitle of the book indicates, my main philosophical guide in this project is the eighteenth-century Scottish thinker Adam Smith. Smith is widely recognized as one of the first people to treat empathy in depth, and he has a distinctive conception of empathy. This conception has many attractive features. Among other things, I will argue, it enables us to answer many of the worries we have about empathy, including the objections of Professor Bloom. But before we can begin to see what is distinctive about Smith's conception of empathy, we will need to survey the variety of other things that go by that name. That will be our task in this introductory chapter. One might regard it as like the opening panoramic shot, surveying a broad landscape or cityscape, that some films employ before narrowing in on a particular home or character. Only after getting some sense of the broad landscape of empathy can we appreciate the features of Smith's particular kind of empathy. We'll get to some of those features toward the end of this chapter.

2. That we have feelings on behalf of others and not just for ourselves has been remarked upon since ancient times. Mencius, a Chinese philosopher writing more than two centuries before the common era, declared that "all men have a mind which cannot bear to see the sufferings of others." "If men suddenly see a child about to fall into a well," he said, "they will without exception experience a feeling of alarm and distress," and they will have this feeling independently of self-interest, including a selfish interest in being praised for virtue.[1]

Mencius gives us here an important corrective against seeing human beings as exclusively self-interested. But it is unclear how to classify the feeling he describes. Is it empathy? Sympathy? And what is the difference between these two things?

Both empathy and sympathy are species of what we might generally call "fellow feeling": feelings that we have on behalf of another, or that incline us to help another. Very different things may fall under this heading. I may feel your pain but not be inclined to do anything about it, and I may want to help you without feeling your pain. On the whole, we use the term "empathy" for the sharing of feelings, and "sympathy" for caring about others. People are not strict about this, however. One who cares about others may be described as "empathetic," and "sympathy" is sometimes used for sharing another person's feelings.[2] Literally, "empathy" means "feeling in" (I feel my way into what you are feeling), while "sympathy" means "feeling with." But etymology gives us only a rough guide to the use of these words.

"Empathy" is a fairly new word in English, introduced in 1909 by the psychologist Edward Titchener, who was translating the German term *Einfühlung*, as used by the German psychologist Walter Lipps and, before him, by the aesthetic theorist Robert Vischer.[3] Vischer was interested in how we "feel our way into" a piece of music or a majestic natural scene; Lipps and Titchener were similarly concerned with feeling our way into things, including inanimate things. Some trace the German word further back, to the late-eighteenth-century writings of J. G. von Herder, who called on us to feel our way into other cultures.[4] Even if that is true, the word was not available to Smith and his friend David Hume, who were the first theorists to develop elaborate accounts of what they called "sympathy." It seems to me, as it does to many writers on this subject, that they probably would have used the word "empathy" for their concerns had it existed in their day.[5] In any case, I prefer "empathy" to "sympathy" as a description of their concerns, and will generally use that term when discussing them. They are interested above all in how we share feelings with one another, rather than how we care about one another, even if they both think that sharing feelings with others generally *leads* us to care about them. Perhaps we had best say that their "sympathy" lies somewhere between our "empathy" and our "sympathy."

Even today, "empathy" sometimes means just the sharing of feelings, while at other times connoting care. Indeed, that understates the ambiguity of the term. The psychologist C. D. Batson, who defines empathy as a kind of caring (having emotions "congruent with the perceived welfare" of another person), discusses seven other definitions as well.[6] The philosopher Amy Coplan says, "Depending on whom you ask, empathy can be understood as one or more of several loosely related processes or mental states," and offers seven alternatives.[7]

On most lists like these, including Batson's and Coplan's, one will find (a) knowing what other people feel; (b) being affected by their feelings; (c) caring about them; (d) catching their feelings, as it were, contagiously; and (e) projecting oneself in imagination into their situations. These are very different things, and if we allow the word "empathy" to range loosely over all of them, we cannot carry out a serious discussion of the nature and effects of empathy; we will just talk past each other, and lose track of what our discussion is supposed to be about. At the same time, one reason why the term has such a wide range of meanings is probably that the different phenomena it is used for are somehow related to one another. We should therefore not settle on one of its meanings merely by stipulation. Our question is whether what we call "empathy" in ordinary conversation—what gets praised and criticized under that name—is deserving of the merits or failings that people attribute to it. So the meaning we give to that term in a scholarly investigation needs to track its common usage; if there is some ambiguity in that usage, we should not simply run roughshod over it.

With these competing concerns in mind, I submit that the core of our common uses of "empathy" is a sharing of feelings that comes about via either contagion or projection: (d) or (e) in the above list. All the other things on that list—caring, knowing what others are feeling, being affected by their feelings—will normally count as empathy only if they involve some contagious or projective sharing of another's experience. If I know what you feel because I infer it from your gestures, but do not feel it myself, we are disinclined to say that I empathize with you. If I am affected by your feelings in the sense that your being angry scares me, without my sharing your anger, then I do not empathize with you. And if I care about you without feeling what you feel, then we normally say that I sympathize with you but do not empathize with you. Contagion and projection seem to be central to our uses of "empathy," our paradigmatic ones at least. There are significant differences between contagion and projection themselves, but both get called "empathy": the common use of that term is ambiguous between these meanings. I will try to disambiguate them by speaking of "contagious empathy" and "projective empathy." The first of these is what Hume, for the most part, has in mind, so I'll also sometimes call it "Humean empathy." The second is what Adam Smith discusses, and I'll often call it "Smithian empathy."

3. We'll get shortly to the differences between contagious and projective empathy. Let's first consider forms of caring that do not involve either of these things. I've noted that we include these forms of caring under "sympathy," and the differences between them and empathetic kinds of sympathy are worth exploring. The particular moral goods that I want to claim for empathetic sympathy, at least where that is driven by projective or Smithian empathy, will be clearer if we place it in relation to nonempathetic modes of caring.

Begin with the scenario described by Mencius: You reach out instinctively to stop an infant from falling into a well. We do have such instincts, and it is well that they suffice to lead us to act in urgent situations, where any pause to reflect on our actions, or to take in how the other person is feeling, could be fatal. There is no need to suppose that we share feelings with the infant in Mencius's case and similarly urgent situations—no reason to suppose that empathy comes into play. That may be a very good thing, as I have noted: it may be important that neither empathy nor reflection slows down our instinct to help.

Instincts are not always reliable, however, and in less urgent cases we do well to make our help more deliberate and more careful. Sometimes we act out of a duty-based caring. You hear that Fatima is in need, and think you should help her. Maybe Fatima is a refugee and you've seen an ad calling for help for refugees, or heard your pastor or rabbi make a pitch for such aid. Here you don't need actually to see Fatima's feelings and catch them from her, nor do you need to imagine yourself into her situation. You may be acting on a principle about helping people—a principle that you think comes from

God, or a principle underwritten by a moral philosophy you favor—or you may have been habituated, from childhood onwards, to feel bad when you hear about certain kinds of suffering, and feel a duty to help the sufferers. In the latter case, you will be acting on a feeling or set of feelings, just as you are if you act on empathy. But the feeling only indirectly reflects the *other* person's feelings. Fatima is only indirectly present in the feelings you have on her behalf in habitual caring, or the feelings that lead you to act on her behalf.

Then there is a kind of caring that stems precisely from very strong feelings that you have, directly, for another. John is your child or lover, or a person you are entranced with or want to be led by. Every success he has is therefore something you want to share, and every misfortune he faces is something you want to make go away. You needn't be aware of what he actually feels in either the good or the bad fortune, nor bother to imagine how you might feel in his shoes—you are simply drawn by your passion for him to identify with him. As many writers point out,[8] there is not enough of a gap between self and other to call this kind of identification "empathetic," and the absence of that gap is not infrequently stifling to its object. But sometimes—when we are caring for a young child, especially—it plays a useful role in our lives.

At the other end of the emotional spectrum, there are cases in which we try to alleviate another's distress with a different feeling of our own. Perhaps you are calm or confident when I am a nervous wreck. Leslie Jamison describes such a case in an incisive set of essays on empathy: "Instead of identifying with my panic," she says of a doctor who mentioned that she might need a pacemaker, "he was helping me understand that even this, the barnacle of a false heart, would be okay. His calmness didn't make me feel abandoned, it made me feel secure. It offered assurance rather than empathy, or maybe assurance was evidence of empathy, insofar as he understood that assurance, not identification, was what I needed most" (17). We can see that Jamison doesn't quite know whether to count her doctor's assurance as empathy; she also remarks that "empathy is a kind of care, but it's not the only kind of care." On the whole, she treats the doctor's assurance as care, thus sympathy, but not empathy. But that may be wrong. The doctor may pick up on her feelings (contagion); or imagine himself into her situation and experience the fear he would feel there (projection), but dampen those feelings, or dampen the expression of them, because he knows that what she most needs—what *he* would need most in her situation—is assurance rather than panic. In that case, his assurance is indeed "evidence of empathy." But it need not be, and Jamison is certainly right to say that empathetic care "is . . . not the only kind of care."

As a final example, consider situations in which you identify with another, or think of yourself as doing that, because you see yourself as identifying with all humanity. Perhaps you are a devout Christian who takes your love for Christ as entailing a love for all humanity; perhaps you are a cosmopolitan who sees caring for everyone as itself the lodestar of your ethical life. In any case, upon hearing that Sunil is upset you feel moved to do something to help him, whether or not you catch his feelings or project yourself into his situation; and upon hearing that he has triumphed over a terrible danger, you feel joy for him—again without going through the preliminary process of contagion or projection. At least that's how you describe yourself: you say that your joy or pain for him is a joy or pain in Christ for all of Christ's creatures, or a joy or pain that you take in the fortunes of any human being.

I am not sure that these scenarios are really possible, and that even if they are, they are truly cases of empathy. Does anyone really love all of humanity via Christ (or Krishna or the Buddha or the Lubavitcher Rebbe)? Does anyone love people, as individuals, via a love en masse for humanity? I am suspicious of such claims, having found that people who make them are often not as loving as they think they are. Or they are quite selective in their love, primarily directing it toward others who share their religion or ideology. But perhaps this sort of love vests itself only in people who believe in it. And perhaps the less-than-fully-caring and the selectively caring people I have met do not really have the faith they claim to have.

A deeper question is whether caring for others via Christ, or a solidarity with humanity, should *count* as caring for any individual person. If I love Sunil just as one of God's creatures, do I really love *Sunil*? Sunil's individuality seems to go missing in this scenario, and with it, Sunil's emotions: everything about Sunil with which I might empathize. Yet a loving Christian or committed humanitarian may do everything for other people that empathy would seem to entail: take in foster children, send care packages to refugees, talk comfortingly to friends. We ordinarily call people who do things like this deeply empathetic. And why shouldn't we? Perhaps the religion or ideology to which they are committed leads them into a contagious or projective empathy with individuals; perhaps it functions like the habitual caring we considered above; or perhaps it is really true, despite my doubts, that a love for Christ, or for humanity as a whole, can of itself spill over into a love for any and every particular person.

For convenience, we can sum up the varieties of nonempathetic caring we have surveyed under the following headings:

- *instinctual care*, an instinctive impulse to take care of others, which need not depend on sharing their feelings;

VARIETIES OF EMPATHY

- *duty-based or habituated care*, helping others out of habit, or out of a habitual sense of duty;
- *vicarious identity*, helping others out of passionate love or admiration; or
- *religious or ideological care*, helping others out of a love for or commitment to a being or principle that you regard as calling on you to care for all humanity.

There are good things about these forms of caring; in some respects, they are indeed superior to empathetic caring. When I help others out of the bald sense that they need help, and an instinct to give help where it is needed (the infant at the well), I may do so more spontaneously and more fully than when my reactions are filtered through a sharing of their feelings. When I act out of habit or duty, my caring may be more reliable than it is if it comes from shared feelings. As Kant pointed out, a care based on duty is more likely to continue even when we aren't in the mood to care.[9] It is, moreover, possible that this kind of caring will extend to a wider range of people than the care that depends on our sharing feelings. At least that is likely if I have been habituated into helping anyone and everyone, or taught that that is my duty. If I am taught instead that "we stay away from *those* people" (blacks, Jews, transvestites), or get into a habit of caring only for a closed circle of kin or religion, then my duties and habits may be precisely what *prevent* me from caring for human beings in general, what limit my caring to a provincial group.

Religious or ideological caring will often direct me explicitly to care for any and every human being. I have indicated that I am not convinced that this sort of caring occurs very often, and have noted that those who claim to care for everyone out of love for Christ or Krishna, or for humanity as a whole, tend to care rather more for those who share their love or ideology than for people in general. But it is certainly true that many devoutly religious people make significant efforts to help the poor and sick all over the world.

So these kinds of care can have some advantages over forms of care that spring from contagion or projection. What they do not do is (1) enable us to share the experience of the people we care for, or, relatedly, (2) give us a window into what exactly those people themselves think, want, or need. It is the particular virtue of contagion and especially projection, as we'll see, to accomplish these tasks, and they are the tasks that most properly fall in the domain of what we ordinarily call empathy. I therefore focus in this book on contagion and projection—and especially projection, the distinctively Smithian form of empathy.

I will also argue, in future chapters, that only projective or Smithian empathy enables us to care for other people as they most want to be cared for.

8   CHAPTER ONE

In a nutshell, that is because only by way of Smithian empathy do we appreciate people in all their differences from us, grasp the ways in which what they want out of life is different from what we want. That is a very significant moral advantage, outweighing some of the advantages that accrue to instinctual or duty-based or religious care.

4. Let's return now to the differences between contagious and projective empathy.

Start with contagious empathy. John seems happy, so you feel happy; Amy seems sad, so you feel sad. You can "catch" other people's feelings in this way without realizing that you are doing that. You are barely aware that Amy is annoyed, but find yourself annoyed nevertheless, having subconsciously picked up on something in her facial expression or tone of voice. You are inexplicably cheerful after seeing John in a cheerful mood, without having recognized that John was cheerful. You don't even need to notice from *whom* you are catching feelings, in order to catch them. You can catch feelings from a crowd, just as you can catch a cold, without so much as exchanging glances with any particular person in the crowd. The crowd sings or dances joyously, and you sing and dance along. Or the crowd roars angrily, and you chime in.[10]

In some cases, you can pick up feelings contagiously without even seeing another person. You walk into a festive room and feel the cheer of the party that is about to start even though no one has arrived yet.[11] You see the trappings of a funeral and find yourself in a somber mood, even though no one is yet around for it or everyone has left.

Contagion thus does not entail that you grasp, even try to grasp, anything about *why* the people whose feelings you share have those feelings. That's not true of projective empathy. In projective empathy, you try to imagine yourself in another's situation, and feel certain emotions as a result. You may imagine the other's situation very roughly, or in close detail. You may imagine (just) being as agonized as Jane, as harsh as Stefanie, as rich or as poor as Myron; or you may imagine what it might be like to have been injured in the precise way that Jane has been injured, to have hurt a friend in the precise way that Stefanie did, or to live in the precise grand apartment or hovel that Myron lives in. As these examples suggest, you may as a result feel joy or pride on the other's behalf, as well as pain or embarrassment; all of these feelings will be empathetic feelings. And unlike the feelings of contagious empathy, you will know *why* you feel them, how the feelings arose, and what they respond to.

Also unlike the feelings of contagious empathy, however, the feelings you have on behalf of the other person may not be feelings that he or she has herself. That means, in the first place, that you may have a far weaker version of the feelings that the other person has. By way of contagion, you may feel as joyous or angry or depressed as the person from whom you catch these feelings (more so, perhaps). By way of projection, and the cognitive work it requires, you are likely always to feel something less intense. As Adam Smith says, "The emotions of the spectator will . . . be very apt to fall short of the violence of what is felt by the sufferer."[12]

In the second place, the feelings you have by way of projective empathy may be entirely different from the feelings of the person with whom you are empathizing. Myron may not take joy or pride in his riches, or feel particularly unhappy in his poverty. You feel what you think the other person is likely to feel in his situation, and perhaps what you think he *should* feel, but you don't necessarily feel what he *does* feel; your empathy for him does not take its start from his actual feelings.

Which brings us to an ambiguity in the phrase "imagining how the other feels in her situation." Does that mean imagining how (you think) *she* would feel in that situation, or imagining how (you think) *you* would feel there? How much of the other person, how much of her specific character or circumstances—her perspective—do you need to take on board in order to empathize with her projectively? I'll take up this question in chapter 2. As we'll see, answering it is of considerable importance for figuring out what is involved in the kind of empathy that Smith describes.

In short, projective empathy, especially as Smith conceives it, differs in many ways from contagious empathy. It has an essential cognitive component, alerting us to the cognitive structure of emotions more generally. It is weaker than contagious empathy. It can lead us to feelings that we think the other *should* have, instead of the feelings that he or she *actually* has. And it requires us to attend to the entire character and perspective of the other person, rather than just her momentary experiences.

Despite these differences, many current writers, including some of the most prominent scholars of empathy, fail to distinguish between contagion and projection.[13] Richard Miller slips back and forth between describing empathy as "a kind of . . . perspective-taking" and describing it as a kind of "mimicry," seeming not to notice the difference between these two things.[14] Paul Bloom begins one article by identifying empathy with Adam Smith's projection of oneself into others' circumstances, but later runs that together with contagion ("flinching" at another's suffering, or "lighting up" at their joy), as if it has not occurred to him that imagining oneself into others' circumstances might lead one precisely to *not* feel as they do.[15] Jesse Prinz similarly runs Hume and Smith together, attributing a contagion view to both.[16] Leslie Jamison more consistently sticks to a projection view, treating empathy as requiring a deep entering of other people's perspectives, but at times she also equates it instead with contagion.[17] And Martin Hoffman writes that "affective empathy seems like a simple concept—one feels what the other feels," but then adds that his research has led him instead to a definition of the term in which what is essential is that one's feelings pertain to the situation that the other is in, rather than mirroring what the other actually feels.[18] He seems to think that this latter definition—what I call projective empathy—merely spells out more clearly what is already implicit in the first definition: as if projection were just a more elaborate form of contagion. Karyn Lewis and Sara Hodges bring some empirical evidence suggesting that this is a mistake.[19] For moral purposes, it seems to me certainly a mistake. In the next two sections, I'll try to show why.

5. Contagion is our most immediate and intense way of sharing feelings with others. It comes over us whether we want it to or not—whether we are *aware* of it or not—and comes over us constantly, whenever we interact with others. There seems to be a biological basis for it (it is contagious empathy that can be explained by "mirror neurons") and a basis that we share with other animals, many of whom seem to catch one another's moods just as we do. We also feel other people's feelings strongly when we pick them up via contagion, getting very angry when they are very angry, feeling on top of the world when they are joyful, and falling into a funk when they are depressed. This mode of empathy thus gives us a strong and direct bond with our fellow human beings: we identify with one another, and experience their emotions much as we do our own. And the pervasiveness and intensity of contagious empathy makes it a powerful tool for explaining social phenomena. Hume, who focused on this sort of empathy, was perhaps the first to demonstrate that. One social phenomenon he did not use it to explain is language, but I think contagion is also the crucial and perhaps sole basis on which we could possibly learn, at least, the language of emotion. More on that anon.

But the advantages of the contagious mode of empathy come with disadvantages. I can't really help catching other people's emotions, but that is to say that I am passive, helpless even, in the face of contagion. Hume captures this aspect of contagion wonderfully. "A chearful countenance infuses a sensible complacency and serenity into my mind," he says, "as an angry or sorrowful one throws a sudden damp upon me."[20] And: "As in strings equally wound up, the motion of one communicates itself to the rest; so all the affections readily pass from one person to another, and beget correspondent movements in every human creature" (*T* 576). The language throughout these passages is passive, describing people among whom emotions travel whether they want those emotions or not, in the way diseases pass from one person to another: "contagiously," as

Hume expressly says at one point (605).[21] So if we want control over the degree to which we share other people's emotions, we have reason to be wary of contagious empathy, and hope there is another way of sharing feelings.

Our lack of control over contagion often goes along with a lack of awareness of the causes of the emotions we are experiencing, and of whether they are appropriate or inappropriate responses to those causes. When I catch your anger or joy, I needn't know why I am catching it—what has angered or pleased you, or in what light you saw the object of your emotion, such that it angered or pleased you. Your neighbor said something that you took to be a sneer. But the two of you have a bitter history that can make any remark seem like a sneer. So I might not feel anger if I heard your neighbor's remark myself. But I didn't hear it. I just saw your anger and, since I like you, reacted similarly.

That last qualification, about liking you, brings out a further feature of contagion that can be problematic. We can catch the emotions of any other human being, but we catch those emotions more readily from people we like or feel close to. Hume emphasized this feature of contagion, using it to explain family relationships, classism, and national characters.[22] And he is right that in these and many other respects, contagious empathy both draws on and reinforces divisions among human beings, helping us form or strengthen "us/them" relationships. Knowing this helps us account for a variety of social formations. But we may well also want to resist or overcome our divisive tendencies as best we can, and look for a form of empathy that does not encourage them.

6. Projective or Smithian empathy improves on contagious empathy in many respects. In order to imagine myself into your situation, I need to do something, not just let your emotions wash over me. Empathy is not for Smith, as it largely is for Hume, something that just happens to me; it is, rather, something I achieve only when I engage in certain kinds of imaginative activity.[23] And because it is active in this sense, I can and must *choose* whether, how, and to what degree to engage in it. I try to imagine, perhaps, how I would feel if I had to live in a one-room shack, or if I won the lottery, or if I had to choose between taking care of a medical need and securing a large business deal. I don't necessarily feel what you feel as a result. Perhaps you are inured to the hardships of life in the one-room shack and don't feel its limitations as sharply as I do for you. Perhaps you are overjoyed at winning the lottery, but I see the many factors that are likely to lead you to lose your winnings in a few years. Perhaps you are enormously upset about your business deal but it seems to me that I would be, and you should be, grateful at having promptly averted a potential health crisis, even at the cost of a monetary loss. But then I wonder

whether I have adequately imagined the details of your situation. Maybe your life in the one-room shack *is* pretty good, and it is class or cultural bias that leads me to think otherwise. Maybe you have wise plans for using the lottery money. Maybe your business deal was so important that you are right to be bitterly disappointed at losing it. What exactly I should be projecting myself into is not easy to say, and I may try and then come to think that I have done it badly, and need to try again.

So projective empathy takes work. We need to set our imaginations in action to engage in it, and may need to extend our imaginations to correct or improve it. Smith says that the empathetic spectator "must . . . endeavour . . . to bring home to himself every little circumstance of distress which can possibly occur to the sufferer" (I.i.4.6, 21). Jamison points out that empathy—by which she means projective empathy[24]—calls on us to *unearth* the full form of the situations in which we are to imagine ourselves: "to bring difficulty into the light." "Empathy isn't just listening," she says; "it's asking the questions whose answers need to be listened to. Empathy requires inquiry as much as imagination."[25]

We are thus not passive when engaging in projective empathy. On the contrary, we are intensely active. And we are not, cannot be, unaware of what gave rise to the feelings we have as a result. On the contrary, we have those feelings only *because* we are aware of a set of circumstances that causes or occasions them. What we share with the other, then, is not just a feeling—to the extent that we do share a feeling—but an understanding of the course of experience in which the other had that feeling: of what her life, or a passage in it, is like.

Projective empathy is also easier to extend beyond people who happen to be like us than is contagious empathy. We do project ourselves more readily into the circumstances of people we know and like—Smith, too, uses empathy to explain familial and national bonds. But the very fact that in Smithian empathy we actively engage our imaginations means that we can, if we choose, put them to work in ways that go beyond our instinct to identify with our near and dear. In projective empathy, we are in any case imagining ourselves into another life; it is just a further extension of that process to imagine ourselves into the lives of people in a different class or culture. Of course, to do that properly we need to gather information about that other class or culture, to inquire into it, asking the questions that "bring difficulty into the light." But as we've seen, that's what we're always called on to do in projective empathy.[26]

Projective empathy is, thus, more promising than contagious empathy if we seek to preserve our freedom while developing fellow feeling, to gain a real understanding of the people with whom we share feelings, and to share feelings widely with all other human beings.

7. But is projective empathy really a form of shared feeling at all? We are certainly less likely to feel as strongly as our neighbor does when we merely imagine ourselves into his or her situation. The very fact that we are experiencing the other's emotion only through our imaginations weakens its impact on us. When you catch my anger or joy by contagion, you simply feel anger or joy. You may feel less anger or joy than I do, but you may also feel these things as much as I do, or more. I am slightly annoyed about something, but you, catching that annoyance and mixing it with a standing bad mood (or a good mood that you are upset to have interrupted), feel enraged. When you feel your anger or joy by imagining yourself into my situation, by contrast, you are aware that you can easily let go of that feeling again by stopping the imaginative process, and returning to your own situation. Smith acknowledges this, indeed makes use of it in developing his moral theory (*TMS* I.i.4.6–9, 21–23).

Worse, as we've seen, you won't always feel what I do at all in projective empathy. I'm numb to the discomfort of my one-room life; I don't even notice it anymore. You, by contrast, feel stifled and enraged when you imagine such a life. I am terribly upset about a small disappointment; you shrug it off when you imagine having the same disappointment. I am drunk, acting like a fool, and wrongly suppose that everyone is entertained by me. You, sober, imagining yourself into my situation, feel nothing but embarrassment. Is this empathy at all? Why call it that, if you do not feel what I feel?

Well, in the first place, if your imaginative projections do lead you to share my feelings, you will share them *as* I feel them—for the same reasons, as part of the same course of experience. If you share my feelings just by way of contagion, there is no reason to think you understand *me* and how *I* live. You may indeed catch my anger or joy, and then rationalize it so that you think you have become angry or joyful because of something that happened to you. In projective empathy, that is conceptually impossible: you share my feelings, when you do, if and only if you see them as appropriately responsive to *my* situation. You are, literally, thinking your way *into* how I feel, which is exactly what "empathy" means.

In the second place, when you arrive by way of projection into my situation at different feelings from mine, you may well have the feelings that I *would* have if I were thinking more clearly about my situation—perhaps even those that I *will* have if I get a chance later on to engage in clearer reflection on it (e.g., what I will feel tomorrow, after I sober up). As you stand by in irritated amusement while I whine over a minor disappointment, I come to think that you represent how I *should* feel, and how I do feel when I am the person I like to see myself as being. I say to you, when I recover from my bad mood, that you recalled me to my better self. Perhaps I add, "I don't know what came over me," or, "I wasn't myself." If, on the other hand, you think I should be *more* upset than I am about some situation—the one-room shack is worse than I think it is, you say, and a symptom and result of racism—I may come to think not just that you stood by me in my suffering, but that you helped me realize who I really am, or helped me become who I want to be. "You stood up for my better self," I say, or even, "You brought me to my real self." We'll discuss these sorts of cases more fully in the next chapter, but I hope the examples I've given already indicate that you can, in some important sense, share my life—even *be* me—precisely by *not* sharing the emotions I feel at a particular moment: precisely by substituting for those emotions another reaction, more suited, in my own reflective opinion as well as yours, to my situation.

8. For Smith, this sort of empathy—this sharing my life without necessarily sharing my occurrent feelings—has a number of features that shape our moral practices.

In the first place, Smith believes that actually sharing other people's feelings is a great and important pleasure for us, so the gap that often exists between what we feel on behalf of others and the feelings that they have themselves gives rise to an uncomfortable tension. When we are spectators of a situation, we are aware that the people principally concerned in it would like us to share their feelings more fully; when we are the people principally concerned, we wish that our spectators would share our feelings more fully. To reduce this tension, spectators try to increase their empathy so that they bring their feelings closer to the feelings of the people principally concerned, and the people principally concerned try to lower, or alter, their feelings so that spectators can enter into them. Both moral judgment and the attempt to achieve virtue take their origin from this process of mutual emotive adjustment, for Smith.

But in order to approximate what others are actually feeling, we need to enter into their situations in as much detail as possible. This brings us to a second morally significant feature of Smithian empathy: it is particularistic. We need to bring home to ourselves "every little circumstance of distress which can possibly occur to the sufferer," to "adopt the whole case of [our] companion with all its minutest incidents." (*TMS* I.i.4.6, 21) Simply feeling in general what it might be like to be a prisoner of war, or to grow up in a poor and crime-wracked neighborhood, is not enough. We need, rather, to enter into the "minutest" details of these situations, and of the people who live through them. It follows (a) that since moral judgment takes its origin from empathy, it will be similarly particularistic,[27] and (b) that since the details relevant to empathy and moral judgment are in principle infinite, our empathy and our judgments will always be corrigible: something on which we can improve.

A third morally relevant feature of Smithian empathy is that it can be cultivated by reading novels or seeing plays. An empathy that is driven constantly to close the gap between what we feel on behalf of others and what they themselves feel is an empathy than can be raised and shaped by the deliberate exercise of our imaginations. As we have already noted, it takes imaginative work to "adopt the whole case" of our companion in all its detail—to ask the questions, conduct the inquiries, that Jamison, in Smithian mode, calls for. But it follows that there is a more obvious role for imaginative literature to play in our empathetic, and hence our moral, development for Smith than for Hume—or for virtually any other eighteenth-century writer on morality. Smith says explicitly at one point that fiction can be of greater moral value than philosophy.[28]

A fourth feature of Smithian empathy with consequences for morality is that we can empathize with ourselves.[29] Once we realize that others empathize with us, we can take up their perspectives and see ourselves through their eyes. Having done that, Smith believes, we can also construct a notional perspective—the perspective of an "impartial spectator"—from which we should properly be seen. And when we look in at ourselves from these real or notional external points of view, we may encounter much the same gap between our empathetic and our actual feelings that we encounter when we empathize with others. This gap, too, is a source of moral judgment—judgment of ourselves now—and of our attempts to achieve virtue. And it inspires us to try to achieve the most full-bodied kind of virtue, in which we aim to have certain emotional configurations simply because we think we ought to have them, rather than because we want others to admire us for them.

Finally, the impartiality that we seek to achieve in self-empathy helps us strive for impartiality in our judgments of others—a crucial point if empathy is to underlie moral judgment. Using our imaginations to empathize just with people close to us can keep us from many duties of humanity, and empathizing just with one party in a conflict can be grossly unfair. We need an *impartial* empathy, for Smith—an empathy that goes out as equally as possible to everyone, and especially to all parties in a conflict. Smith explains how we empathize both with agents and with those benefited or harmed by an action, noting that when we empathize with the recipient of a benefit or harm,

16   CHAPTER ONE

we assess these things in accordance with the intention of the agent who bestowed them, and not just with their effect upon the recipient. (*TMS* I.ii.3, 34–38; II.i.5, 75–78) This can get complicated when we consider a series of actions—a feud, for instance—in which agent and recipient keep switching roles, and the motivation for the person who undertakes each new action depends on what he thinks motivated the harm he received in the last round. There are added complications when a feud takes place between groups and each participant sees him or herself as representing a larger body of injured people. All of these complications lead us to set up systems of justice in which conflicts can be resolved by impartial judges, acting on general rules.

From the gap between projective empathy and the "concord" of feeling (*TMS* I.i.4.7, 22) that we seek to achieve with others, Smith thus spins out a series of consequences that allow that gap to ground a rich and plausible account of moral judgment and moral development. The tension between the empathy we actually have and the empathy we seek to have with others underwrites our search for common moral standards, for self-improvement, and for impartiality. These are moral advantages of Smith's projective empathy, above and beyond its compatibility with the free, active direction of our minds discussed above in sections 5 and 6.

9. But even if Smith's projective empathy has moral advantages over Hume's contagious empathy, we cannot write off the latter. Humean empathy does certain things that Smithian empathy cannot. This comes out especially clearly if we consider a bad argument that Smith makes for preferring his sort of empathy to Hume's, and the presupposition that makes that argument seem appealing.

Smith thinks he has an argument against Hume's conception of empathy that Hume himself should accept—a sort of "gotcha" argument, using Hume's own philosophy against him.[30] Hume had described our minds as having two kinds of content, "impressions" and "ideas," with impressions being direct imprints of experience while ideas are the less vivid thoughts that our imaginations and memories form from impressions. He added that every idea must derive from a prior impression: every thought must be traceable to a prior experience. On this basis, Hume denied any meaning to what philosophers called "substance" (an unchanging form or material that underlies all change), to the self as we usually conceive it (an unchanging thing: a subjective substance), and to causality as we usually conceive that (a necessary connection between two events). The ideas in all these cases point to something that cannot possibly be experienced, Hume said: everything in our experience changes, and we never experience any necessity in the link between

VARIETIES OF EMPATHY

two events. Smith borrows Hume's language and uses Hume's reasoning to insist that we cannot possibly experience another person's emotions: they are locked up in the other person, and we can't get an impression of them. "As we have no immediate experience of what other men feel," writes Smith on the opening page of the *Theory of Moral Sentiments*,

> we can form no idea of the manner in which they are affected, but by conceiving what we ourselves should feel in the like situation. . . . [Our senses] never did, and never can, carry us beyond our own person, and it is by the imagination only that we can form any conception of what are his sensations. Neither can that faculty help us to this in any other way, than by representing to us what would be our own, if we were in his case. It is the impressions of our own senses only, not those of his, which our imaginations copy (*TMS* I.i.1.2, 9).

We can form "no idea" of other people's emotions, says Smith: Hume was wrong to suppose that another person's expressions and speech can convey even what he called an "idea" of what they feel (*T* 317). On Hume's own terms, we can't assume that we ever catch other people's feelings—we have no "impressions" of those feelings, no "immediate experience" of them; and we cannot know, by way of our experience, that other people even have any feelings to catch. Nor can we infer those feelings from their countenance or gestures. We never experience what lies behind those external signs, so we never know that they represent in others what we feel when we display them. Other people's feelings *must* then be represented in us by way of imaginative projection; Hume's alternative model relies on what he himself should regard as a violation of the principle that ideas need to be traceable to immediate experience.

The presupposition behind this critique is what today would be called a private access model of the mind (a model that Smith and Hume shared, it should be said; that's why Smith could take his criticisms to be ones that Hume should accept).[31] Only I can know what is in my mind, on this model; you can't possibly know what it is like to be me. I may see entirely different colors from you when I call something "red" or "blue"; I may feel something entirely different from you, perhaps something you would call pleasant, when I describe myself as "in pain." At best, you can *guess* my feelings. Only I can *know* them, and I know the contents of my mind in a radically different way from the way I know everything else.

This is a common model of the mind in popular discourse even today. Indeed, it seems to many people unquestionable that we have access only to our own minds. And a model along these lines was held almost universally among early modern philosophers. Not until Ludwig Wittgenstein's classes and writings of the mid-twentieth century did it come under direct and forceful attack. Today, however, most philosophers would be embarrassed to be caught suggesting that they believe in this model.

Why? Well, for one thing, it renders language for sensations unintelligible. (It renders language for any mental content unintelligible, but let's stick to sensations.) If I alone have any idea what my pain is like, how on earth did I learn that that feeling was called "pain"? To borrow a metaphor that Wittgenstein himself uses,[32] suppose that everyone had a box with different contents. Nobody can ever see the contents of another person's box, or describe them to others. Some of the boxes may even be empty. How could we have a word for the contents of such boxes? We would have no criteria for distinguishing between right and wrong ways of referring to the boxes' contents, hence no way of giving a word for these contents a function in our language. Which is to say, it could not *be* a word, could not communicate anything. It would, literally, have no meaning. If our feeling-language is like that, if what I call "pain" and "anger" and "cheerfulness" refers to something entirely unavailable to you, and that may be entirely different from what you call that, then these words lose all meaning: cease even to *be* words.

The basic point is that words are social entities, even when we use them privately, and that they must accordingly function and be taught with reference to publicly available things. That applies to our feelings as much as it does to anything else. When you say to your four-year-old, "Look, your sister is upset; go over and comfort her," you presuppose that he can *see* his sister's pain, that it is readily available to him. When you then say, "See how happy she is now?" you presuppose that happiness is similarly available. And that is how we all learn feeling-language—learn what to call, even in our own cases, "pain" and "happiness." If the presupposition were false, our feeling-language would be meaningless. We would not know, even in our own case, what counted as "pain" or "happiness"; we would have no language for describing these things—even for the purpose of saying, "I know my own pain better than others do."

This doesn't mean that people always display their feelings. One of the things we learn, when we learn feeling-language, is that sometimes people hide their feelings, or repress them, or act cheerful when they are really angry or humiliated. We also learn that some people are better at doing this than others—that some people display few feelings vividly, and that others give off strange signals about how they are feeling. But all this takes place against a background in which we know what it normally looks like for a person to be anxious or envious or pleased.

Now the best explanation of *how* we know these things, and therefore come to understand feeling-language, seems to me to depend on the pervasiveness

VARIETIES OF EMPATHY

of contagion. I know what it means for my little sister to be upset, because *I* feel some of her upset as I watch her. I know what it means to be cheerful or anxious—in my own case and that of others—because I pick up some of these feelings when I watch others with them, at least in the paradigm scenarios in which we learn such words.[33] It is contagion that best explains how feelings are publicly shared: even if, once we learn feeling-language, we may figure out how another is feeling in other ways. If I had never experienced the pain of others and thus learned what "pain" means, just looking at someone crying out in agony could not tell me that she was in pain. But once I know what pain is, I can sometimes know that another is in pain without feeling anything of that sort myself. Concentrating on my rounds, as a busy doctor walking the wards, I suppose that Jones has a stomach ache without feeling a thing on his behalf. I infer the pain, here, from what Jones tells me or how he acts. But that sort of inference would tell me nothing if I had never learned pain language. And to learn that, I need first to have shared the pain experience of others, via contagion.

Similarly, once I have pain language I can know what someone is feeling, or likely to feel, by projecting myself into his or her situation. You tell me you have passed a kidney stone and I say, "Oh, that must be awful," without necessarily picking up on your actual feelings or inferring them from your expressions. I suppose—rightly this time, let's say—that living in a one-room shack is miserable for you, because I think it would be miserable for me, and thereby share your feelings even if you did nothing to express them to me. All these things are possible, but they are possible only once we know what "pain" means, and projection alone could never tell us that. It could only refer us, as Smith says—wrongly supposing that this is an advantage of his account—to what lies hidden in our own inaccessible mental boxes. And *that*, as we have seen, would not be enough for us to know even that there is something in those boxes, let alone what it was.

I have tried to simplify Wittgenstein's elaborate and difficult arguments for the public nature of meaning, and I fear that in doing so, I have left out much that gives those arguments their power. But it will be sufficient for our purposes in this book if it is clear that the public nature of meaning entails that feelings, too, need to be publicly shareable. And it is the contagion model of empathy, not the projection model, that best explains how that is possible.

10. That said, a Wittgensteinian understanding of language can also help us see the place of the projection model in our lives. We hear our parents say, "It must be wonderful to live in a house like that." They say, "Oh, that must hurt so much!" when we have certain bruises or have been humiliated by

our best friend, and "Oh come on, it can't be that bad," when we have other bruises or have undergone other, more minor kinds of disappointment. We learn with some precision, and make clear to the children we raise, what sorts of emotions tend to be aroused by what sorts of situations, and what sorts of emotions are appropriate to what sorts of situations. The descriptive and the normative are here blended promiscuously with one another. We say:

"Big children don't get upset about little scratches."

Or:

"I'm glad you're so pleased with your new video game; I just wish you were half so pleased when we go out together as a family."

We describe Uncle Jack as "whining" if he makes too much fuss over a minor setback at work, and Aunt Molly as "stoic" or "numb to her suffering" if she seems calm ("*too* calm!") after a string of tragedies. Ralph, we say, is "ecstatic" over his new marriage, and we are pleased for him or worried about him, depending on how healthy we think the marriage is. We may also be expressing our approval of his devotion to his new wife, or our concern that he is losing sight of other priorities. Evaluative language is mixed into all of these descriptions, and the function of the descriptions is to bring about a social world in which everyone knows what people *ought to* feel in various circumstances, as well as one in which everyone knows how people *actually* feel in those circumstances. Our emotional language gives rise to norms for feeling,[34] which are crucial to how we interact with one another. (We help the *rightly* suffering and rebuke the *wrongly* angry.) These norms, in turn, regulate how we express our feelings and, to some degree, what we feel. If I am ashamed to make too much fuss about a minor injury, I will also try to *feel* less upset about it, and sometimes succeed. Certainly, maturity consists in learning, more or less automatically, not to have quite the capricious responses to things that a small child has.

I'll discuss these processes more in the next chapter, but I hope it is evident that they would be impossible without projection, and that the emotion language we use in them presupposes that we can project ourselves into other people's situations. Again, I want to stress that we could not learn a vocabulary for emotions at all without contagion. But in the course of learning that vocabulary, we also learn how to project ourselves emotionally.

This projective language captures a peculiarly human way of experiencing emotions and sharing them. It is readily imaginable that other animals can pick up emotions by contagion, and many of them in fact seem to do that. It is not readily imaginable, not even clearly intelligible, how any creature without language could imagine itself into the situation of another and determine whether that situation would normally bring on irritation or grief. Frans de

Waal describes chimpanzees, orangutans, and even ravens who seem capable of knowing what other animals are likely to believe, and playing on those beliefs to fool their rivals.[35] He points out, however, that this cold perspective taking does not yet amount to experiencing how other animals' situations feel to them.

But de Waal also describes a young chimp who whimpers and looks back plaintively at his limping brother when their mother moves too fast for the brother to keep up.[36] We might want to describe this behavior as implying that the whimpering chimp imagines how his brother feels, limping along without his family. De Waal does not draw that conclusion, however, and it is just as easy to suppose that the whimpering chimp has simply "caught" his brother's pain and feels pity for him. So at best we have here a *possible* case of projective empathy in a nonhuman animal, and it is hard to imagine how one could even set up an experiment to test whether an animal without language could make sense of the distinction between appropriate and inappropriate anger, or project itself into a counterfactual situation and figure out what that might feel like. Language seems necessary to these exercises.

And it is these exercises that allow us not only to share a rich emotional life with our fellow human beings, but to *have* such a life. Moreover, we define ourselves by the kinds of emotions we have and the situations that provoke them: by what we like and dislike; what humiliates us or makes us angry; what puts us in awe, soothes us, exalts us, makes us yearn with sexual excitement or weep with love or nostalgia. These are the things that make us the particular individuals we take ourselves to be—Melody or Julio or Felicia—rather than just anyone, a generic rational being. Projective empathy is thus essential to our identity. It is also essential to our humanity—to what we value in our humanity, at least. What we care about when we care about being human is not so much membership in a particular species, but the opportunity to be a distinctive Melody or Julio or Felicia: to have a distinctive perspective on the world. But projective or Smithian empathy is essential to having such a perspective. (We'll discuss this point further in the next chapter.)

Which should help explain why Smithian empathy, far more than contagious empathy or the instinctive, habitual, duty-based, or ideological kinds of caring that can do without shared feelings, is of great importance to our ethical life. As we learn to think about how we would feel if someone did this or that to us, we develop our powers of imagination and learn ways of controlling our emotions: we bring our emotional life into the sphere of reflection and deliberation. This helps make us active rather than passive beings—helps us free ourselves from the blind impact that emotions in the first instance have on us. We can now choose to empathize, or not, with a particular person, or to empathize with her to a particular degree, and we can choose whether and how to act on our empathy. The particularizing nature of empathy also helps us focus our choices on the details of our own and others' lives: to distinguish finely and delicately in our feelings and judgments, and to develop patterns of feeling and judgment that respect what is distinctive in other people and in ourselves. Smithian empathy thus helps shape everything else we do in the course of structuring a nuanced ethical life. It is for this reason that I focus this book on that kind of empathy. Some of the problems that empathy's critics have identified will not apply to Smithian empathy; many of the advantages that empathy's friends have attributed to it apply to this kind of empathy alone.

2

Smithian Empathy

1. It's time now to explore Smith's notion of empathy in depth. I'd like to begin by returning to the debate between Hume and Smith on this subject.[1] Recall that Hume construed empathy as being passed from one person to another mostly by way of contagion: I "catch" your feelings from your expressions. You look sad, so I feel sad; you are cheerful and that cheers me up. Exactly how this contagion works, for Hume, is not entirely clear. Sometimes he indicates that I infer what you are feeling from your expressions (*T* 319, 516); sometimes it seems there is no intermediary inference, and your feeling, or your expression of your feeling, has a direct impact on me (317, 386, 576, 592, 605). In either case, I wind up with the bare idea of your feeling. I then associate this idea, in my imagination, with the idea of my self—I imagine myself feeling what you feel—and I thereby come to experience your feeling.

For Smith, by contrast, we feel what others feel by projecting ourselves into their situations and imagining how we would feel there.[2] Smith allows that sometimes it "may seem" as if empathy arises merely by contagion. Strong expressions of joy and grief, especially, can light up or dampen the feelings of others.[3] But even here, he says, the joy and grief transfer over "because they suggest to us the general idea of some good or bad fortune that has befallen the person in whom we observe them" (*TMS* I.i.1.8, 11): we imagine ourselves in the situation of having experienced good or bad fortune.[4] Moreover, even as regards grief and joy, and certainly as regards most other feelings, we do not empathize with any depth or nuance unless we know more about what is going on with the other:

> General lamentations, which express nothing but the anguish of the sufferer, create rather a curiousity to inquire into his situation . . . than any actual

sympathy [Smith's term, remember, for empathy] that is very sensible. The first question which we ask is, What has befallen you? Till this be answered, though we are uneasy both from the vague idea of his misfortune, and still more from torturing ourselves with conjectures about what it may be, yet our fellow-feeling is not very considerable. (*TMS* I.i.1.9, 11–12)

Smith concludes: "Sympathy . . . does not arise so much from the view of the passion, as from that of the situation which excites it" (I.i.1.10, 12).

This difference between Hume and Smith has the consequence that for Smith, but not for Hume, it may often be the case that I feel something different from what you feel, when I empathize with you. Hume acknowledges that this happens sometimes, as when we "blush for the conduct of those, who behave themselves foolishly before us," without seeming to realize that they are doing that (*T* 371). But for Hume this is a hard case to explain, while for Smith it follows readily from how empathy works in paradigm cases.[5] On seeing someone insulted, I imagine I would feel angry, but not *as* angry as she seems to be—or, on the other hand, more angry (I admire her stoicism, or think she has insufficient respect for herself). On seeing someone receive an award, I think I would be rather less pleased with myself, or rather more, than she seems to be. In other cases—Smith gives the example of a madman who "laughs and sings" before us (*TMS* I.i.1.11, 12)—I may have entirely different feelings from the person with whom I empathize. This last scenario may be rare, but it is common for my empathetic feelings to differ to some degree from those of the target of my empathy. Smithian empathy opens up a *gap* between the feelings we have when we empathize with another and the feelings that she has herself. That gap means that it is something of an achievement if the person empathizing and the person empathized with are able to reach a harmony or concord of feelings. Smith says we strongly desire to achieve such a harmony, which motivates us both to try to understand the feelings of others and to change our feelings when people around us fail to empathize with them.

2. A second point to note about Smith's account of empathy is that it consists not simply in feeling *what* another might feel, but in being aware that that is how things feel *for* him or her. Stephen Darwall lays out the difference between these two things in a beautiful essay. The first can be illustrated by a scenario famously presented by Daniel Kahneman and Amos Tversky:

Mr. Crane and Mr. Tees were scheduled to leave the airport on different flights, at the same time. They traveled from town in the same limousine, were caught

SMITHIAN EMPATHY

in a traffic jam, and arrived at the airport 30 minutes after the scheduled depar-
ture time of their flights. Mr. Crane is told that his flight left on time. Mr. Tees
is told that his was delayed and just left 5 minutes ago.[6]

Most people (96 percent of Kahneman and Tversky's subjects) respond
to this scenario by thinking that Mr. Tees will be far more upset than
Mr. Crane—because they think *they* would be far more upset in Mr. Tees's
situation than in Mr. Crane's. They don't think about what it is like to be
Mr. Tees or Mr. Crane in general, however; they just imagine themselves in
their situations.[7] The story could be retold with "you" in place of the characters' names and have the same effect. It would be quite different for us to be
told something about Mr. Tees that distinguishes him from other people—
that he is on the verge of being late to a wedding, or, on the contrary, that he
is reluctant to get to his destination and has plenty of reading to do in the
airport—and to then be asked what it might be like to be him in his situation.
And that, as Darwall points out, is how Smith frames empathy:

> When I condole with you for the loss of your only son, in order to enter into
> your grief I do not consider what I, a person of such a character and profession,
> should suffer, if I had a son, and if that son were unfortunately to die: but I
> consider what I should suffer if I was really you, and I not only change circum-
> stances with you, but I change persons and characters (*TMS* VII.iii.1.4, 317).

Darwall offers a nuanced explication of this passage. "Consider the difference," he says, "between the instructions: (a) imagine what someone would
feel if he were to lose his only child, and (b) imagine what it would be like for
that person to feel that way." Under (a), Darwall says, I will think, "What a
terrible thing—a precious child is lost." Under (b), I will think, "What a terrible thing for him—he has lost his precious child."[8] The latter thought requires
me to consider "not just a person with the relevant feelings, but someone
conscious of his feelings, their phenomenological textures, and relevance for
his life." Let's call the feelings that arise from this latter thought "perspectival"
or "Smithian" empathy, as opposed to the plain empathy we have for Mr. Tees
and Mr. Crane. Smithian empathy involves the awareness that the other has a
distinct kind of consciousness from mine—a distinctive perspective—and an
attempt to enter his situation from that perspective.

3. A third point about Smith's account of empathy. For Smith, mutual empathy is always a source of pleasure. Hume famously criticized Smith on this
score. Writing to Smith in response to the first edition of the *Theory of Moral
Sentiments*, he said,

I wish you had more particularly and fully prov'd, that all kinds of Sympathy are necessarily Agreeable. . . . It would appear that there is a disagreeable Sympathy, as well as an agreeable: And indeed, as the Sympathetic Passion is a reflex image of the principal it must partake of its Qualities, and be painful where that is so. . . . An ill-humord Fellow; a man tir'd and disgusted with every thing, always *ennuié*; sickly, complaining, embarrass'd; such a one throws an evident Damp on Company, which I suppose wou'd be accounted for by Sympathy; and yet is disagreeable. . . . [If] all Sympathy was agreeable[, a] Hospital would be a more entertaining Place than a Ball.[9]

Smith responded to this critique by drawing an important distinction, in a footnote he added to the second edition. While it is indeed painful to share the pains of others, he says—we would hardly be "sharing" them otherwise—the *awareness* that I share another's feelings, of whatever sort, is always pleasurable. And it is this awareness of shared feelings that constitutes the sentiment of approbation:

. . . In the sentiment of approbation there are two things to be taken notice of; first, the sympathetic passion of the spectator; and secondly, the emotion which arises from his observing the perfect coincidence between this sympathetic passion in himself, and the original passion in the person principally concerned. This last emotion, in which the sentiment of approbation properly consists, is always agreeable and delightful. The other may be agreeable or disagreeable, according to the nature of the original passion, whose features it must always, in some measure, retain (*TMS* I.iii.1.9n; 46n).

Now one might complain that Smith is changing the subject. He seems to be granting that empathy is not always pleasurable, while insisting that a different feeling, approbation, is pleasurable. For Smith, however, approbation consists in our "observing the perfect coincidence" between our empathetic passion for a person and "the original passion" in that person herself, and feeling a pleasure in that coincidence. So approbation is itself a kind of shared feeling—a kind of empathy. And indeed, elsewhere in the *Theory of Moral Sentiments*, Smith speaks as if the pleasurable awareness of shared feeling is what he had in mind by what he calls "sympathy."[10] Strictly speaking, then, Smith is here acknowledging that empathy, on his view, has several components, which he had not previously distinguished. Nor does he make entirely clear in this footnote how these components go together, although presumably he sees our projection into the circumstances of others as being always aimed at the pleasurable sharing of feelings that we achieve in approbation.

So one might legitimately complain that Smith's response to Hume shows that his account of empathy is somewhat muddy. Otherwise, however, the response seems to me an effective one. Other commentators disagree, on the grounds that your bad feelings, and my bad feelings on your behalf, cannot add up to a good feeling.[11] But this misses Smith's point. The awareness of empathy is not for him a matter of *adding* your feelings to my feelings: it is a *new* feeling, separate from both your original feeling and my empathy for you. It is a second-order feeling, we might say, taking as its object the concord between our two first-order feelings, rather than the objects of those feelings themselves.

In addition, for Smith a sympathetic passion is not a mere "reflex image of the principal" passion in the other person, as it is for Hume. Hume reads his own account of empathy too much into Smith, as if Smith too were a contagion theorist, assuming that my empathetic feelings straightforwardly mirror your feelings. For Smith, however, my empathy arises from thinking myself into your situation, and it is an open question whether I will then feel as you do. If you are "ill-humord" and constantly complaining, I may *not* share your feelings. And if I do feel as you do, there is a new element to the situation— the harmony between us—about which, if I am aware of it, I will also have feelings. The sentiment of approbation emerges from that new element of the situation; not from your feelings alone, nor from my empathetic feelings for you alone. There is no reason why this new feeling has to have the character of the feelings whose concord gives rise to it. And in cases where the original feelings were painful, says Smith, it does not: it is, rather, "always agreeable and delightful."[12]

The remaining question is whether this point is true. Smith notes that empathy "alleviates grief by insinuating into the heart almost the only agreeable sensation which it is at that time capable of receiving" (I.i.2.3; 14). We take comfort at funerals from the grief of our friends, even if we continue to mourn our loss. In addition, whatever Hume may have thought, sometimes a hospital *is* more entertaining than a ball. Imagine walking through a hospital and feeling very much in synch with the suffering of the patients. Now imagine being at a ball while feeling very *out* of synch with the delight that the other people seem to be having. Where would you rather be? Experiencing a ball as an outsider to the fun others are having can be sharply painful, and not a few of us will leave a ball like that for a place where people are suffering. Sometimes, we agree with Ecclesiastes: "It is better to go to the house of mourning than to the house of feasting" (7:2).

This is especially true where we *disapprove* of "the house of feasting." Imagine being at a ball in the middle of a world crisis, when you think people should not be celebrating. You might very well prefer to be at a hospital then, or in any case somewhere dominated by the darker-hued sentiments you consider suited to the time. Cheerfulness of which we disapprove tends to be depressing, and anger or grief of which we approve tends to instill in us at least a modicum of pleasure: by way of the solidarity we feel with the person experiencing it.[13]

And it is that sense of solidarity, I suggest, that Smith most wants to bring out. The reason why awareness of mutual empathy is always pleasurable is that in it, we are reassured that we participate in a common humanity. We find that our feelings are characteristic of the human community, and we experience that as comforting and encouraging. We don't want to be idiosyncratic in our feelings. Sometimes we are regarded that way, and worry about it. A friend or colleague disapproves of my anger, my self-pity, my joy in my accomplishments, even my good cheer, and I fear that I am weird, cut off from other people, emotionally malformed in some way. So it is a relief to find that others *do* share in my feelings.[14] Finding that others feel as I do signals my membership in the general human community. That is always a pleasure.[15]

4. But even if we grant that empathy with unpleasant feelings can have an element of pleasure in it, is it really true that empathy is always pleasurable? Are there not people who don't *want* us to empathize with them, who are indeed annoyed or upset if we do?[16]

There are, it seems to me, two main kinds of case in which it at least seems as if others don't want our empathy. On the one hand, there are people who pride themselves on their sophisticated artistic taste, and are irritated if you tell them that you share their fondness for, or aversion to, a film or novel or piece of music. On the other hand, there are people who are very private about their emotions and would rather not have others grieve or rejoice with them.

The art connoisseurs fall in turn into two subcategories. Some are simple poseurs, putting on an air of having superior tastes because they think that others will admire them for that. Hungry for the approval of others with refined tastes, and tickled by the idea that the riffraff around them are whispering, "Oh, he knows so much about art—nothing pleases him!" these people *crave* empathy. So they merely appear to provide a counterexample to Smith's thesis that empathy is always pleasurable; in fact, they confirm that thesis.

But not all art connoisseurs are poseurs. Some people devote their lives to developing a rich and deep knowledge of music or film or literature, and are sincerely annoyed when less knowledgeable people claim to share their tastes. You have just seen Brian de Palma's *Scarface* and were delighted by the references in it to *Macbeth*; a week later, you're still mulling over the way that *Macbeth*'s "none of woman born" prophecy structures its final scene. You tell me that you loved the movie and I say, "Oh, I loved it too!" adding perhaps that

I love gangster movies, or movies with Al Pacino in them. But my attempted sharing of your feelings irritates you, because you don't love *Scarface* because it is a gangster movie (you may indeed hate gangster movies, generally) or because it stars Al Pacino. So my empathy is not a pleasure at all, for you: you don't want empathy, on this matter, from me.

But am I really offering you empathy? What you are likely to think is that I don't in fact share your feelings. I like *Scarface* because it is a gangster movie, and you are not taking that sort of pleasure in it; your pleasure in it is of an entirely different variety. Were it to turn out, on discussing the matter further, that the fact that *Scarface* is a gangster movie was not the main factor in my love for it, and that I too picked up the allusions to *Macbeth* and can discuss them thoughtfully—were it to turn out that I am indeed as thorough and erudite a film buff as you are—then you almost certainly *would* come to take pleasure in the empathy I have expressed. But that's because you would now regard me as sharing your feelings: you would regard the erudite film-connoisseur version of me as having very different feelings from the crude version.

So there is a straightforward explanation of the art connoisseur cases that is perfectly compatible with Smith's view. We might add that both the poseur and the sincere art connoisseur limit their pickiness about shared feelings to a narrow band of responses to art. They are unlikely to reject offers of comfort after they have been fired or lost a loved one, or congratulations offered to them after they have gotten married.

Let's turn now to the intensely private people, who may not want comfort after a loss or congratulations after an achievement. But what exactly are they rejecting? At the funeral for your mother, I exclaim, "It's so hard to lose a parent!" and try to give you a hug. You cringe and step away. Are you upset by the fact that I recognize how hard it is to lose a parent? No, you are upset by the fact that I don't recognize that your particular version of that pain involves not wanting others to give you a hug. Had I instead come up and said, "I know this is a hard time for you but I also realize that you'd like to be left alone," you would probably have been grateful, and pleased by the fact that I was capable of entering your feelings precisely enough to know that I should not hug you. More generally, I think it is fair to say that most people who dislike warm expressions of shared feeling are put off by the *expression* and not by the shared feeling itself—and that they think that a friend who really shares their feelings will recognize this feature of their personalities and express her empathy by keeping her distance. So once again, the purported exception to Smith's "pleasure in empathy" thesis turns out to be someone who does find shared feeling pleasurable—but thinks that fervent expression of it signifies that others do not really share their feelings.

30 CHAPTER TWO

I don't mean to say that there are no cases of people who hate empathy itself—that there *could* not be such cases, at least. Perhaps Ted Kaczynski, the Unabomber, came to hate anything that smacked of community with other human beings; perhaps that is true of many psychopaths, whether or not they go on a killing spree.[17] But it is important that the examples that come to mind here are of human beings who lack or have renounced their connection to other human beings: who have cut themselves off from humanity at large. That supports rather than undermines the overarching thesis I am attributing to Smith and defending in this chapter: that empathy is essential to humanity, that the pleasure we take in shared feeling is precisely a pleasure in a sense of shared humanity.

5. On this view, we have a felt common humanity rather than a reasoned one: in the sense both that our common humanity consists in certain shared feelings or shared dispositions to have certain feelings, and that we recognize our common humanity by way of feeling rather than reason. Perhaps this is too sharp a dichotomy. Insofar as Smithian empathy depends on a reflective process of putting ourselves in another's situation, it requires a certain amount of reasoning. But the shared sentimental humanity that arises from this process is still sharply different from the shared rational humanity of a Plato or a Kant.[18] Reason alone neither constitutes nor makes us aware of Smith's common humanity. Nor, on the other hand, is Smith's common humanity a purely biological one, or a religious posit, something that depends on our having a God-given soul.

And one thing that distinguishes Smith's common humanity from these alternatives is the degree to which it consists in what makes us *different* from one another. As we have seen, in Smithian empathy we are aware of the fact that the person with whom we are empathizing has a distinctive perspective from which she experiences her feelings. If she comes into fellow feeling with me, she is likewise aware of my distinctive perspective. That we have such perspectives, and therefore differ, is precisely one of the things we share and enjoy sharing. Which is to say: What unites me sentimentally with the rest of humankind is not just a disposition to have certain feelings in certain circumstances, but an ability to be aware of those feelings, in myself and others, *as from a distinctive perspective*. Only because we have distinctive perspectives do we worry about our differences from others; only because we worry about that do we take pleasure in discovering that we are not so different after all. But that discovery, fully spelled out, amounts to the realization that *we are similar while distinct*, that we retain our uniqueness even as we have similar reactions—that, indeed, one of the main things we have in common is our ability to be unique. In Smithian empathy, we hold two thoughts together: (1) "For all our differences, we yet share these reactions," and (2) "For all that we share, we yet remain different people." Both thoughts are sources of pleasure, and the distinctive pleasure of Smithian empathy is one we take precisely in their combination. They delineate, together, the *kind* of common humanity in which we want to participate.[19]

So Smith's sentimental conception of humanity is at the same time a perspectival conception of humanity. To be human is for Smith not at its core to be rational, or to have a God-given soul, but to develop and sustain a perspective, a point of view: a mesh of opinions and attitudes that respond to the situations we have lived through in the past and shape the way we live through future situations. And because the situations I live through are different from the ones you live through, my perspective will differ from your perspective. What we share, what makes us all human and differentiates us from other animals, is *that* we have a perspective. We can also enter one another's perspectives by way of empathy. Indeed, only by way of doing that do we come to see that, and how, we differ from others: only by empathetically understanding that others have perspectives different from ours do we come to recognize that we ourselves have a perspective. Our sense of common humanity thus consists in our ability to empathize as much as it does in our having a perspective; there is no way to separate these two things. What it is to be human, on this view, is to have and maintain a perspective, but we can maintain a perspective only if we can engage in Smithian empathy. We are, at the same time and by the same token, empathetic and perspectival beings.

6. What is a perspective? As I am using that term, it refers to a more or less coherent network of opinions and attitudes, formed in response to events in the world around us.[20] It contrasts with a mere jumble of feelings, with momentary feelings that vanish in the next moment, and with feelings that are disconnected from the world—feelings, like those induced by a drug, that are *caused* by something in our environment but do nothing to *represent* that cause to us. It also differs from a set of beliefs that we arrive at independently of feeling. The beliefs to which pure reason might bring us will not be a perspective, nor will a collection of arbitrary Humean feelings, representing nothing beyond themselves. A perspective is a *subjective take on the world.* Many philosophers do not give us an account of mental functioning that yields such an idea.

Smith does. In explaining his conception of empathy, Smith interweaves emotions and opinions: "To approve of another man's opinions is to adopt those opinions, and to adopt them is to approve of them.... But this is equally the case with regard to our approbation or disapprobation of the sentiments or passions of others" (*TMS* I.i.3.2, 17). Smith's view of how we approve and disapprove of sentiments or passions indeed depends on viewing them as like opinions, with objects they can fit or not fit. "To approve of the passions of another . . . as suitable to their objects," says Smith, "is the same thing as to observe that we entirely sympathize with them" (I.3.1, 16). So our passions, like our opinions, represent the world; they are not, as they are for Hume, enclosed within themselves, incapable of representing anything.[21]

Our passions and opinions, for Smith, are also interwoven with one another. He illustrates his fittedness account of approval with a variety of cases: sharing another's resentment, "keep[ing] time" with another's grief, admiring the same poem or picture that another admires, and laughing at the same joke. These examples mix moral with aesthetic reactions, sentiments that respond to an event with sentiments that respond to an action, and sentiments that endure over considerable time—resentment and grief—with momentary feelings of admiration or hilarity. And in the next chapter of the *Theory of Moral Sentiments*, he brings our shared reactions to art, science, and philosophy together with our reactions to one another's grief, happiness, and indignation. So for Smith our intellectual and emotional experiences are all of a piece, all in some way representative of the world around us, and all likely to vary with the different experiences we have of that world. They add up to a general *way* in which we experience the world.

Now I don't entirely agree with Smith here—I think he brings sentiments and opinions too close to each other.[22] Our opinions can affect our sentiments and our sentiments can influence our opinions, but opinions have a different sort of fittedness to the world than sentiments do. In our more reflective moments, at least, we share other people's opinions only when we are persuaded by the arguments for them, while it does not make much sense to speak of an "argument" for an emotion. Our opinions are far more directly under our rational control than are our sentiments; and if another person's perspective was just a collection of opinions, we would share or fail to share it by examining the reasons for those opinions, not by trying to enter into his experience emotionally. What most distinguishes us from one another, moreover, are more the unarticulated attitudes and habits of seeing and reacting that underlie our various beliefs and judgments than those beliefs and judgments themselves. It's hard to pin down exactly what this web of attitudes and habits amounts to (ex hypothesi, it lies below the level at which clear conceptual articulation is possible). But we might describe it as an individualized version of the pre-doxastic "being-in-the-world" that Martin Heidegger tries to capture in *Being and Time*, or the "whirl of organism" with which Stanley Cavell identifies Wittgenstein's forms of life:

> ... routes of interest and feeling, modes of response, senses of humor and of significance and of fulfillment, of what is outrageous, of what is similar to what else, what a rebuke, what forgiveness, of when an utterance is an assertion, when an appeal, when an explanation.[23]

Cavell's point is that we must share these things in order to communicate. But we don't always or fully share them; and I submit that when we do, we do so precisely by way of Smithian empathy—that it is indeed the prime function of that empathy to enable us to enter into the different "whirls" by which we each move through the world. Many of our explicit beliefs, especially the ones (religious, aesthetic, political) that we cannot fully defend rationally—to which, as we say, we are "emotionally attached," rather than being, first and foremost, convinced of them—will depend on their embeddedness in these pre-doxastic webs. So it will be true, in part, that we are each who we are because we believe in Jewish or liberal or modernist principles. But it is the embeddedness of these beliefs in our affections, routes of interest, modes of response, and so on, and not their rational content alone, that makes them central to our identity.[24] We hold many beliefs simply on logical or perceptual or testimonial grounds, and give them up when we are dissuaded of those grounds. But some beliefs, especially on religious, political, or aesthetic matters, have a close tie to who we think we are, and therefore do not come and go so easily. That is because they are nested in a way of living and feeling that precedes belief[25]—an attitudinal and practical web, or perspective.

The kind of perspective to which Smithian empathy gives us access will thus include opinions, but will not for the most part be constituted by them. It will mostly consist instead of sentiments and other similarly pre-doxastic materials: of great relevance to the way we *form* many opinions, but not themselves opinions. To say that we have distinctive perspectives, then, is to say that we are individuated by our pre-doxastic whirl of organism, in which our beliefs are nested.[26] This makes better sense of Smith's intuition that opinions and sentiments belong together than his own simple comparison between the two.

That said, I think Smith is right to see opinions and sentiments as belonging together, and he indeed seems at times to be reaching for an interweaving of them along the lines of the holistic "whirl of organism" I have sketched. This is especially clear when he speaks of our "chang[ing] persons and characters" with others. A "person and character" seems very much to be a holistic subjective take on the world, shaped by experience and social relationships

34   CHAPTER TWO

but not reducible to these external factors. Elsewhere, Smith talks about types of characters—the "prudent" man, the "vain" man, the "proud" man, in the *Theory of Moral Sentiments* (VI.i.7–13, 213–16; VI.iii.35–36, 255); the "uncouth" but judicious ploughman, the idle and prodigal aristocrat, the bold merchant, in the *Wealth of Nations* (I.x.c.24, 143–44: III.ii.7, 385; III.iv.3, 411)—as having whole patterns of feeling and thinking and acting that differ from one another. These patterns are shaped by external factors while at the same time providing their bearers with a distinctive way of taking in and responding to such factors.[27] In all these respects, Smith talks of people as having not merely character traits but *a* character: a comprehensive pattern of feeling and acting that shapes their outlook on the world. That is what I have been calling a perspective.

7. We have seen that there is a connection between engaging in Smithian empathy and being aware of perspectives: being aware, even, of our own perspective. Only if you can enter into the perspective of others can you recognize that you have a distinctive perspective of your own. I would now like to suggest that the connection between empathy and perspectives goes deeper than this: that you cannot even *have* a perspective unless you can enter empathetically into other perspectives. The connection between empathy and perspectivalism is, we may say, a metaphysical and not just an epistemological one. Who we each are is intimately bound up with who we think others are— and with who they think we are. To put the point starkly: There is no sharp line between being me and being you. I will try to make a case for this claim by way of a problem in the account of empathy I have presented thus far.

I have been taking for granted that there is a clear distinction between plain empathy and perspectival empathy. Most writers on empathy do take this for granted. Darwall does, as we have seen. Peter Goldie distinguishes between empathy and "in-his-shoes-imagining," where the former involves imagining myself as another in his or her situation,[28] while the latter requires me to figure out how *I* would feel in that situation.[29] Coplan marks a similar distinction with the phrases "self-oriented" and "other-oriented" perspective taking.[30]

These distinctions seem intuitively plausible, but they presuppose that we can have stable and sharply delineated perspectives independently of empathy. I would now like to question that presupposition. Is there really such a thing as "my perspective" and "your perspective," independently of empathy? Consider what it means for me to enter another's situation *as* me. Suppose I am trying to feel my way into the shoes of a black person who has been subjected to a racial insult, or a poor person who has lost ten dollars. Can I really enter so much as their situations without thinking about what it is like to be them in that situation? *My* being subjected to a racial insult is unlikely to have the practical consequences or emotional impact that such a thing would have on a black person, and my being deprived of ten dollars will have a much smaller effect on my life than a similar loss would have on the life of a poor person. So even to enter the other's situation properly, I must become her to a significant degree. I can't so much as try on her shoes if I remain wholly me in imagination.[31] There is, moreover, no clear limit to how much I must take on board to get her situation right. The effect of a flight delay on an impatient person's life is different from the effect of a delay on a calm person's life;[32] the effect of a setback on the life of a person with a fragile ego is different from the effect of a setback on a person with great self-confidence. What counts as a person's situation cannot be neatly separated from how she feels about those situations, nor can her feelings be separated from her history, including her psychological history. The situations we are in *include* our dispositions to react emotionally to various things, and the histories that have bred such dispositions in us. Accordingly, we can't really enter other people's shoes without also imagining ourselves, to some degree, as them.

At the same time, we can't really imagine ourselves as them without also imagining what it might be like to be in their shoes. How can I figure out what it is like to be you without imagining what it would be like to occupy your historical and social position or to live through your experiences? Who are you, apart from all these things? Your characteristics—a cheerful or cynical attitude toward life, athletic skill or the lack of it, self-respect or self-hatred, charm or irritability, ease or anxiety—are, after all, largely the product of your position and experience.

On the other hand, if I try to take on *all* your experiences and characteristics, leaving nothing of myself behind, I will no longer be empathizing at all, merely attempting to merge with you. Actually merging with you is impossible,[33] and even holding up such a thing as an ideal obscures the fact that *I* must do the imagining, and must draw on *my* experiences and feelings in order to feel my way into you. I could, of course, simply mimic what you say or do, but this would no longer be a way of feeling myself into you at all. In none of these ways can I imagine *myself* in your perspective or character. I instead lose sight of myself altogether—and consequently lose the ability to have feelings of my own for you.[34]

If I try to merge with you, I will certainly fail to achieve what Smith thinks we seek to achieve by way of imaginative projection: I will fail to reach a position from which I can judge your feelings morally, in which I can assess them as appropriate or inappropriate to the situation that gives rise to them. To assess feelings as appropriate to a situation, one needs a certain distance from the perspective of the person who has those feelings. One needs to be able to abstract from those factors in the other's emotional state that lead him or her to react too strongly, or not strongly enough—or to react, as in some of Smith's own examples, like a lunatic, a child, or an "impudent and rude" fool (*TMS* I.i.1.10–12, 12).

It is, moreover, intrinsic to empathy, independent of its relationship to moral judgment, that we manage this distance from the other. For the lunatic and child and fool, were they fully aware of what they were doing, would probably *also* react differently than they do. They may indeed be trying to do that even as we watch them; certainly people with greater control over themselves often try to do that. We misjudge others if we take them to be stuck in the current form of their perspectives, if we don't recognize the degree to which they themselves are trying to peer beyond the limits of self-awareness that their habits or history have placed upon them. We all constantly try to see ourselves as others see us, and change ourselves in response to that view. Something frustrating happens to me, and I gather from my friends' responses whether I am overreacting to it, or not reacting strongly enough. I am unexpectedly successful in something and take a quick surreptitious glance around the room before determining whether I should be bursting out in joy or feeling something more modest and expressing it in more measured tones. Or my responses are shaped by an inward glance at how I think an impartial spectator might react.[35] These efforts at self-understanding and self-transformation are part of what it is to have a perspective; one who strives to empathize with me will fail if she assumes that every detail of who I am is fixed in that form. Empathy requires of us that we not freeze the perspective of the people with whom we are empathizing, not lock it into one determinate form.

Finally, in some cases the very effort that others are making to empathize with us may change our perspective. Realizing that another is trying to empathize with me may change my view of him or her, and thus change the situation to which I am reacting.

All of which is to say that I am, and the other is, and we all are creatures who are constantly trying to feel as other human beings do.[36] But if that is so, then someone who assumes that I will necessarily react with excessive fear or jealousy to a particular situation because I have tended to react that way in the past underestimates the degree to which I try to change my responses to things—underestimates what Smith would call my self-command. I am in central part a being who tries to control and change his reactions; part of my very perspective is an effort to alter elements of that perspective. So if you are trying to be me, you will miss something if you fix my dispositions

SMITHIAN EMPATHY

and attitudes and assume that they cannot become like yours, or like those of an impartial spectator. Putting too much of the other's affective and cultural background into her situation is a way of misconstruing her, of not taking her self-command seriously enough.[37]

By the same token, I should not assume, when attempting to understand *myself*, that my reactions or perspective are fixed. I am a wilting wallflower, say, and you are forthright and fearless. I watch you take a heroic stance on an issue and think, "I would never have the guts to do that." But do I really know that about myself? My very admiration for you bespeaks some motivation to become like you. And if I can enter empathetically into the circumstances and practices that have given you courage, I surely have some understanding of what I need to do in order to achieve it myself. In a future situation I might well think, "What would you do?"—and do that. I misconstrue myself—*my* self-command—if I think I am incapable of this. I need instead always to assume that the other could be me, and that I could be her. That possibility is precisely what is entailed by the view that human beings are capable of "fellow feeling," and that locates their shared humanity in that capacity. But then there will be no sharp line between being me in your shoes and being you in your shoes. Our best sense of who we are is a constantly moving target: a perspective whose contours we come to understand and control only insofar as we engage in a constant process of empathizing with other perspectives. We do not have a perspective independent of empathy, and our attempts at empathy change our perspectives. Our selves are determinate, to the extent that they are, only by way of empathetic relationships with other selves, which move constantly between what we have in common and what differentiates us. We do not merge with one another, but who we each are depends inextricably on how we see others.[38]

So to sharply distinguish imagining myself in your shoes from imagining myself as you obscures the degree to which our situations depend on who we are, who we are depends on our situations, and our perspectives include an effort to go beyond their own limitations. Goldie's distinction between "empathy" and "in-his-shoes imagining," and the parallel distinctions in Darwall and Coplan, cannot be clearly made out.[39]

8. This brings us to Smith's conception of the self, which arises from the process of empathy. I have no self independent of having a perspective, for Smith, and I have no perspective independent of my empathetic interactions with others.

To elaborate: For Smith we are driven to reflect on ourselves, which for him means entering our own perspectives as if from the perspective of an outsider, only after realizing that others are doing that to us:

Our first moral criticisms are exercised upon the characters and conduct of other people. . . . But we soon learn, that other people are equally frank with regard to our own. We become anxious to know how far we deserve their censure or applause, and whether to them we must appear those agreeable or disagreeable creatures which they represent us. We begin, upon this account, to examine our own passions and conduct, and to consider how these must appear to them, by considering how they would appear to us if in their situation. We suppose ourselves the spectators of our own behaviour, and endeavour to imagine what effect it would, in this light, produce upon us (*TMS* III.2.5, 112; see also 129).

So our notion of ourselves arises in the first instance from our response to how others see us. Indeed, Smith says explicitly that we can arrive at this notion only in and from society:

Were it possible that a human creature could grow up to manhood in some solitary place, without any communication with his own species, he could no more think of his own character, of the propriety or demerit of his own sentiments, of the beauty or deformity of his own mind, than of the beauty or deformity of his own face. All these are objects which he cannot easily see, which naturally he does not look at, and with regard to which he is provided with no mirror, which can present them to his view. Bring him into society, and he is immediately provided with the mirror which he wanted before (110).

A person who was "a stranger to society" would attend only to "the objects of his passions, the external bodies which pleased or hurt him"; it would never occur to him to notice his "passions themselves, the joys or sorrows, which those objects excited." (110) Without the mirror of society, we would not become aware that we had a self.

That puts the point too weakly, however. Without the mirror provided by society, we would not just be *unaware* that we had a self; we would in fact *not have* a self. [40] The metaphor of the mirror is misleading. I have a body before I see it in the mirror. The mirror gives me a way of becoming aware of my body, but my body exists whether I am aware of it or not. On the Cartesian and Lockean views of the self from which early modern philosophers begin, however, my self does not exist if I am not aware of it; the self, on these views, is by definition something that reflects upon itself. [41] So Smith's self cannot so much as exist until it is awakened to such reflection by society. Society brings the self into existence and at the same time provides the standards guiding its characteristic acts of self-reflection—which for Smith are first and foremost acts of moral self-reflection. Smith responds to Hume's deconstruction of the self in Book I of the *Treatise* much as Kant does (and as Hume himself has been said to do in Books II and III of the *Treatise*):[42] by positing a continuous self for moral purposes. But unlike both Kant and Hume, Smith sees the social construction of the self as necessary to that moral posit. Hume had himself concluded his chapter on personal identity by suggesting that the identity we attribute to the self, like the identity we attribute to a church that is rebuilt in a new style, may serve social purposes.[43] For Hume, however, this was just evidence that the self is a fiction. There is nothing fictional about the self for Smith. It is a posit we cannot do without—cannot think away or see beyond—and is as real as anything else whose existence we need to posit. Nor is there anything worrying about the fact that that posit results from a process of social construction. That is just how posits arise, both in science and in morality.

But on this conception of the self, constructed for moral purposes out of our acts of empathy with others, and with ourselves as if we were another person, I will have no self prior to my acts of empathy.[44] I come to determine who you are by distinguishing your perspective from mine, and I come to determine who I am by distinguishing my perspective from yours. What I take to belong properly to you, and what I take to belong properly to me, may change as I proceed with this imaginative and interpretive process. It follows that there will be no "natural," pre-empathetic self to which I might turn in order to ground a distinction between imagining being myself in your situation and imagining being you in it. That distinction will arise, rather, *from* the process of empathy.[45]

More precisely, I come to determine who both you and I are by contrasting our perspectives with that of the impartial spectator. The impartial spectator is of course the centerpiece of Smith's moral system. It is a device that, Smith says, we build within ourselves in response to the fact that people often judge us out of misinformation or bias. We want to know how we would look, instead, to someone who knew all the facts relevant to what we have done, and who did not have reason to favor either us or the people with whom we are interacting. Smith says that what this impartial spectator approves and disapproves of will set the standard for what we ourselves should approve or disapprove of. But my focus at the moment is not on Smith's moral theory. I want to stress instead the role that the impartial spectator plays in the way we determine our identity: in our construal of who we and other people *are*. The impartial spectator tells me how a human being in general—"anyone"— would think or feel in a particular situation.[46] So to the extent that you don't seem to think or feel that way, I take you to occupy a distinctive perspective on the world. And I come to see myself as having a distinctive perspective by way of *my* differences from the impartial spectator. At the same time, the impartial spectator is also constructed, out of the various actual spectator perspectives I encounter as corrected for bias and misinformation. So, in figuring out my own identity, I am constantly thinking about yours, and comparing both identities to that of a notional, general human being. But all these positions are constructed out of a process of interpretation, and are subject to constant reinterpretation. There is no stable, essentialist conception of the human self to be found here. We are instead constantly making sense of ourselves and others by way of a triangulation among self-perspectives, other-perspectives, and a notional impartial spectator perspective.

In practice, it seems to me, we engage in precisely such a triangulation to determine our identities. As I try to figure out what is peculiar to my take on the world, I constantly note ways in which I react to things differently from you. At the same time, I conduct a comparison in my mind's eye of both of our reactions with the reactions that "anyone"—a vague "anyone," which reflects everyone I know—might have to such behavior. I also note your differences from me, and from "anyone," when I try to figure out *your* take on the world. You are an observant Jewish academic like me, let's say; but you are always calm and accepting when fellow academics schedule events on Jewish holidays, while I get upset. I think to myself: "Why this difference between us? Is she more generous-minded or stoic than I am, recognizing wisely that the Christian world we live in can't be expected to accommodate itself to our needs? Or is she conformist or cowardly, unwilling to speak up for her rights?" By the same token, I wonder whether my indignation is a mark of self-respect and courage, or just of spleen and self-indulgence.[47] And to settle these questions, I think: How might an impartial spectator react? What would be the response of an unbiased and well-informed "anyone"? The impartial spectator thus guides—disciplines—the process of construction by which I interpret who you are and who I am: provides norms, standards, for that process, a benchmark of how "people in general" feel or act, against which I can recognize and assess your peculiarities and mine. At the same time, this "anyone" is itself constantly under construction, a product of how I interpret the many "you"s I encounter and "I"s I imagine myself to be.

This is a complicated and fluid conception of selfhood. But it is also a phenomenologically accurate one, and a useful one for moral purposes. It explains nicely how and why our notions of who we are are deeply tied up with our notions of who we think we should be, and how and why we tend to try to change ourselves in the course of trying to understand ourselves. Selfhood, on this picture, is not a fiction, as Hume would have it. It is instead a necessary and ineliminable component of our moral and psychological reflections.

But it is indeterminate, ever-changing, and a reflection of and response to our social environments.

If I am reading him correctly, Smith's answer to the problems we considered in Darwall's, Goldie's, and Coplan's accounts of empathy is thus, in effect, to eat those problems—to say that there is no stable conception of the self by which we could definitively resolve what counts truly as you and what belongs instead to your situation, or what counts as your perspective and what belongs instead to mine, when I try to imagine myself in your shoes. Instead, we need to recognize that these positions are constantly in motion, shifting in accordance with the interpretation that seems best to us at a given moment, of what is peculiar to you or me and what "anyone" would feel. Recognizing this indeterminacy in who we are, and the dependence of our identity on how we interpret ourselves, should lead us also to realize that it is a mistake to assume that the self precedes its perspective. Finally, recognizing the crucial role that the conception of "anyone," or an impartial spectator, plays in how we interpret ourselves should help us see that *that* perspective, although a notional one, is essential to our psychological identity, and not just to our moral virtue. As Christine Korsgaard likes to stress, moral virtue and psychological identity are inseparable from one another.[48]

9. A word on the interpretation of Smith I have been employing here. Some readers of Smith might complain that he never explicitly identifies the awareness of empathy with an affirmation of our common humanity. But that reading fits the phenomenological facts, I think, and makes sense of why this awareness would always be pleasurable. It also makes sense of Smith's repeated claim that, when I strive for empathy, I must see myself as "one of the multitude, in no respect better than any other in it" (*TMS* II.3.5, 137; see also II.ii.2.2, 83). Why is human equality a presupposition or consequence of the achievement of mutual empathy? Because empathy captures the aspect of ourselves in which we *are* in fact all the same: our shared modes of emotional response. In empathy, I recognize what I share with others, and feel solidarity with them on that basis.

Other readers of Smith might complain that Smith never himself ties empathy to a fluid conception of our selves. Charles Griswold, for instance, sees just a sharp tension between the empathy of Part I of the *Theory of Moral Sentiments*, in which I place myself in your situation, and the empathy of Part VII, in which I "change persons and characters" with you. Griswold argues that there is an internal contradiction in what Smith wants out of empathy. I have been arguing, to the contrary, that Smith intends these to be flip sides of the same process, or perhaps ends of a spectrum that includes both exercises. Does Smith *say* that they are two facets of the same process, or place them along a spectrum? No. But I think my reading of him fits well both with his account of the self and with the phenomenology of empathy. These are reasons to favor my interpretation over Griswold's.

Relatedly, I think Griswold's reading of Smith on empathy misses its interactive quality. Smith, says Griswold, presumes that we can share other people's feelings *exactly*, can wholly grasp how another feels. "The transparency of the agent to the impartial spectator, the definitiveness of the latter's knowledge and judgment, . . .—these are among the views that Smith's [account of empathy] . . . seems to require according to Smith himself."[49] Griswold derives this understanding of Smith in part from Smith's frequent use of ocular imagery to characterize empathy—we "see" other people's suffering, "look" at their situation "through their eyes," and so on.[50] And it's characteristic of vision, says Griswold, or at least of philosophical construals of vision, that the objects we see are wholly before us. By contrast, Griswold thinks that empathy should be understood as "an interpretive process expressed . . . through narrative, or probably narratives whose competing claims must themselves be adjudicated somehow."[51]

But that *is* how Smith presents empathy! Griswold is right that it would be a mistake to think that others are transparent to us, or that we definitively grasp how they feel, and he is also right that Smith's ocular language can push us toward such a model. Smith's primary account of empathy, in Part I of the *Theory of Moral Sentiments*, does not make these mistakes, however. On the contrary, Smith says that we ask for a narrative—"What has befallen you?"—before empathizing with even the most basic emotions of another (*TMS* I.i.1.9, 11), that we need to "adopt the whole case of [our] companion with all its minutest incidents," before we can properly empathize with him or her—and that even when we do this, our emotions "will still be very apt to fall short of the violence of what is felt by the sufferer" (I.i.4.7, 21): the feelings of agent and spectator "will never be unisons," although "they may be concords" (I.i.4.7, 22). This is precisely a narrative account of empathy, governed by the reciting of a "case" (note that the imagery here is legal, not ocular), and in which the goal is explicitly said to stop short of perfect harmony. Smith's frequent use of detailed vignettes (e.g., I.ii.1.10–11, 30; I.ii.5.3, 42; I.iii.1.15, 49–50; II.ii.2.3, 84–85), and allusions to the value of literature (e.g., III.3.14, 143; III.6.12, 177), also suggest a view of empathy as "an interpretive process expressed through narrative." And when Smith considers the conflicting empathies we experience when one person is angry with another (I.ii.3.8, 38; II.i.5.5,

75–76), he brings in "narratives whose competing claims must themselves be adjudicated somehow." So while Griswold characterizes the workings of empathy astutely and beautifully, he is wrong to suppose that his account differs from Smith's.

These disagreements with Griswold are related because an account of empathy which works through narrative rather than vision is much more open to the complex formation and re-formation of the self who is empathizing, and the self who is empathized with, than would be either a placing of my self, taken as a fixed entity, into your situation or an attempt to transform myself into you (taken, again, as something fixed). The open-ended interpretive process that constitutes empathy, for both Griswold and me, allows and at times requires each of us to reinterpret who we take to be the narrator of the tales we imagine, hear, or tell about our own and other people's situations: who exactly you are, and who exactly I am. A narrative interpretation of what Smith means by empathy will therefore buttress the case for reading the *Theory of Moral Sentiments* such that the self-oriented empathy of Part I belongs together with the other-oriented empathy of Part VII.[52]

I submit that this is the best way to interpret what Smith is up to. Smithian empathy is indeed a narrative process, which doesn't sharply distinguish between who we are and what situations we inhabit, which shapes and reshapes how we understand ourselves and others as we go along, and which therefore allows for a fluid movement between entering your situation, in imagination, as me and as you.

10. But is there not something circular in the relationship between empathy and selfhood that I have developed and attributed to Smith? Don't I need to have a self before I can imagine myself into the perspective of others? How, then, can my conception of myself arise *from* empathetic encounters?

My answer is that there is indeed a circle here, but it is not a vicious one. Of course I need some awareness of a distinction between myself and others if I am to engage in empathy at all. But this awareness may lack any clear content—any clear idea of who exactly I am. Initially, it may well be too tenuous to warrant so much as the description, "a sense of self." Only by way of empathy do I give content to this vague idea—begin to make it precise—while at the same time giving content to my conceptions of other people. With these richer, clearer ideas of myself and others in hand, I then engage in further empathy, and give the ideas more or different content. I reshape them even as I use them. I thus build a conception of my self by interpreting my similarities and differences with others. And the circle involved in this process is a version of the circle involved in all interpretation: of what philosophers of interpretation like Wilhelm Dilthey and Hans-Georg Gadamer call the "hermeneutic circle."

This is, in fact, one of several respects in which the view I have been presenting allows for a rapprochement between Smithian empathy and the mode of understanding others favored by the hermeneutic tradition of philosophy. Writing in that tradition, Hans Kögler makes a strong case for the dependence of our ability to grasp the idea of a perspective on our ability to grasp norms of communication.[53] Drawing on a famous psychological experiment, he argues that our understanding of how and why others maintain false beliefs—our ability to follow their train of thought when they make mistakes—not coincidentally arises just when we learn how to follow a conversation. In the experiment, children are shown a scene in which a puppet named Maxi puts some chocolate away in a box and goes out to play, whereupon Maxi's mother takes the chocolate from the box and puts it in a cupboard. When asked where Maxi will look for the chocolate upon returning, two- to four-year-olds say, "in the cupboard," while slightly older children say, "in the box." But the transition point between these ages is just the stage at which most children learn "the supposedly simple mechanisms of responding, listening, . . . emphasizing, explaining . . . and so on in response to another's speech acts": learn the process of "*Mitgehen*," or "following along," in conversation. And this amounts to learning how "to look at things from another's perspective" (208–9). Kögler suggests that the very notion of a perspective is a linguistic one, and that even our awareness of our own perspective—our self-consciousness—should be understood as "reflexive" or "dialogical." In self-consciousness, we are always engaged in "a dialogue with [ourselves]," a relationship between "'I' as [a] thinking self to 'me' as the 'object' of my reflection." Thus, "the very possibility of self-knowledge [is] derived from a socially shared and intersubjective source" (210). Among other things, this entails that other people can help me figure out who exactly I am: I never have "an absolutely privileged position vis-à-vis the meanings that make up [my own] sense of self" (211). It also entails that there is no definite end to the process of interpreting either myself or the other; every such interpretation is open to further challenge and revision. Finally, according to Kögler, it entails that our conceptions of our selves and others are culturally mediated from the get-go. As we are socialized into communicative practices, we are ipso facto socialized into specific cultural modes of communication.

Kögler's divided, dialogical self is very close to the self I have attributed to Smith.[54] I think it also fits well with Smith to see our capacity for both empathy and self-consciousness as thoroughly dependent on language.[55] The fur-

SMITHIAN EMPATHY

ther point Kögler wants to make, that these processes must therefore vary with culture, is more questionable. Undoubtedly, there are different conversational norms in different cultures—different norms about taking turns to speak, for instance, or deferring to authority figures—and it makes good sense to suppose that these differences will affect some *formal* features of the process by which we understand one another. But no *substantive* cultural norms need come into that process. On the contrary, the fact that all cultures carry on conversations suggests that empathy, if it comes along with the learning of communicative practices, will be a human universal, much as Smith supposes. At any rate, an argument for the claim that culture colors or channels the emotions and thoughts we attribute to one another will have to come from other premises.[56]

We will return to the claims of culture in chapter 4. I think Smith would insist—as I will on his behalf—that there is some level of human shared feeling that cuts across culture. That is enough to keep any view that emphasizes empathy, even in its Smithian form, somewhat apart from the hermeneutic tradition for which Kögler speaks. Nevertheless, Smithian empathy, as I understand it, has more affinities with that tradition than one might have expected.

11. I'd like to close this chapter with a historical point. If I am right about Smith's linking of empathy to perspective, and his construal of our humanity in terms of empathy and perspective, he is one of the first philosophers to explore a theme that has been central to literature, popular culture, and politics ever since his time.

The eighteenth century is notable for its emphasis on both empathy and perspectivalism. The centrality of empathy to eighteenth-century moral thought is well known. Lynn Hunt and Thomas Laqueur have demonstrated how much it shaped not just moral philosophy, but everyday moral thought and the ideas that went into movements for the abolition of slavery or the proclamation of human rights. Laqueur says that the "humanitarian narrative" of the eighteenth century—he gives the realistic novel, the autopsy, and the clinical report as examples—inspired political change by speaking in an "extraordinarily detailed fashion about the pains and deaths of ordinary people [while making] apparent the causal chains that might connect the actions of its readers with the suffering of its subjects."[57] (I have argued elsewhere that Smith's *Wealth of Nations* belongs among these humanitarian narratives.)[58] Hunt asks whether it can be merely "coincidental that the three greatest novels of psychological identification of the eighteenth century—Richardson's *Pamela* (1740) and *Clarissa* (1747-48) and Rousseau's *Julie* (1761)—were all published in the period that immediately preceded the appearance of the concept of 'the rights of man.'"[59] She also details the many ways in which the art and music of the eighteenth century aimed at the arousal of empathy in their viewers and listeners.[60] And the idea that empathy, rather than reason or our creation in the image of God, is the main source of our ability to see others as fellow human beings is new in this period.

Less well attended to, but implicit in what Laqueur and Hunt have to teach us, is the fact that the eighteenth century also saw the invention or discovery of the idea of a perspective. Hunt describes how people marveled at the ability of Richardson to immerse his readers in the worlds he created, to "create the impression that you are present" in those worlds, and how Rousseau defied the conventional complaint that novels seduce us into living vicariously in "an estate that is not [our] own"; he thought we should revel in that fact instead.[61] But this is a seduction into other people's perspectives. Novels give us entry into *subjective* worlds or estates other than our own: the objective world as seen through the eyes of people different from us. We enter the head of a Moll Flanders, a Pamela, or a Julie, as we would later enter the head of Dickens's Pip, Tolstoy's Pierre Bezuhov, or the various unhappy Buddenbrook siblings. This entering the head of another, learning to appreciate their psychological perspective in great detail, is the stock-in-trade of novelists, and something rarely to be found in ancient or medieval literature. Famously, despite a few forerunners in other places and times, the novel is an eighteenth-century European invention which enables a new kind of sentimental identification among people.[62] But that identification is inextricable from a new appreciation of the subjective differences among us, and the degree to which our subjective features come together in a distinctive whole: a perspective. A subject with such a distinctive perspective amounts, indeed, to a new "I." Consider, in particular, first-person novels. We get glimpses of the inner workings of Iago and Hamlet by way of their monologues, but we are not invited to enter their subjective worlds holistically, or to consider how their passions and attitudes add up to a subjective whole. And in earlier literature, the first person was generally an exemplary "I," standing in for any of us. The first person in the Psalms, or in Paul's letters or Augustine's *Confessions*, is meant to represent the religious experience or journey of any human being: we are meant to see ourselves in it. By contrast, the first person in Dickens's *Great Expectations* or Dostoevsky's *Notes from Underground* is a distinctive human being who is emphatically *not* the same as the reader, but whose subjective world we are meant nevertheless to enter. (It's worth noting that it may take a full novel to lay out a person's perspective.)

I suggest that it is no more coincidental that an emphasis on empathy came together, historically, with an emphasis on distinctive perspectives than that it was followed by the proclamation of human rights. Empathy and perspectivalism belong together. It becomes important for me to empathize with you only if you have a distinctive perspective that I cannot learn about simply by looking to common human reason, or to a general theory of human nature. I understand *that* you have such a perspective, however, and even that *I* have such a perspective, only by way of empathy. This is Smith's position, as I understand it. But Smith was just expressing, more clearly than his peers and predecessors, a view that was coming to the fore throughout the literature, politics, and moral practice of his time.[63]

12. So Smith helped develop a new conception of humanity as consisting in the having of distinctive perspectives that are accessible to one another by empathy. There are some very attractive features of this conception. In the first place, I suspect that most of us simply feel that we are "most ourselves" in our having a distinctive perspective on the world. To say that my "proper self" consists in occupying this perspective, and being aware of it as such, rings much more true than saying, as Kant does, that pure reason is my proper self.[64] Saying that my proper self consists in my having a God-given soul, on the other hand, tells me little. Even if I am a devout theist, I am likely to be unsure what this means.

In the second place, the notion of a perspective, as I have been describing it, arises from my reason as well as my feelings—it is shaped by how I reason about the situations I am in, and the poems or systems of philosophy I admire; not just by my unadorned feelings. So it can take on board much that is plausible in Kantian as well as Humean views of human nature. It can give much the same weight to reasoning over coercion that Kantians do; it is just as egalitarian as a Kantian view; and it can demand the same sort of respect for others that Kantians do. Indeed, by requiring us to respect the *differences* between ourselves and others, and not just our commonalities, it may do a better job of capturing what we mean by "respect" than Kantians do.

Relatedly, while Smithian empathy may not be quite the same thing as caring for others, it is a condition *for* respectful, sensitive, and nuanced modes of caring. We are likely to care badly when we don't care out of Smithian empathy: we are likely to care in a way that does not reflect an awareness of the difference between our own perspective and the perspective of those we care for.[65] Which is to say—if I am right about the links among empathy, perspectivalism, and humanity—that we are likely to care in a way that does not adequately reflect an awareness of the other's *humanity*. When we make sure that Smithian perspectival empathy directs our caring, we care as one unique human being to another: we respect our differences from others as well as our commonalities. In Kant's terms, we respect the humanity in others and display the humanity in ourselves. Or, in the terms of the modern Kantian John Rawls, we show how seriously we take "the distinction between persons."[66] Kant and his followers have never made good sense of that distinction, however. Smith does. His perspectival conception of humanity, and the empathy that underlies it, capture perfectly what we take to be most valuable about ourselves—what defines and explains why we are, each and all, of absolute and intrinsic value.

3

Updating Smith

1. Smith may be a rich theorist of empathy, but he wrote more than two centuries ago. How realistic is it to use him as a model for thinking about empathy today? There has been an explosion of empirical research on empathy in recent decades, and moral theory has developed in many new directions, some of it making use of empathy. Shouldn't we turn to this more recent literature, rather than leafing through the pages of an eighteenth-century philosopher?

In one sense, there is a simple reason why I draw on Smith. Smith is *an* influential and thoughtful theorist of empathy, much cited even in contemporary literature, and I have devoted much of my scholarly writing to Smith for almost thirty years. So the contribution I can best make to our thinking on empathy (my "comparative advantage," as an economist might say) is a book on Smith. And that should be a useful contribution, even if it will not cover everything there is to say on the subject.

Still, there are important points that Smith missed or dealt with inadequately. There are also ways in which modern empirical and theoretical work backs Smith up better than he did himself. It is in any case valuable, when asking after Smith's contemporary relevance, to consider whether modern scholarship can shed light on Smith's views of empathy, and vice versa.

The burden of this chapter is thus to bring Smithian empathy into conversation with empirical work and moral theories that have arisen since his time, and to develop or refine it accordingly. I take up a somewhat disparate array of topics, beginning with the relationship of Smith's work to contemporary theories in cognitive psychology and the philosophy of mind. From there, I turn to empirical work on novel reading and empathy, psychotherapy and empathy, the nexus between empathy and altruism, and the question of whether animals have empathy. I conclude with some normative questions

50   CHAPTER THREE

about how Smith's account can illuminate, or be illuminated by, contemporary moral theory on care and on epistemic justice.

2. It may seem that Smith can be neatly aligned with certain contemporary scientific and philosophical models of the mind—that he anticipated what is today called "simulation theory." Cognitive psychologists and philosophers of mind have been sharply divided over how in ordinary life we explain and predict one another's responses and behaviors. The "theory theorists" suppose that we glean a set of causal regularities from what we hear and observe in childhood about how people behave: a folk theory of human behavior that bears the same sort of relationship to scientific psychology as folk theories about how things move do to physics.[1] "Simulation theorists" maintain that we instead put ourselves in the position of others, and, after adjusting for relevant differences between ourselves and those others, expect them to feel and do pretty much what we would feel and do in their situation. Simulationists are said to take their cue from a remark of Quine's on how we attribute beliefs: "We project ourselves into what, from his remarks and other indications, we imagine the speaker's state of mind to have been, and then we say what, in our language, is natural and relevant for us in the state thus feigned."[2]

Now Quine's remark bears obvious affinities to Smith's account of empathy, and Smith is often described as a protosimulationist. I think we should preserve some distance between Smith and both camps in the theory/simulation debate, however.[3] For the overwhelming concern of both camps is to figure out how we *predict* one another's behavior—even when they talk of "explanation," they have in mind the sort of explanation that makes for good prediction—and it is not at all clear that this is Smith's concern. Prediction is a mark of good science, part of the triplet of criteria—explanation, prediction, and control—by which we assess scientific theories, especially in the modern age.[4] It is suited to the worldview that gave birth to and nurtures modern science: a view on which our goal is mastery over the objects in our environment. It is far less well suited, as philosophers of many stripes have pointed out, to our interactions with our fellow human beings.[5] To begin with, it may be best not to regard our fellow human beings as "objects" at all. That is, there are ethical problems with a prediction-and-control-driven model of understanding our fellow human beings. And Smith's account of empathy is meant to play more an ethical role in our lives than a scientific one.

What interests, other than prediction and control, might an account of empathy serve? Well, we might care about empathy insofar as it plays into the triangulated reflections on identity described in the previous chapter: we might be concerned with how to work out who exactly we are, and who our friends and loved ones are, as part of figuring out what we should do. But figuring out what I should do is not the same as figuring out what I am *likely* to do; *deliberating* over my actions is not the same as *predicting* them. So, insofar as empathy enters my deliberations, it is not a tool for prediction.

Relatedly, insofar as empathy structures my relationships with the people around me, it may not be a tool for predicting *their* behavior. For in my relationships with people around me, especially people with whom I am intimate or need to work closely, I seek much of the time to *deliberate together with them* over what we should do, jointly or in interaction with one another, not to treat them as objects to be moved around for my own ends. I seek relationships of mutual respect, which is to say a mutual regard for each other as beings with our own loci of agency. That agency, in turn, depends on what we see as reasons for action from our different attitudinal perspectives. But we access one another's perspectives via empathy. Empathy, then, plays a central role in structuring our ability to respect each other.

None of which is to deny that in the course of respectful relationships with others, we need to do some predicting. Peter Goldie talks of predicting "what the wedding guests will be amused by, how my close friend will respond to this tragic news, what birthday present Amanda will be thrilled by, or what compliment will most put Stewart at his ease."[6] These kinds of predictions are integral to ethical practice; I can't claim to care for you if I make no effort to find birthday gifts that please you, or to avoid ways of speaking that offend you. But consider two different ways in which I might settle the question about the birthday gift. On the one hand, I might project myself imaginatively into your perspective, using the rich detail I've gleaned about you from our relationship over the years, and try to see whether I, if I were you, would like this gift. On the other hand, I might check statistics about what people of your class, occupation, age, and so on tend to like—perhaps a very smart set of such data, like the ones that go into the lists that Amazon comes up with—and give you something in accordance with these criteria. Let's say that the second route yields more successful predictions about what you like. (Perhaps you are a gourmet cook; so, using empathy, I decide you'd like a good knife. But you tell me that you prefer to buy your own knives. Your Amazon list might have let me know that.) Would it not often nevertheless be true that a person who proceeds in the first way would be perceived as a better, closer friend—would *be* a better, closer friend—than the person who proceeds in the second way? Of course, over time, the empathetic procedure had better yield pretty good predictions about gifts (et cetera); otherwise real concern for you should lead me to try something else. And there is every reason to think that a sensitive and careful employment of empathy *will* yield pretty good predictions. But the point is that acting out of empathetic projection into your perspective will be better, on the whole, for my friendship with you than relying on cold facts in which you appear as just one of many undifferentiated people.

A sharper version of this point appears if we turn our attention to negotiations between people who are not friends: strangers or even enemies. Here the *goal* of the process, the distribution of goods that the negotiations are intended to reach, is often a moving target, dependent in large part precisely on the intentions with which the parties engage in the negotiating process. If you show real respect for me, and a real willingness to reach a compromise that reflects my interests, then I am likely to be more willing to cut back on what I ask of you, to make more of an effort to satisfy your interests. If, on the other hand, you regard me as an object to be manipulated for your own ends, then I am likely to harden my position or make it more extreme. I once heard a participant in the failed 2000 Camp David negotiations between Israel and the Palestine Liberation Organization say that Ehud Barak—an outstanding chess player, apparently—used to come into the negotiating room and tell his Palestinian counterparts, "I figured it all out last night! We've offered you x, so your best countermove is to offer y, and after that we'll compromise on z. So why don't you just propose z?" Upon which the Palestinian negotiators, exasperated, would respond, "Why don't you go negotiate with yourself, Ehud?"[7] Greater empathy might have done more for these negotiations than Barak's skill at prediction.

Finally, our aims in understanding one another may be in part to reconcile ourselves to facts about our society that we cannot control, rather than to help us gain control over those facts. This is a large part of Smith's own purpose in his *Wealth of Nations*: showing politicians and would-be politicians how *little* they can expect to control their nations' economies and imperial projects. The last line of the book is telling. Having sketched a somewhat utopian solution to the struggle Britain was engaged in with its American colonies (the *Wealth of Nations* was published in 1776), Smith suggests that British control over those colonies had always existed more in imagination than in reality, and that if Britain could not resolve the problems it was facing, it should "endeavour to accommodate her future views and designs to the real mediocrity of her circumstances." (*WN* V.iii.92; 947). This Stoic adaptation to reality is also a large part of what Smith teaches us to aim for in his *Theory of Moral Sentiments*. The "wise and virtuous man," in the *Theory of Moral Sentiments*, becomes that way by adjusting himself to his surroundings, including his human surroundings, rather than trying to get them to adjust to him. In this context too, empathy is a tool for accepting others rather than trying to control them.

There are therefore a number of reasons for developing accounts of empathy that do not fit the program of any contemporary scientific or scientifically-oriented theory about how our minds work. I think Smith's reasons for discussing empathy are largely of this other, ethical kind. We should accordingly be wary of aligning Smith with any side in the debates in modern cognitive psychology, or among philosophers who take their lead from cognitive psychology.

3. With that caveat in mind, let's consider the possible bearing of some contemporary scientific work on Smith's conclusions.

On the relevance of imaginative literature to our capacity to empathize, Smith anticipated modern developments closely. We noted in chapter 1 that Smith recommends novelists and dramatists over philosophers for teaching certain aspects of morality (chapter 1, section 3), and that that recommendation fits in nicely with his emphasis on the active role of the imagination in raising and shaping empathy. Since Smith's day, several novels—*Oliver Twist, Uncle Tom's Cabin, A Passage to India*—are thought to have had an enormous impact on the changing of social attitudes, precisely by inspiring empathy with a type of suffering that readers of these books had hitherto ignored.[8] Whether these novels in fact had quite the impact claimed for them is hard to say—the causes of a large-scale social change are always difficult to pin down—but a number of scholars who have looked into the reception of these books think there is something to the claims.[9] A recent study indicates that even reading Harry Potter stories, whose central character is a wizard from a humble background struggling to find his place amid the wizarding elite, "changes the attitudes of children and young people toward people from disadvantaged backgrounds: specifically refugees, immigrants and gay people." Shankar Vedantam, describing this last study on National Public Radio, drew a general conclusion: "The most effective way to [fight prejudice] is not through rational thinking and conscious effort, but through narrative and story-telling. When stories allow us to empathize with people who lead very different lives, or come from very different backgrounds, [that] allows us to get into their shoes in a way that no amount of preaching could accomplish."[10] Smith would surely welcome this conclusion.

No single study can establish such a claim, of course. And Suzanne Keen, who has examined in depth the relationship between novel reading and empathy, warns against attributing any single type of emotional reaction to novel reading, and notes that the evidence that novels increase our empathy for others is mixed.[11] But she does suggest that the very fact that a text is fictional may "release readers from the obligations of self-protection through skepticism and suspicion" of people they ordinarily fear or contemn,[12] and thereby open them to an empathy they have hitherto resisted. This seems plausible, and it extends Smith's claims for the power of literature in an intriguing way. Peter Goldie's association of empathy with "centrally imagining" oneself into the narrative of another's emotion[13] also suggests that novels may be particularly helpful in learning the skills of empathy. Perhaps for that reason, Goldie makes extensive use of *War and Peace* to explain his views.

4. Nancy Sherman praises Smith's psychological acuity, and draws on him for her own view of empathy, but remarks that what he says about empathy "tends to get compromised by being nested within an . . . account of the emergence of moral judgment." Empathetic understanding, she says, "all too quickly becomes incipient moral judgment" for Smith—Smith thinks that our "ultimate interest" in empathy lies in "the *reasonableness* of another's joy or sorrow, the *credit-worthiness* of another's generosity." He also thinks that our empathy toward ourselves is intimately bound up with our desire to be worthy of approval: to win a favorable judgment of our actions and characteristics from others, and from the impartial spectator in ourselves.[14] According to Sherman, this feature of Smithian empathy blocks us from seeing how valuable a nonjudgmental empathy can be. "Empathy toward oneself and others is easily thwarted," she says, "by both the urge to judge and [the urge] to defend against that judgment." But this feature of empathy was brought out only by "psychoanalytic and, in general, psychotherapeutic exploration" (91). Accordingly, Sherman moves from Smith to a discussion of the rich tradition of reflection on empathy in therapeutic practice, in writers like Carl Rogers and Heinz Kohut.

Sherman is quite right that for Smith, empathy is bound up with judgment; we are constantly asking ourselves what emotion is properly fitted to the situation of the person principally concerned. She's also right, I'm sure, to say that such judgment needs generally to be suspended in psychotherapy. "The therapist's role is to communicate with sensitivity her understanding of the patient's world," says Sherman, explaining in this context Rogers's insistence on "acknowledging" what the patient is thinking or feeling, and Kohut's technique of "mirroring" the patient's thoughts and feelings back to herself. For both Rogers and Kohut, and for the psychoanalytic tradition more broadly, it's crucial that this mode of helping the patient think through her own beliefs and attitudes—this mode of empathy, and of encouraging self-empathy—be nonjudgmental. Especially where strongly "disavowed wishes and thoughts" are in play, judgment can easily lead a patient to freeze up, deploy the punitive or defensive mechanisms that led her to disavow these wishes and thoughts in the first place, and halt the explorative process, refusing to recognize the wishes and thoughts in question as her own. One does not have to accept the entirety of Freudian orthodoxy to find this concern immensely plausible, and to see how judgment could undermine the therapeutic process. If people are ever to come to grips with their mental conflicts, their sources of self-loathing and anxiety, they need at some point to understand and accept themselves without judgment. And the appropriate role of their therapists is to help them along in a similarly nonjudgmental way. The fact that the psychoanalytic tradition has emphasized this point and used it to develop nonjudgmental forms of empathy is a real advance on Smith.

But psychotherapy is not all of life. It is indeed, by design, *uncharacteristic* of how we live most of the time, a practice that takes us "offline" from our usual modes of interacting with others. So the fact that judgment is out of place in therapeutic empathy does not entail that it is out of place in the empathetic exchanges of ordinary social life. Sherman implies that the judgmental context into which Smith places empathy skews his account generally. There are also many other people, today, who say that we should get away from judging each other and ourselves. Some of them see empathy as a *replacement* for judgment. We should just try to feel with each other, they believe, to share each other's experience without judging it.

I think this is a mistake. When I try to feel with you in the Smithian, projective way that normally constitutes deliberate empathy, I am constantly judging. If I think I would feel as you do in some situation, I approve of your feelings, just as Smith says; if I do not, I disapprove of them. This is inevitable. It is part of how we form social bonds, and it is essential to our reflections on identity and our modes of caring for one another. I think I would feel outrage in response to the insult you have received, even when you do not feel outrage. But then I ask myself how an impartial spectator might react. The answer to that question will lead me to judge either myself or you as having the *wrong* reaction, and I need to do that in order to work out which reaction is fitted to this situation. That in turn helps me figure out whether I am overly irascible or you are overly stoic. And I need to figure these things out if I am going to help you, or myself, wisely.

Of course, there are occasions in which the wise person will say that two people fighting with one another would do better to withhold judgment—that both are at fault or neither one is, and that recognizing that fact would lead them to make peace with one another. But making this point is also a judgment. The wise person in this situation judges that the two *wrongly* blame each other for their conflict, and that withdrawing these judgments would be *better* for both. Many of the "no judgment" advocates in our contemporary society judge the rest of us in precisely this way—while failing to see that there is a performative contradiction in judging that no one should judge.

Now there are some circumstances, even outside of the therapeutic context, in which we should try to withhold judgment. Conflict resolution sometimes works through methods that resemble therapy, encouraging the parties struggling with one another simply to try to understand each other's views nonjudgmentally; only that, it is thought, will enable the parties to find a solution that can satisfy all of them. Method acting, and writing a psychologically astute novel, may similarly require entering the mind of another without judgment, as may the rehabilitation of addicts and criminals. In all these contexts, however, as in the therapeutic context, the point of the nonjudgmental method is to prepare the agents in question for actions that will be subject to judgment: a resolution to a conflict, a successful bit of acting or writing, the turning of a former addict or criminal into a functioning and happy member of society. There is a discipline in each of these cases that involves suspending our normal modes of interaction, so that agents can gain affects or skills that will enable them to re-enter those modes of interaction more successfully. Nonjudgmental empathy serves as a special practice that helps us function in a social world in which empathy draws on and feeds into judgment. So Sherman and the psychoanalytic tradition she describes are right to say that empathy need not always be judgmental. But judgment is always in the offing when we engage in empathy, and empathy normally functions to guide our judgments, to ensure that they are properly sensitive to the people we are judging in their particular circumstances. Empathy cannot replace judgment; the two are, normally, inextricably intertwined.

5. Smith does not so much as raise the question of whether animals are capable of empathy. Many contemporary writers do. There has been a good deal of research in recent years suggesting that empathy is not limited to human beings, and can instead be found in a wide variety of animals—from rats to chimpanzees. If correct, that would shake up the identification of humanity with the capacity for empathy that I developed in the previous chapter, and that I argued is implicit in Smith.

It should be noted that much of the empirical work in question here has no bearing on the kind of empathy that Smith talks about. As we saw in chapter 1, many things get called "empathy," most of which do not involve the projection and perspective taking central to Smithian empathy. When scientists get excited about mirror neurons, for instance, which fire in animals both when they feel a certain way or do a certain thing and when they see other animals feeling that way or doing that thing, this at best attests to the existence of *contagious* empathy in a variety of species, not projective empathy.[15] And when a chimpanzee whimpers because his injured brother is being left behind on a walk, that may just show pity.[16]

Closer to our topic is a striking case described by Stephanie Preston and Frans de Waal, in which a bonobo seems to understand what it is like to be a bird:[17]

> Kuni, a female bonobo at the Twycross Zoo in England, once captured a starling. She took the bird outside and set it onto its feet, the right way up, where it stayed shaking. When the bird didn't move, Kuni threw it a little, but it just fluttered. Kuni then picked up the starling, climbed to the highest point on the highest tree, and carefully unfolded the bird's wings, one wing in each hand, before throwing it into the air.

Lori Gruen cites this passage as a possible example of empathy in a nonhuman animal, but notes that "there are . . . explanations for [Kuni's] behavior that don't require positing empathy. . . . Kuni may see the bird not as a creature with a wellbeing but as an object or toy that isn't doing what it normally does."[18] De Waal himself says that "fully developed sympathy is unlikely to be found in rodents, and is probably also absent in canines and monkeys," and allows just that "some large-brained animals *may* share the human capacity to put themselves into someone else's shoes."[19]

Gruen talks of some of the unreflective ways in which nonhuman animals share feelings, or engage in limited perspective taking, as "precursors to empathy"; I think that is a good term for most of the empathy-like traits we see in such animals.[20] De Waal distinguishes "pro-concern"—"an attraction toward anyone whose agony affects you," which doesn't require thinking yourself into the other's situation, and which even a one-year-old may feel—from the various "layers of complexity [that make this] response . . . more discerning." What de Waal calls "full-blown sympathy" requires a rich understanding of the situations that others are in, and de Waal thinks that high levels of this understanding are peculiar to the human species: "Our species is special in the degree to which it puts itself into another's shoes. We grasp how others feel and what they might need more fully than any other animal."[21]

Christine Korsgaard makes a stronger point. Drawing in part on Smith, Korsgaard argues that the "capacity to take responsibility for ourselves, to give shape and form to our own identities or characters," is unique to human beings: that it indeed cannot arise except in creatures with the particular kind of self-consciousness (an awareness of our own attitudes and beliefs, above all) that we have.[22] Given that this capacity is central to the Smithian variety of empathy, there is good reason not to expect that kind of empathy of non-human animals.

6. Given the tight links I have proposed between Smithian empathy and perspectivalism, it would seem that we should also not expect to find distinctive perspectives in nonhuman animals. But can that possibly be true? One colleague has suggested to me that a perspective is simply a way of seeing. If so, animals must have perspectives.

I want in the end to grant this, but let's consider first what we mean by a "way" of seeing. If I survey a scene sometimes from right to left and sometimes from left to right, if I sometimes focus on red objects and at other times on blue objects, or if I sometimes pay close attention to things while at other times letting everything blur into one another, then there may be various quirks in my sensory perception, but they don't form a consistent enough pattern to speak of a "way" of seeing.[23] Now most animals do have patterned ways of seeing—what flies see differs from what dogs see—although the patterns seem generally to vary just by species, and not from individual to individual, as they do among us. But a patterned way of seeing is still not enough for a perspective. Consider sentences like "You have to see things from her perspective." If my way of seeing differs from yours *just* in starting from the left rather than the right, or in attending more to bluish than to reddish items, then there is not enough here to speak of "a perspective" in the sense that sentences like that call for. When we invoke differences in perspective, what we need are patterns that have significant cognitive or affective implications—that affect how we understand the world, what we think is going on and likely to go on in it, and/or how the world affects us: how it makes us feel, react, plan. Depending on how much we build into words like "understand" and "plan," we may well hesitate before attributing a perspective in this sense to most other animals: to animals with low-level mental capacities, certainly.

But I don't want to insist on this. If we are willing to give "understanding" and "planning" thin meanings, and look for patterns of sensory perception that affect cognition and affection in a weak sense, then there surely are animals to which we can attribute a perspective: chimps and dolphins, elephants and dogs, mice and bats. What we cannot do, in any of these cases, is suppose that they are *aware*, to any degree, that they possess or occupy a distinctive point of view. For that, they would need to be aware of how other animals know and feel, and it is hard to imagine how they could have *that* awareness without being able to talk. As we've noted, we need grant even to Kuni, the bonobo who tried to make a bird fly, just a sense of the mechanical differences between her and a bird, not of how the bird feels or how the world looks from the bird's perspective. I suspect that an awareness of perspectival differences comes along with the learning of language,[24] and that any fine-grained awareness of that sort—any sense of the particular things others see or feel, and the particular ways in which their seeing and feeling differs from one's own—is impossible without sophisticated linguistic capacities.[25]

What most distinguishes us from other animals will, then, be that we are or can be made aware of the differences between our perspective and the perspective of others, and therefore can identify ourselves by way of those differences. And it is this capacity for and interest in identifying ourselves as distinct individuals that I believe most importantly characterizes the human animal from an ethical point of view. "Humanism," in the sense I use that term, is an ethical orientation that gives supreme importance to our capacity for individualization, our ability to develop and maintain distinct perspectives. A humanist can, however, recognize that in some sense many nonhuman creatures also have a perspective, albeit a less finely individuated one. So it can be, as I think it should be, a part of humanism to care for nonhuman animals, especially when those animals approximate our own capacity for perspectivalism and empathy.[26] But human beings have that capacity to a supreme degree, and humanists will value human beings over nonhuman animals when a choice needs to be made between them. No decent ethical system should call on us to be neutral between the death of a human being and the death of a wolf, let alone to kill the human in order to save the wolf.

Nor do even enthusiastic defenders of animal rights deny this. They also recognize other differences between even the most decent ("humane") treatment of animals and the way we ought to treat our fellow human beings. We do not cull human beings from the herd, for instance, even in cases of gross overpopulation—while culling a herd of deer is widely considered good practice, for the sake of the deer themselves.[27] We do not expect justice or great generosity from animals, and do not punish them when they fall short of those virtues.[28] Above all—and lying behind these points—we do not expect animals to make anything remotely like free choices, reflecting on what they do in the light of either rational principles or the sorts of sophisticated imaginative exercises that, on Smith's view, go into a human being's moral judgments. These reflective capacities are bound up with the possession of language and the awareness that one inhabits a perspective different from those of other people. Both of these are uniquely human capacities.[29] And both are conditions for the level of moral responsibility that we expect from our fellow human beings, and for our sense that each individual human being has an intrinsic value that cannot be sacrificed for the good of the species.

So our awareness that we occupy different perspectives, and the rich differences in outlook that follow from this capacity, have wide-ranging ethical implications. They explain why we see each human being as unique and think that destroying any human being is a crime or tragedy, while in the case of other species, we are content to value the *kind* of life that the species represents, without worrying too much about culling the species if that will help it survive. They also help explain why we place so much importance on individual choice, rather than assuming that what goes for one of us should be good for everyone else. They explain, in short, why we care about "the distinction between persons."

7. The empirical work we've looked at thus far mostly either buttresses Smith's view of empathy or is compatible with it. Empirical evidence lends much more equivocal support to another point of importance to Smith: that empathy with others leads us to care about their well-being. Smith recognizes that empathy can breed certain pathologies. For instance, the fact that it is more pleasant to put ourselves in the place of happy rather than unhappy people leads us to admire the rich and have contempt for the poor. Smith calls this tendency "the great and most universal cause of the corruption of our moral sentiments" (*TMS* I.iii.1; 61). He is also aware of the tribalist tendency of empathy, binding us into small groups rather than encouraging us to be concerned equally for every human being (*TMS* VI, section 2; we'll take up this subject in chapter 5). But he seems never to recognize the possibility that empathy may be a tool for cruelty and manipulation. It seems possible for a torturer or a con artist to be richly empathetic, however: they indeed would seem to need empathy to achieve their goals.[30] A good salesperson needs similar skills, and may be perfectly willing to use them to sell shoddy goods (good salespeople are not always sharply distinct from good con artists). And actors or novelists might be interested in figuring out how people feel for the purposes of their art, without actually caring about them.[31]

Smith never mentions such cases. There are no con artists or torturers in the *Theory of Moral Sentiments*, nor even self-absorbed actors. But these cases suggest that one feature of his conception of empathy is incorrect: empathy need not breed care. Increasing people's empathy for one another might then seem a mistake, or at least something that comes with considerable risks. We might simply enable potential con artists and torturers to wreak greater harm on their victims.

Now it may be that we are shortchanging Smithian empathy. We might distinguish, as many theorists do, between cognitive and affectional empathy, where the first is a grasp of how other people think and feel that need not involve feeling anything of the sort oneself—a cold perspective-taking—while the second, which Smith has in mind, involves precisely an attempt to feel as the people one imagines do. Some people seem quite capable of grasping how others feel without experiencing those feelings themselves. This may indeed be what successful con artists or torturers or novelists do. If so, however, they do not engage in Smithian empathy. Cold perspective-taking, without an attempt to feel what it would be like to be another,[32] cannot do the ethical work that makes Smithian empathy so important.

But warm perspective-taking, if we may call Smithian empathy that, does seem likely to incline most people, most of the time, to care about the well-being of the people they feel for. There is reason to think that this link does not hold universally, however. The friend or family member who plots to defraud or kill his beloved, after years of sharing the same joys and sorrows, is hardly an unknown figure. It also seems likely that some novelists and actors manage to share other people's feelings quite thoroughly, while using that experience just to feed their art.

So intuition and everyday experience do not settle the question of whether empathy, even in its full and warm Smithian form, will lead us to care about others. Can we settle that question with empirical studies? There has been a good deal of work in recent years on the "empathy-altruism nexus." The psychologist C. D. Batson, especially, has explored this nexus richly, asking in many ways whether empathy—or "empathic concern," which he defines as "other-oriented emotion elicited by and congruent with the perceived welfare of someone in need"[33]—leads us to be inclined to help others. In his most famous experiments, he gave his undergraduate subjects descriptions of fictional young women in difficult circumstances. "Katie Banks" was presented as struggling to support her siblings after the death of their parents; "Carol" needed help with class notes after breaking her legs in a car accident. When the subjects were told to think about what it was like to be in Katie's or Carol's circumstances, or when their attention was drawn to the similarities between themselves and Katie or Carol, they were far more likely to offer help than when they merely heard an objective description of what had happened to Katie or Carol. This is evidence for what Batson calls "the empathy-altruism hypothesis," which other experimental psychologists have confirmed.

But Batson's empathy is not Smithian empathy. Smithian empathy does not necessarily reflect the other person's welfare, and is not aroused solely by someone in need. It is both wider and narrower than that: wider in that it encompasses vicarious joy and pride and anger as well as vicarious distress; narrower in that it is elicited by what we think we would feel in other people's circumstances, and not by other factors that might attune us to their welfare. A sense of duty, a habit of performing charity, or an instinct leading us to help people in distress (recall Mencius's infant at the well), can all give us feelings congruent with another's welfare. But feelings raised in this way will not be Smithian empathy.

Batson is aware of these differences, and lists projecting oneself into other people's situations and imagining how one would feel in another's place among the alternatives to his own definition of empathy.[34] For him, these things are precursors to empathy proper. But that means that the empathy-altruism hypothesis, as he construes it, is weaker than what we would need to establish a nexus between *Smithian* empathy and altruism. Batson's empathic concern already presupposes that the other person's well-being matters to us. In order to establish a connection between Smithian empathy and altruism, we would need to show that projecting ourselves into other people's lives leads us to *take* an interest in their well-being: to care about them.

Smithian empathy thus starts one step further from altruism than does Batsonian empathy.[35] Still, Batson's experiments do lend some support to the idea that Smithian empathy conduces to altruism.[36] Many of these experiments arouse feeling for a person by having subjects imagine themselves into her circumstances, and that projection does seem to increase the subjects' willingness to help. Moreover, Batson cites studies showing that people are willing to help the target with the *particular problem* they have imagined themselves into, and not with other problems he or she may have.[37] That gives empirical evidence for the idea that Smithian empathy can guide the way we care toward precise problems of other people, as they themselves are likely to see those problems, rather than leading us to impose our own vision of their welfare upon them. This will be a point of importance to my defense of Smithian empathy as a tool for moral theory, in chapters 7 and 8.

8. So we can draw from Batson's experiments some support for the idea that most people, most of the time, will care about a person for whom they develop Smithian empathy. We should remember, however, that Batson has worked exclusively with subjects with no predisposition *against* helping the people they were asked to empathize with; his subjects were unlikely to have the interests of a con artist or a torturer. So while it may be true that what Batson calls "empathic concern"—what I call "caring about" another (as opposed to caring *for* them: we'll see the difference shortly)—generally flows

from empathy as Smith describes it, Batson's evidence tells us little about the conditions needed to establish that link, or how and why it has exceptions.

Michael Slote argues that, since feeling pain and being distressed about it "automatically count[s]" as being motivated to alleviate it, empathizing with someone else's pain must count similarly as being motivated to alleviate it. "On strictly conceptual grounds," he says, "empathy involves sympathy with and motivation to help another person."[38] But this is surely too quick a conceptual route to what should be an empirical conclusion. Sometimes people react to other people's pain by turning away from it. Jonathan Glover cites a letter from a woman who lived near the German camp at Mauthausen in 1940s. Upon seeing prisoners taking several hours to die after being shot, she wrote a protest letter saying that the sight made "such a demand on my nerves that . . . I cannot bear it," and asked that the killings either be discontinued, "or else be done where one does not see it."[39] What would Slote say about cases like this? (They are not uncommon.) That on some level the woman *must* be motivated to alleviate the pain she sees? Nothing in her letter indicates that, and it may just not be true. Or would Slote say that the distress she feels does not count as empathy? But that would seem an arbitrary stipulation, designed to preserve the thesis that empathy gives rise to altruism, rather than to fit the empirical facts at hand.

Lori Gruen delineates a more plausible position. "Cognitive empathy is thought to generate an altruistic motivation," she says, because "when one is . . . trying to understand the perspective of the other, to feel the other's subjective experience," one is *inter alia* trying to share her goals."[40] But does "trying to understand the perspective of the other" necessarily involve trying to share her goals? Consider, again, the con artist and the torturer. To succeed in their aims, they must try to understand the perspective of their targets— but only in order to further their *own* goals, which are quite different from the goals of their targets. Perhaps we can concede that they need to "share" their targets' goals in the sense that they need to *understand* those goals. But in that case they share the goals only as an imaginative exercise: their sharing is bracketed by a suspension of belief, an "as if" mode that allows the empathizer just to taste what it would be like to have such goals, without actually committing himself to them. The sharing is offline, as it were—not something the con artist or torturer does *in propria persona*.

Now I myself am inclined to suppose that the con artist and the torturer are anomalies, and that normally we do move from empathy to caring about others, but I see no way of decisively establishing this supposition. The abundance, if not of con artists and torturers, then at least of self-centered novelists and manipulative salespeople, who use empathy for ends that do not

64   CHAPTER THREE

align with their targets' well-being, also tells against it. Rather than worrying further about a defense for the intuition, therefore, I recommend adopting a proposal made by Olivia Bailey in a recent article on the motivation for empathy in Smith.[41] Bailey suggests that we see Smithian empathy as motivated *by* a concern for others, rather than seeing that concern as the result of empathy. The point of Smithian empathy will then be not to raise concern for others in us, but to "serve an informational function" once that concern is already in place:

> [The feeling I have when I imagine being you] cannot spontaneously generate previously non-existent basic concern for you. But what if I am *already* concerned about you? . . . What if your feelings matter to me *before* I have experienced an echo of them? In that case, it makes sense that I would be motivated to put the feelings I derive from imaginative projection to use. In particular, I can infer that you are experiencing something like the grief that I am experiencing (faintly) in virtue of my imaginative engagement with your situation. And now that I have some idea of what your experience must be like, even though I cannot directly experience it myself, my general concern for you is better informed. This will help me to demonstrate my understanding of your plight and otherwise condole with you.[42]

Bailey acknowledges that this placement of concern before empathy reverses Smith's own account of how we come to care about others, but argues that her proposal is psychologically plausible and makes more sense than Smith does of how our feelings for others can be truly unselfish.[43] She also allows for the possibility that the empathetic process can "intensify the benevolent interest" we take in another, or alter its shape. The "basic concern" with which we begin "need not be the fully developed and well-informed concern that characterizes our relationship with those with whom we empathize" (270). Care might thus take a cyclical form, beginning with "a quite general regard for other people as beings whose inner lives matter to us" (270), and developing from there, via empathy, into something more robust and nuanced.

Bailey does not present her proposal as a solution to the problem of the con artist and the torturer, but I think it does solve that problem. Instead of worrying about why, in some people and some situations, Smithian empathy fails to arouse concern for others, we work instead on the hypothesis that empathy can improve the aim and depth of the caring of those who already care about others. Perhaps empathy also often inspires such care. It does seem to do that in kind or good-natured people who have no stake in harming the targets of their empathy. But the main moral advantage of Smithian empathy is not that it leads us to care about others, but that, if we do care, it improves

UPDATING SMITH   65

the quality and direction of that care. Empathetic care, where the empathy in question is of the Smithian variety, is a better guide to benevolent action than other kinds of moral motivation. Notoriously, acting on principle alone can generate cold and dehumanizing ways of giving aid, and can go along with arrogance. We can get too attached to our principles and pay too little attention to the concerns or circumstances of the people those principles are supposed to help. But even aid motivated by empathy can be problematic, if the empathy is not of Smith's perspectival kind. Suppose I come to feel as you do by way of Humean contagion—laughing and cheering because you laugh and cheer, or crying because you cry, without understanding what is making you laugh or cry. Then it will be a matter of luck if I am able to care for you in a way that you will appreciate or that is good for you. Or suppose I share your grief and joy simply because I feel some sort of solidarity with you. I empathize with all my fellow Frenchmen or Arabs or Jews, let us say, or with all workers. Again, my empathy is likely to be shallow and ill-informed. It will be a matter of luck if I care for the objects of my empathy in the manner that they would like to be cared for, even if I want to do that.

In short, we have reason to expect only a caring based on Smithian empathy to be well-informed and apt. That is the main moral advantage of Smithian empathy, not its ability to lead us to care in the first place.

9. Before moving on, we should note that there is a further step from caring *about* the happiness of another to caring *for* that other. I might care about you but be unable to care for you: you might live too far away, or be in a situation I cannot alleviate. Or I might care about you, but be too lazy or selfish to take any steps to help you. It is difficult to see how I could count as caring about you unless I am at least *disposed* to care for you, but that disposition may not be actualized, for one reason or another. We may reasonably assume that caring about someone necessarily gives rise to an inclination to care for him or her, but not that one who cares about another will actually care for her. Smith does not say much about this point, but he seems aware of it, given his extensive discussions of *akrasia* and self-deception (*TMS* III.4).

Even caring for others is not necessarily a good thing—sometimes our care is misdirected. Smith is fully aware of this point. He stresses that we tend to care excessively about the well-being of the rich and insufficiently about that of the poor; if we act on these feelings, we will help others who do not need our help more than those who do. He also indicates that we may empathize with a wrongdoer rather than his victim.[44] Acting on that empathy can again be a moral error. To correct for these errors, we need to empathize only as an impartial spectator would do, and to constrain even the empathy of the impartial spectator by way of certain general rules (*TMS* III.4.12, 160–61). Peter Goldie writes that neither empathy nor sympathy "is . . . the high road" to morality.[45] Smith is well aware of this, and makes empathy central to his moral system only after hedging it about with various conditions.

10. The empathy-altruism nexus has led us into a discussion of care, a topic that has received rich attention in contemporary moral theory, especially among feminists.[46] Care is usually understood as an emotion-driven, particularistic mode of attention to people. It is contrasted with the abstract concern for people required by rules of justice, and is recommended as a complement or alternative to the dryly rationalistic, principle-governed mode of moral decision-making characteristic of abstract moral theories like Kantianism and utilitarianism. Care theory is a recent development, but it's tempting to call Smith a care theorist avant la lettre. Is that true?

To answer that question, we'll need to spend a little time on Smith's moral philosophy as a whole. I haven't said much about that so far—this is a book on Smithian empathy, not on Smith's moral philosophy as a whole—but some aspects of his broader moral views affect how we understand the role that he gives to empathy, and especially to empathetic care. I will lay out those aspects in the rest of this section and the next. I'll then return in section 12 to the question of Smith's relationship to modern-day care theorists.

First, we need to consider what exactly goes into his impartial spectator. When I give talks on Smith to general audiences, the main objections to his views that I tend to hear concern the idea of the impartial spectator. If this figure is meant to represent just a calm and unbiased version of our local society's values, then it would seem to push us into a conformism that can leave untouched everything morally troubling about our society's views: affirming slavery or racism and sexism if our society holds slaves or is racist and sexist—and opposing these things, if it does, only when our society happens to oppose them, not on principled grounds. If, on the other hand, the impartial spectator is something more idealized, representing a universal moral standard of some sort, then it is hard to see (a) how we can ever access that spectator, and (b) why Smith did not simply lay out his favored moral standard (the utilitarian calculus? the categorical imperative?) rather than getting at it so indirectly.

These are vexed questions over which Smith interpreters disagree to this day.[47] My own view is that the impartial spectator is meant to be an unidealized common-sense device that tracks what we do in common life when we try to judge situations fairly. We gather as comprehensive a grasp as we can of the facts about the situation we are judging, and abstract from the passions we feel in response to it and the stake we may have in it. We ask, "If I weren't so angry, what would I think?" or "If it weren't my son who hit that boy, what would I think?" In this sense we always seek to judge as an impartial spectator.

But if that's how the impartial spectator works, it will always in the first instance express local norms, with all the prejudices they may contain. It can, however, also be turned *against* those prejudices—when, for instance, someone asks questions like, "What would an impartial spectator, standing above the feud between Britain and France, think of our British attitude toward the French?" (compare *TMS* VI.ii.2.4, 229), or "What would an impartial spectator, thinking herself into the situation of the Africans we enslave, think of our attitudes toward them?" (compare V.2.9, 206). Better information about a group we contemn can also shake up a standing prejudice against it. We learn more about the poor, say, and realize that they are not the lazy shirkers we took them to be.[48] So the impartial spectator can improve over time in a more or less Hegelian fashion: turning on itself, in the face of new reflection or experience, so as to widen the scope and deepen the kinds of empathy it allows for.[49] None of these exercises *guarantee* that social attitudes, and the corresponding norms of a local impartial spectator, will change. But they at least make it possible for the threat of uncritical conventionalism to be overcome. I don't think Smith's moral theory does worse in practice, in this regard, than explicitly universalist theories like utilitarianism and Kantianism. Notoriously, these theories often have also been interpreted to confirm local prejudices rather than to challenge them.[50]

But a reader need not accept this reading of the moral role of the impartial spectator, or my endorsement of its adequacy, in order to accept the role I give that device in the workings of empathy. For the point of the introduction of the impartial spectator into the triangulated process of reflection on identity I described in the previous chapter is simply that that process is a moralized one. I don't simply compare how I imagine I would feel in a situation with how the person principally concerned seems to feel; I ask myself how *anyone*—a generalized human being independent of both of us—would and should feel about it. And while that "anyone" is of necessity a moralizing figure, it can represent a variety of moral views. If you think that morality is determined by a utilitarian calculus or categorical imperative, then the "anyone" you appeal to will be the voice of utilitarian or Kantian morality. If you think that the "anyone" to whom human beings should appeal is a faithful Christian or Muslim, then you will insert a Christian or Muslim view. If you think of yourself as a cultural relativist (we need not here settle whether such a position, in its strong forms, is coherent), then you will appeal unabashedly to a local impartial spectator, without feeling the need to correct that figure by further moral reflection. The point, for

68   CHAPTER THREE

the purposes of an account of empathy, is simply that you will moralize your willingness to share others' feelings, and your correspondent account of who they are and who you are. That's all we need from Smith's impartial spectator for the purposes of this book.

11. A second and related point to make about Smith's moral theory is that Smith himself carries it out without delineating any general principle for determining goodness or rightness. He does not urge us to look to the greatest happiness of the greatest number of people, nor does he sketch any alternative rule for moral decision making. Instead, he refers us to the judgment of the (empathetic) impartial spectator, which he does not further elaborate.

Why not? One possibility is that Smith was what today we call a moral particularist.[51] Moral particularism is an approach to moral theory, identified above all with Jonathan Dancy,[52] according to which general rules are never adequate for moral thinking; reason instead requires of us at least potentially different decisions in every new set of circumstances. I indicated in chapter 1, section 8, that Smith can be seen as a particularist, and he says some things that strongly encourage a particularist reading of his view of moral judgment. He insists, for instance, that all general moral rules "are ultimately founded upon experience of what, in particular instances, our moral faculties . . . approve or disapprove of" (*TMS* III.4.8, 159). He maintains that the "first perceptions" of good and bad are grounded in "immediate sense and feeling" (VII.iii.2.7, 320), which can only be directed to particular instances. There are differences here from Dancy, who sees *reason* as particularist rather than tying moral judgment to the particular by way of "sense and feeling." But these are not differences that would show in practice. So it seems reasonable to see Smith as anticipating particularism.

Yet to identify Smith with particularism would occlude the fact that Smith gives general moral rules an important role in his theory, both in combating self-deception and in establishing systems of justice (*TMS* III.4–5 and II.ii). The point of his insistence that such rules are grounded in particular judgments is not to *dismiss* the rules, just to show their origin. In fact, he thinks we go wrong if we try to judge every case on its own: we are liable to get carried away by passion, and to hold people in similar situations to unfairly different standards. As regards certain kinds of things (keeping promises, protecting property), the impartial spectator *demands* that we rely on general rules. Smith indeed sounds proto-Kantian when describing the importance of these rules.[53]

It is by no means impossible to square the generalist with the particularist elements of Smith's moral theory, but I am inclined to think that these

UPDATING SMITH

various elements are instead symptoms of a fundamental eclecticism. Smith first gives us an account of immediate moral judgment, based on empathy and the impartial spectator.[54] He then makes room for rules to override some of these immediate judgments. He adds in a limited role for custom to shape aspects of our moral norms and practices, and he also gives a role to utility in governing how we assess moral systems as a whole.[55] What is this but an eclectic system, attempting to accommodate the disparate elements that in fact enter into our moral decision making?[56] Smith seems, moreover, to believe that any normative account of moral judgment—any prescription for how we should judge—needs to be drawn from a phenomenology of how we actually judge.[57] So this eclectic result is just what we should expect of him.

Now I endorse both the phenomenological presumption and the eclectic result that I am attributing to Smith. I think that the attempt to develop single-principle or single-method moral theories inevitably distorts elements of our moral practices, and that those practices are more reliable than the theories that try to systematize them. And I would point to John Stuart Mill and Bernard Williams as other examples of moral eclectics, whose writings on morality gained precisely from this eclecticism.[58] But I am aware that these views are controversial, and one need not accept them to find Smithian empathy morally useful. For Smithian empathy is a module that can find a home in many different kinds of moral theories. If Smith *is* a moral eclectic, however, then that would explain how empathy can sit together with a rule-based conception of justice for him, and how the dangers of empathy, so stressed by its critics today, can be overcome.

12. Back now to justice and care. On any reading of Smith, but especially on the eclectic one, he finesses the debate between justice and care theorists. Smith is generally described as a moral sentimentalist rather than a moral rationalist, and hence a care rather than a justice theorist. But even a cursory reading of the *Theory of Moral Sentiments* reveals that he attributes great importance both to care and to justice, and to both the particularist, sentiment-driven mode of attending to people that goes with care and the rule-governed, reason-driven mode of attending to people that goes with justice. To be sure, he says that justice provides only the "foundation" of society, not its content (*TMS* II.ii.3.4, 86), and that it is compatible with lives void of the "mutual love and affection" (ibid.) that he describes as the chief part of human happiness (I.ii.5.1, 41). But he notes that societies "crumble into atoms" without a foundation (II.ii.3.4, 86), and adds that it is justice that enables us to treat every human being as our equal (II.ii.2.1 83; III.3.4, 137; this is also a theme that runs through the *Wealth of Nations*). So these two virtues, or types of virtue,

are complementary: Smith gives neither one absolute priority over the other. We may say that this is because he is an eclectic, or we may say that he sees justice as itself a modification of care: a system that we need to employ if we want society to survive, as we must if we care about the people around us. Caring, on this latter view, leads to justice and underwrites it, even if justice calls on us in particular cases to suspend our caring feelings.

Either way, the both/and approach Smith takes to care and justice enables him to avoid some of the pitfalls that recent critics of empathy have attributed to that phenomenon (more on this in chapter 6). If one associates care and sentiment especially with women, and justice and reason with men,[59] Smith's account will also have the advantage of avoiding the criticisms that some feminist philosophers have made of moral systems like Kant's, which prioritize justice and reason over care and sentiment. I do not myself think that associating justice with men and care with women is useful: I agree with the critics of this literature who maintain that they play into stereotypes that we should be trying to overcome.[60] They also undercut the call of feminists, in many political struggles, for justice. So I consider it an additional advantage of Smith's approach to morality that it attributes both justice and care to women and men alike.[61] That said, Smith emphatically agrees that we need empathetic care and not just abstract rules (whether of justice or of any other kind) to guide us in our moral decision making.

13. But even a combination of empathetic care and justice can lead us badly astray. That's because much of the work that goes into making decent moral decisions depends on first getting the facts straight, and a variety of prejudices and ideologies can block us from doing that. Neither care nor justice will operate properly if, for instance, we refuse to listen to what black people or women tell us, or misconstrue the facts so as to favor people we like, and ignore or distort what happens to people we dislike. This brings us to the topic of epistemic justice, originally raised in the context of feminist philosophy.[62] It turns out that Smithian empathy can be a useful tool in helping us overcome epistemic injustice. But it also needs itself to be corrected by a respect for objectivity, stripped as much as possible of all emotional coloring, including empathetic coloring. In the remainder of this chapter, I'll elaborate this point.

In her pathbreaking book *Epistemic Injustice*, Miranda Fricker proposes two ways in which people can be wronged epistemically: testimonial injustice and hermeneutical injustice. We commit testimonial injustice when we reduce the credibility we attribute to someone because of their membership in a group against which we harbor prejudices. Fricker gives two examples: Marge Sherwood, in the screenplay drawn from Patricia Highsmith's novel

The Talented Mr. Ripley, whose correct opinion about a murder is dismissed on the grounds that she is speaking from "woman's intuition" rather than a grasp of the facts, and Tom Robinson in *To Kill a Mockingbird*, whose testimony, when he is wrongly accused of rape, is dismissed on the ground that he is black. Hermeneutical injustice arises when there are inadequate resources in our language for making sense of the experience of members of an oppressed or underprivileged group, and a major reason for the paucity of our resources is an interest, on the part of the privileged, in preventing the development of such resources. Fricker gives the example of sexual harassment, the experience of which was ignored or dismissed until it came to be named as such by a group of women who had experienced it.[63]

Fricker also argues that the source of these epistemic wrongs lies mainly in modes of perception that lie below the doxastic level:[64] we simply see certain types of people, more or less automatically, as less worthy of our credence than others, or are disinclined to enter into their ways of understanding their experience. She argues further that these modes are largely structured by general social patterns rather than the actions of individual agents.[65] The result remains grossly unjust, and a crucial element of practices that keep people oppressed more generally. But this injustice cannot be attributed solely to individual agents. Fricker's view thus fits well with a Foucaultian approach to power and its effects on knowledge, while eschewing the epistemic relativism that plagues Foucault's own writings.

Finally, Fricker lays out the long-term effects that the denial of epistemic justice can have: a loss of confidence in one's cognitive faculties, and consequently—given how central cognition is to our identity—in one's equal worth as a human being. She suggests that being subject to epistemic injustice is a kind of "epistemic objectification," not unlike sexual objectification in its effect on one's self-image.[66] And she proposes virtues of testimonial and hermeneutic justice to counter this objectification. Both of these virtues involve something much like Smithian empathy.

To see this, we need first to take a step back. Fricker roots the epistemic virtues she proposes in basic features of our epistemic functioning, as developed by Edward Craig and Bernard Williams in their state-of-nature approach to knowledge and truth.[67] Craig holds that the search for necessary and sufficient conditions for knowledge is hopeless, and that the puzzles inspired by Gettier are irresolvable as long as we insist on searching for such conditions. He proposes, instead, an account of knowledge that starts by asking after the *function* that attributions of knowledge play in our lives. To get at this question, he imagines a state of nature, in which we first rely for information on our "onboard" resources: perception, memory, inference, and so on. In this condition, we would appeal to others for information if and only if we see them as extending our onboard resources—if they occupy a better position than we do, literally (if they are up in a tree) or figuratively (if they have better eyesight or are quicker at calculations). "Knowledge," then, is what we attribute to those informants who we think can help us come to reliable conclusions about the things we are trying to figure out. And skeptical puzzles about whether these informants are brains in a vat or have come to justified true beliefs by a perverse causal route will rarely if ever arise.

Williams takes up Craig's account and adds to it the thought that contributors to the communal storehouse of knowledge need above all the virtues of sincerity and accuracy:[68] they need to intend to convey the truth rather than to lie or mislead, and to do what they can to make sure their reports reflect the facts they are reporting. What Williams overlooks, according to Fricker, is that to make effective use of our communal cognitive storehouse, we also need a virtue for how we *take up* claims in that storehouse: how we respond to purported truth tellers. Truth-accepting is also an activity that can be done more or less well, and it accordingly has distinctive virtues. Fricker proposes testimonial justice as the virtue of believing people to the extent that they have earned that trust, and hermeneutical justice as the virtue of being alert to the possibility that the difficulty a person is having in communicating something is "due . . . to some sort of gap in [our] collective resources."[69]

There are some obvious ways in which Smithian empathy enters into this account and contributes to the cure for epistemic injustice. First, empathy comes into the informant-inquirer relationship quite generally, above all in establishing trust between the speakers. Fricker makes this point, citing an essay by Karen Jones.[70] In addition, central to the case Fricker makes for the existence of testimonial injustice is an exercise in Smithian empathy—an invitation to enter, in imaginative detail, into the cases of Marge Sherwood and Tom Robinson. Not coincidentally, these examples come from works of imaginative fiction: a prime vehicle for raising empathy on the Smithian view.[71]

Finally, Smithian empathy would seem to provide the antidote for hermeneutical as well as testimonial injustice. If we can overcome testimonial injustice by imagining ourselves into the perspective of speakers we unjustly dismiss, we should surely be able to overcome hermeneutical injustice by imagining ourselves into the perspective of those whose experience we fail to understand. Indeed, empathizing with a person in the Smithian sense would seem just to *be* doing them hermeneutical justice.[72]

But there is a problem. Where epistemic injustice is in place, we are likely either to block ourselves from engaging in the empathetic exercises needed to rectify it, or to infuse our empathetic exercises with prejudices of precisely the sort we need to overcome. On being asked to enter the perspective of a woman he thinks of as relying excessively on intuition, a sexist man may simply imagine what it would be like to be guided by intuition all the time. On being asked to think themselves into the perspective of a black person they regard as dishonest and confused, racists may simply try to imagine how they themselves might wind up dishonest and confused. Or they may engage half-heartedly in empathy, enough to pity rather than condemn the people they are prejudiced against, but not enough to recognize that the failings they attribute to their targets are not there at all. Moreover, it may be that the prejudices they hold contain a germ of truth—if only because, as Fricker points out (55–58), a society that treats a group of people as epistemically incompetent is likely to stunt or distort the epistemic development of those people.

The same limitations apply to the likely effectiveness of empathy in correcting for hermeneutic injustice. Unless I am already inclined to listen openly to someone who claims that I don't understand her experience properly, and to look out for ways in which that might be true, I may well suppose I am "entering her perspective" when I am really only reading *my* perspective into the way I think she should view what has happened to her. A male listener thinks, perhaps, "*I* wouldn't mind it if women made sexual remarks to me in the office," and therefore dismisses a woman reporting sexual harassment as being overly sensitive. Or a staunchly secular person, seeing nothing in religion but superstition, can imagine only how he might come to lose his critical faculties when asked to put himself in the situation of a religious Jew or Muslim who is concerned to avoid pork.

The work of Smithian empathy may thus come too early or too late to overturn our prejudices. Testimonial and hermeneutical injustice are likely to infect our empathy, if we have not already recognized them as a problem. That doesn't mean that empathy is useless in countering epistemic injustice. Sometimes the "release . . . from . . . skepticism and suspicion" that we experience in reading novels (see section 3, above) may finesse our testimonial prejudices or compensate for our hermeneutical ones, and enable us to empathize with a kind of person or suffering that we have hitherto dismissed. In general, I think, we should say about the problem of blinding prejudice something similar to what we said earlier about the relationship between empathy and altruism: that empathy will not always lead to epistemic justice, but that *if* a person is already inclined to struggle against her tendencies to epistemic injustice, Smithian empathy can help her in that effort. This is most obvious as regards hermeneutical injustice. As noted above, trying earnestly to understand another's experience as if from her perspective just *is* hermeneutical justice. And if, in a case like that of sexual harassment, a kind of experience regularly gets slotted into categories that distort it ("He's just flirting," "That's just how guys are"), then we will probably need an energetic effort at Smithian empathy to come up with a more suitable category. A conversation in which I say, honestly, "I don't understand exactly what has upset or offended you; tell me more," or perhaps, "You mean it was something like _____?" (in which the blank is filled by an event I have gone through), is precisely what is needed to help me conceptualize the harm you are describing, and to help you articulate it. Smithian empathy can thus play a useful role in overcoming the hermeneutic gap, even if we cannot expect it to operate effectively unless the people involved are already alert to that gap, and are trying to overcome it.

The case is a bit trickier as regards testimonial injustice. Fricker uses Smithian empathy to excellent effect in order to help us see that there is such a thing as testimonial injustice, and that it can have devastating effects on people. But in any particular case, the question of whether we should believe a person cannot turn only on what we think we might have said had we occupied his circumstances from his perspective. For his perspective may be laden with prejudice, misinformation, or poorly developed cognitive capacities. Entering the perspective of climate-change deniers may be valuable in many respects, but it should not lead us to accept their views. Or take a poor person who recounts the dangers of his neighborhood while describing the source of those dangers as "black drug dealers"—or who, in the course of describing the horrors of the building he lives in, mentions the machinations of his "Jew landlord." Instantly, we are or should be alerted to the danger that his account has been skewed by racism or anti-Semitism. And that may lead us not only to doubt the *explanation* he gives for the problems he describes, but to wonder about his reliability in describing the problem itself: perhaps bias has led him to see more evil around him than there really is.[73] To resolve these doubts, and sift the true from the false in his testimony, we will want in a case like this *not* to share his perspective, but to turn to neutral observers, statistical information, and other more objective sources of information. Empathy will play at most an indirect and limited role.

In other cases, empathy may indeed help correct for testimonial injustice. Entering into the perspective of Tom Robinson in *To Kill a Mockingbird* should make it seem highly unlikely that he is lying, or that he committed the crime of which he was accused. Entering the perspective of Marge, whose reasons for thinking that her lover was murdered get dismissed in *The Talented Mr. Ripley,* will make it difficult for anyone to think that she could really be so wrong about the intimate details she mentions. More generally, as Fricker and Jones stress, empathy is essential to the trust we put in witnesses. We think witnesses are reliable when, upon putting ourselves in their shoes, we think our reports would likely resemble theirs. And empathy may be precisely what we need to overcome the sorts of biases that, on Fricker's account, lead us to lower the credibility of people whom our society systematically oppresses: biases that operate at a perceptual rather than a doxastic level, leading us "instinctively" to dismiss what they say.[74] Notoriously, merely *believing* that women are equal to men, that black people are equal to whites, or that Jews are as honest as other people need not translate in practice into treating members of these groups equally. And that is just as true in connection with crediting their testimony as it is in connection with hiring them, acquitting them of crimes, or showing them respect in everyday life. But to combat this sort of bias, one needs not more antiprejudicial beliefs, but a sense of how the people against whom one is biased experience the world—of what it is like, among other things, to be disbelieved even when one is honest, clearheaded, and well informed. One also needs a sense of where, in one's own modes of perception, implicit bias is likely to lurk. But for this too, empathy is needed: empathy with oneself, the ability to enter one's own perspective as if one were someone else.

So empathy can play a role in combating testimonial as well as hermeneutical injustice. We just need to remember that its role in regard to testimonial injustice is a limited one, and that it may itself need correction where the perspective we are trying to enter is skewed by misinformation or prejudice. And as regards both kinds of epistemic injustice, empathy can help us only where we are already inclined to try to overcome such injustice. Otherwise, it may operate in a distorted or perverse way, reinforcing the prejudices we already have. This is not different, however, from the use of empathy more generally. Empathy is a tool for directing and focusing beneficent inclinations we already have. It need not give rise to those inclinations.

14. In this chapter we've considered contemporary work on novel reading, psychotherapy, empathy in animals, the empathy-altruism link, the relationship between care and justice, and the need for epistemic injustice. In some cases (e.g., in regard to novel reading), we found that Smith's account of empathy can be buttressed and expanded by developments since his time. In other cases (e.g., in regard to nonhuman animals), we've defended Smith's views with arguments he does not himself make. And in still other cases (e.g., in regard to the empathy-altruism link), we found reason to revise what Smith says. On the whole, however, it seems clear that we still have good empirical reason to suppose that we have a capacity for empathy of much the sort that Smith describes, and that that capacity is more or less peculiar (thus far) to the human animal. It also seems clear that we continue to have good normative reasons for supposing that that capacity does important ethical work for

us. In the course of our considerations we have, however, somewhat altered the notion of empathy as Smith describes it—as we already began to do in the previous chapter when drawing out the complex triangulation of perspectives that is at most implicit in Smith's own work. We'll go forward with a Smithian empathy that descends from Smith's own account of empathy but is not in all respects identical with it.

4

Empathy and Culture

1. I'd like now to add a cultural layer to the picture I've drawn. I've spoken thus far as if empathy is something anyone can engage in regarding anyone else. If I try to empathize with you, I may need to take into account the fact that your personal history will lead you to emotional dispositions different from mine, but I can come to understand your dispositions by imagining what it would be like to live through that history. Cultural difference would seem to be just one instance of a difference in history, however, so it should provide no special obstacle to empathetic understanding. On the contrary, empathy should *enable* us to understand people in any and every culture. And that seems to be Smith's view. This will come as no surprise to most readers, given the universalism we expect from philosophers in the eighteenth century. There would seem to be little place in Enlightenment thought for cultural barriers to interfere with our understanding of others.

Charles Griswold has criticized Smith on this score. Thinking through the example in the *Theory of Moral Sentiments* in which we are to condole with a man who has lost his son, Griswold notes that the way the son died will affect our reaction—whether the son was killed in battle, or instead committed suicide, died in prison, or was run over by a drunk driver—and he adds that "different cultures will promote varying norms about what it is that one is to feel in the relevant context."[1] For Griswold, we might say, there is a kind of empathetic understanding of others that goes via culture, rather than appealing directly to universal human reactions. Griswold draws here on a long tradition that goes back at least as far as Smith's contemporary, Johann Gottfried von Herder, who is said to have coined the word "empathy."[2] Let's therefore call the culturally inflected kind of understanding "Herderian empathy," by contrast with a universalistic "Smithian empathy." I am not convinced that

Herderian and Smithian empathy should be sharply contrasted with one another, but these labels will at least help us set up a debate over such issues.

2. It is a mistake to suppose that Smith was blind to cultural difference. It is indeed a mistake to read eighteenth-century thinkers generally this way. Montesquieu, Voltaire, Lessing, and even Hume and Kant were deeply aware of the degree to which people's emotional dispositions and moral, religious, and political views varied in accordance with their different upbringings and history. Indeed, they were fascinated by these differences. They also acknowledged the difficulty of making moral judgments across such differences, sometimes approaching the sort of cultural pluralism identified with Herder.[3] Smith is among the most appreciative of these differences. He explicitly allows for notions of virtue to vary from one country to another (*TMS* V.2.7, 204), goes to great lengths to explain infanticide in ancient Greece (V.2.15, 210), and gives thoughtful accounts of why and how the "magnanimity and self-command" of aboriginal people in North America and Africa are "almost beyond the conception of Europeans" (V.2.9, 205–6). He indeed employs his notion of empathy to good effect throughout these accounts, urging us to see how we would hold the same attitudes and views as people in these distant groups if we inhabited their circumstances.

But one might complain that this approach reduces human difference *solely* to differences in circumstance. If we think, upon imagining ourselves into the circumstances of people in a different culture, that we would not react as they do, then we will put down what they feel to a mistake of some kind. Perhaps they have false religious beliefs, or have been indoctrinated in a way that makes them dogmatic about their beliefs. Smith, like Hume, blames religious dogmatism for many social ills (*TMS* III.6.12, 176–77), and says that people were "led away by . . . established custom" when they continued to practice infanticide long after it ceased to be socially necessary (V.2.15, 210). These modes of explanation sometimes serve a laudable moral purpose. For instance, they enable Smith to suggest that some *European* practices, including slavery, result from a blind following of established custom. But we might worry that it is too easy to write off everything puzzling in other cultures as a consequence of confusion or error—to assume that cultural difference does not go deep.

This is the objection that Herder makes to theorists like Smith. Human nature is a "flexible clay," says Herder, "forming itself differently" in different situations, such that "even the image of happiness changes with each condition and region."[4] He also stresses that each group of people has its own "circle of conceptions" or "circle of thinking and sensing."[5] The ideas and attitudes

EMPATHY AND CULTURE 79

of each group form a holistic system—a circle—which gives meaning to each of its elements, and frames how members of the group experience everything. To speak of a *universal* way of sensing or thinking is empty, or virtually so.[6] So we can't expect to understand culturally different others just by imagining how we would react in their circumstances; we must instead first "feel our way into" their circle of conceptions.[7] Writing off the differences between us and them as a matter of error or indoctrination shows that we have not sufficiently felt our way into that circle, that we have mistaken the "horizon" of our own thinking for the horizon of human thought in general.[8]

This view has recognizable descendants among modern cultural pluralists. Wittgenstein complains that James Frazer, in the *Golden Bough*, makes "the magical and religious views of mankind . . . look like errors,"[9] and urges us instead to interpret those views in accordance with the differing "world-pictures" of each human group.[10] This strand of Wittgenstein influenced Peter Winch's *Idea of a Social Science*, which in turn helped give rise to the strong program in the sociology of knowledge proposed by David Bloor; all echo Herder's emphasis on varying circles of conceptions. So does Clifford Geertz's method of "thick description," which works out as much as possible from within the "imaginative universe" of each group being studied.[11] We find echoes of Herder too—and often his direct influence—in Franz Boas, Margaret Mead, and Ruth Benedict; in the Sapir-Whorf hypothesis and the work of Lucien Levy-Bruhl;[12] in the *Verstehen* method of Max Weber and Georg Simmel; and in the hermeneutics of Wilhelm Dilthey and Hans-Georg Gadamer. For all their differences, these figures come together in their resistance to the universalism of a Smith or Hume—to the Enlightenment tendency to reduce human difference to differences in situation, or to error.

This is but a rough sketch of a rich and complex position with many variants, but it is sufficient to set up a contrast between Smithian and Herderian empathy. The former, we may say, assumes that all we need to do to make sense of another is project ourselves into her circumstances and determine which of her reactions are appropriate and which are excessive or based on error. The latter insists that projection of this sort is the wrong starting point—that in making sense of others we need first to figure out each culture's systematic view of the universe, and imagine ourselves into other people's situations only after we have done that. Understanding others, for a Herderian, must first and foremost be a matter of interpreting their culture; for a Smithian, interpreting culture is itself something we do via a more universal empathy.

3. What is there to be said for and against these different kinds of empathy? The Herderian generally launches three main arguments against the Smithian.

80 CHAPTER FOUR

First, the Herderian says that if we use *just* the universalist kind of empathy, we will often find in practice that we fail to understand another. We see a person engaging in an elaborate ritual feast, think of how we ourselves feel at Christmas dinner or at a Passover seder, and say, "You are enjoying the chance to spend time with your family." "No," he snaps back, "I'm hoping that the feast will please the rain god." We think that a woman who accepts a custom of arranged marriage must be conforming to her family's expectations or making the best of a bad situation. But she insists that she considers arranged marriages to be healthier than love matches. In these and many other cases, says the Herderian, we miss how other people actually think and feel if we simply imagine how we would react in their situation. And the charge rings true. People working from universalist accounts of human nature often do a bad job of rendering religious commitments intelligible, or of making sense of cultural practices very different from their own. We fail to fully grasp the other's perspective, in many cases, if we refuse to look out through her cultural circle of conceptions.

The second charge is that all feelings and attitudes, including the ones that go into Smithian empathy, are culturally shaped.[13] There is plenty of evidence for this claim, and it should shake our confidence that our reaction to any situation, even if corrected for misinformation and bias, represents a universally human response. Will everyone be upset by the death of their child? Or might some people feel that their child "has gone to a better place," or experience relief at having one fewer mouth to feed? Does everyone want erotic love, or hate slavery? The fact that Herderians can raise doubts in us about even such seemingly clear cases suggests that Smithian empathy, as a stand-alone way of understanding others, is in trouble.

Finally, the Herderian notes that the idea of a universal human nature has often provided a justification for Western imperialism. If just one way of life is suited to everyone, and we in the West have done our best to figure out what that way of like looks like, then we should have no qualms about trying to institute that way of life universally. Thus have many agents of imperialism thought, at least. Smith did not himself approve of imperialism,[14] but his universalist mode of empathy can easily be enlisted in its defense. This is, we might say, a moral version of the Herderian's second charge: not only are our supposedly universal ways of feeling not in fact universal, but thinking that they are leads us to a condescending and oppressive paternalism.

4. To these charges the Smithian advocate of universalist empathy has several responses.

First, the Smithian can grant that culture infuses much of human life but insist that there is nevertheless a universal human empathy that cuts across cultures. Anyone who has traveled widely or lived in a cosmopolitan city will recall many occasions on which she has experienced a bond of warm fellow feeling with people from very different cultures over such things as the delights of a beautiful day or the frustration of a delayed train. More generally, movements like communism would not spread across the world, and businesses would not acquire vast global markets, if people did not share needs, interests, and attitudes across cultural borders. And of course we have evolutionary reasons to suppose that we share such things.

Second, the Herderian's first charge gains its power from Smithian empathy. We may well acknowledge that in many cases we fail to understand culturally distant others when we merely imagine how we would feel in their situations, but that is because we know we have often failed at this task in the past. And how did we know that? Well, we looked at the other's disappointed or frustrated face and felt ourselves into her shoes—because *we* have also experienced the disappointment and frustration of failing to be understood. We understand why people might be upset when we try to fit what they do too neatly into our own categories because we ourselves don't like to be slotted that way. The Herderian's case that we need his kind of empathy depends, here, on some of our experiences of Smithian empathy. It may be true that we need the Herderian as well as the Smithian kind of empathy, but we come to know that only via the Smithian kind.

A third response is also directed against the Herderian's first charge. This consists in pointing out that "feeling oneself into" an alien circle of conceptions is itself largely a matter of using Smithian empathy. Herderian theorists have stressed that we cannot adequately explain individual emotions and intentions except via their cultural and historical context, and that to understand that context we need to analyze texts, artifacts, institutions, languages, and courses of history—not just to imagine how members of the culture might feel.[15] But our analysis of these objective factors, according to many Herderian theorists themselves, requires us to see *why* people wrote these texts, set up these institutions, and so on. We need to grasp their *reasons* for doing these things. And to grasp a person's reasons for acting, as Karsten Stueber has argued, we need to reenact their thought processes in our imaginations;[16] we need Smithian empathy. R. G. Collingwood put the point this way: "[The historian's] work may begin by discovering the outside of an event, but it can never end there; he must always remember that the event was an action, and his main task is to think himself into the action, to discern the thought of its agent."[17]

Herder would surely agree. He did not himself explain what he meant by "feeling oneself into" a circle of conceptions, but presumably he had in mind very much what Collingwood describes. In any case, in practice understanding the worldview of another culture very much involves an imagining of oneself into the circumstances in which one might come to hold that worldview. A course of experience of this sort is how I might come to believe in a rain god, I think, or how I could welcome an arranged marriage. Novels and other empathetic narratives enable us to enter the world of a devout Hindu, or that of a Brahmo struggling with his community.[18] Ethnography does something similar, especially when it reads like a novel. Clifford Geertz is perhaps the anthropologist who has most strongly emphasized the similarities between good ethnography and good novel writing, but he is far from the only one to employ detailed, empathetic storytelling to help us imagine ourselves into another culture. There is more to cultural understanding than such Smithian projection, but the process is guided by it, and we are unlikely to be able to engage in sensitive cultural interpretation without it.

A fourth response is directed at the second Herderian charge: that all attitudes and perceptions, including the ones we bring to Smithian empathy, are determined by culture. Responding to this charge, the Smithian starts by noting that the Herderian picture itself presupposes a universalist account of human nature: it asserts that culture shapes the attitudes and perceptions of all human beings.[19] But on what basis can the Herderian make such an assertion? If she assumes a Cartesian or Lockean picture of our selves, most of our beliefs and attitudes will be grounded in reason or personal experience, and there will be little room for culture to shape us. Far better to start with Smith's account of the self as arising in social interaction. And this is in fact the sort of account to which Herderians normally appeal. But, as we have seen, this account amounts to a view of human nature as consisting centrally in our being able to enter and being interested in entering one another's perspectives.[20] So according to this view, some attitudes and abilities *are* shared across cultures. Once again, then, the Herderian kind of empathy depends on the Smithian kind.

Finally, the moral charge that universalist accounts of human nature have helped underwrite European imperialism also rings true, where it does, because of exercises of Smithian empathy. We read Forster's *Passage to India*, and squirm with embarrassed recognition at the incidents it recounts in which Westerners seem unable even to notice the feelings of Indians. Or we enter the worlds of Wole Soyinka's *Death and the King's Horseman*, or Graham Greene's *The Quiet American*, and experience the frustration and anger of indigenous people as Westerners try to "do good" for them while ignoring how

EMPATHY AND CULTURE

they feel. Empathy of this sort also gives us the ability to see the tendency in ourselves to assume too quickly that we know what everyone else really wants. So this third charge of the Herderian again gains its power from Smithian empathy.

In a variety of ways, then, Herderian empathy depends on Smithian empathy. That is not to say that we can do without Herderian empathy, It may indeed be true that if we focus on Smithian empathy alone, we will fail to recognize deep differences between cultures, and falsely think we are understanding many of our fellow human beings. Even if we need both kinds of empathy, however, there is an asymmetry between them. We can have Smithian empathy without Herderian empathy, but not Herderian empathy without Smithian empathy. Given a clash between the two, therefore, we have some reason to favor the latter. Smithian empathy is the more basic of the two, and the Herderian kind of empathy, where it adds to the Smithian kind, nevertheless makes use of the latter.

5. We have, in addition, moral reasons for favoring Smithian over Herderian empathy.

In the first place, Smithian empathy amounts to a feeling of common humanity; Herderian empathy does not. Now we have some reasons to avoid relying entirely on any sort of feeling, in our relations to others, even a feeling of common humanity. We need to respect each human being as having equal and absolute value—to treat each human being as an end and not merely a means—whether we feel anything warm for him or her or not. Kant made this point powerfully, locating our absolute value in our capacity for agency (our freedom). And from a respect for agency we can derive a series of basic rights: to freedom of speech and conscience, for instance, or to a fair trial if accused of a crime, and to freedom of movement if not accused of a crime (freedom from arbitrary arrest and search and seizure). On the Smithian conception of agency I have been proposing, our choices will depend in large part on our attitudinal perspectives rather than our reason alone, but that does nothing to derogate from the idea that respect for one another's capacity for choice is fundamental to morality.[21] So we need to respect the rights of others regardless of whether we care about them in any way.

But this is precisely to say that respect alone builds relationships of noninterference which can otherwise be entirely cold: relationships in which we regard the space of choice around others as sacred, but have no interest in working together with those others or helping them achieve their ends. The humanism I have been expounding is richer than that, aspiring to a world in which we see no human being as alien to ourselves and we can take an interest in, learn from, and care for anyone and everyone. Herderian empathy might seem an essential tool for such humanism, enabling us to understand how and why other people develop cultures different from our own. But it is Smithian, not Herderian, empathy that allows us to feel an *emotional* connection to people in other cultures. I may explain another culture's customs by entering its circle of conceptions without coming to feel any common bond with members of that culture. This is obvious if their customs include infanticide, marital rape, and the like; I will in that case not even respect them, not even think they have a right to maintain their practices. But suppose their system of beliefs leads them simply to a more reserved way of expressing affection than I am used to, or a more boisterous way of eating. I may *understand* the reasons why they do this quite fully without feeling anything like the rush of common humanity that comes of thinking, "That's just what *I* would do in their circumstances!" The absence of that latter feeling is what distinguishes Smithian from Herderian empathy. But it is that feeling that enables us to experience fellow feeling with others: to see them as like ourselves, as parts of a single human community. It is that way of seeing others that leads us to care about them.

A second point is related to the first one. Consider the moral reasons we have for respecting cultural difference, as the Herderian wants us to do. Some people deny that we have any such reasons. Cultural difference, they say, is trivial where not pernicious, and should never obstruct the application of the categorical imperative or utilitarian calculus.[22] But many of us find this bald universalism wrongheaded. We make our case against it, as Herder did, by pointing to the value that people place on their cultural identities, and by arguing that universalistic approaches to ethics, including those of Kant and the utilitarians, tend to render life flat and shallow. We appeal, that is, to reasons why the nonrational myths or rituals or kin connections offered to us by a culture may seem to *anyone* an attractive complement to what Kantian and utilitarian moral systems have to offer. Thus do most communitarians and liberal nationalists tend to argue; that is how I myself have in the past defended the importance of both culture and religion (two things that are not sharply distinguishable, in my opinion).[23] But this sort of defense is convincing only if we can see how culture does admirable ethical work for people: how it enhances people's lives. So the advocates of culture, in making these defenses, presuppose that their readers or listeners can project themselves empathetically into the perspective of a person attached to his culture and see the good it does for him. They presuppose, that is, some general notion of a good way of living, to which culture or religion can contribute. And they show how it can contribute to that by way of Smithian empathy.

EMPATHY AND CULTURE

A universal humanism, informed by Smithian empathy, thus underwrites the case for respecting the various cultures people develop, rather than just their individual rights. But it follows that we have no good reason to respect cultures except insofar as they cohere with this universal humanism. That does not mean that what is good about cultures must be *derived* from a theory of universal human nature. The value of cultures, insofar as they have value, may lie precisely in aspects of them that are opaque to such theories: religious practices or forms of art, say, that can be appreciated only by people who have grown up in a particular culture. Cultures may indeed have ethical value for people *because* they are opaque; their opacity may make them fascinating to us, and bestow a sense of depth and mystery on our lives.[24] We may, that is, be able to provide a universalist justification for human beings to have shared ways of life that are not themselves, in every respect, open to universalist justification—not themselves, in these respects, mutually intelligible. But a value that is opaque to universalist justification can deserve our respect as a cultural norm only so long as it does not clash with the practices and attitudes that we consider basic to all human life. Arranged marriage may deserve such respect; cold modes of greeting and loud ways of enjoying one's food certainly do. Infanticide, marital rape, and joy taken in killing innocents do not; there can be no humanistic reason to respect such practices and attitudes. To give Smithian empathy priority over Herderian empathy is, however, one way to give humanism priority over the importance of culture. We have every reason—even insofar as we value cultures—to maintain these priorities. Because it cuts through cultural levels that cloud our equal concern for each human being, Smithian empathy is in the end more admirable, and more basic to who we are, than our efforts to respect cultural difference. We want to hold on to the power of Smithian empathy because it establishes our common humanity with everyone. Only this kind of empathy, not the Herderian one, gives us hope that we can cut through cultural differences when they make for injustice and violence.

6. Still, a doubt lingers: Who exactly is this "we" that cares so much about common humanity? There certainly seems to be a "we" that does *not* feel drawn to such an idea.[25] There is for one thing the "we" of various religious fanatics, who consider everyone who lacks their faith to be beyond the boundaries of humanity. There are also racists who feel solidarity only with people who share their own skin color.

Now it is by no means obvious that even religious fanatics and racists are uninterested in common humanity. Many fanatics say that those who lack their faith should be brought into it, that they can *become* fully human if they convert; and some racists say that members of *all* races should fraternize only with others in their race, that racism is good for humanity as a whole. These views may be frustratingly dogmatic or perverse, but they do not give up on the idea that what is good should in some sense be shareable with all human beings.

But what about people who do seem to draw the limits of moral respect and concern well short of humanity as a whole? What do we have to say to them? *Why* care about universalism; why suppose that morality requires of us a concern for each and every human being? What is my argument for universalism?

Well, I do not have an argument for universalism. My exploration of the moral value of empathy starts instead from the *assumption* that morality makes universalist demands of us. Various arguments (Kantian, religious, intuitionist) have been given for universalism, but I don't find any of them particularly persuasive. Even the most philosophically rigorous of them are subject to cogent objections, regarding both their foundation and their proper formulation. Nevertheless, it seems to me that the universal reach of at least our basic moral claims is essential to their being moral claims at all. And it seems to me that it seems that way to most other people as well. Most of us feel comfortable saying that extreme racists or religious fanatics who rule some people out of humanity are simply not advancing a moral claim, whatever they themselves may think: that norms and attitudes by which some people count for nought, or may be subordinated to the whims of others, just do not count as moral norms and attitudes. In this we are perhaps constituting ourselves as what Hume calls "the party of humankind,"[26] and are willing, if necessary, to combat parties who dismiss our universalism with force, if we cannot persuade them. Hume is more clearheaded about the limits of moral argument than are most philosophers. His position on this issue should be at least an acceptable fallback for those of us who are committed to the intrinsic and equal value of all human beings without being convinced of any argument for that value. We can constitute ourselves the party of humanity and simply insist, to those unwilling to join our party, that we will not count their views as moral ones. They can, after all, give us no reason why we should accept *their* norms: we do not share a starting point for moral argument with them.

One might object that if I am simply assuming a link between morality and universalism, my investigation into cultural diversity cannot have been in good faith. To that I would say that my point has been to explore the degree to which a universalist can endorse the importance of cultural diversity: to show, in particular, that an outlook that emphasizes Smithian empathy is more open than other moral views to a rich appreciation of culture, even if it

EMPATHY AND CULTURE

does not allow for the relativism espoused by some Herderians. For the flip side of arguing that Herderian empathy depends heavily on Smithian empathy, in its workings and for its appeal, is that Smithian empathy can lead us to see the appeal and understand the workings of Herderian empathy. This should not be surprising. If Smithian empathy centrally involves an appreciation of the differences in perspective among people, then it is well suited to appreciate differences in cultural perspectives as well as individual ones.

7. I'd like to close this chapter by returning to the three-way model of interpretation that I introduced in chapter 2 (section 8). I said there that we figure out both what others are like and what we ourselves are like by comparison with the perspective of an impartial spectator—a notional "anyone" that is constructed out of the people around us. Transfer this model, now, to the cultural case. We figure out both what other cultures are like and what is distinctive about our own culture by interpreting them against the background of how we think human beings in general think and feel—a notional impartial spectator perspective that is itself constructed out of both what goes into the impartial spectator in the individual case, and our best understanding of the human attitudes that cross cultures. What we count as peculiar to the other culture, and as peculiar to our own, will therefore change as we go along—in response both to the discovery of greater similarities or differences between us and the other culture, and to changes in our conception of general human nature. (Our culture and the culture we are trying to interpret will also themselves change, in part as a result of our interactions.) What we count as a mistake or moral corruption on the part of other cultures or our own will also depend on our conception of how human beings in general should act and react: our impartial spectator conception of human nature. Once again, that conception disciplines our interpretation of one another and provides it with norms, as well as helping to make it possible. But our impartial-spectator conception of human nature will likewise be shaped by our efforts at cultural interpretation. We will come to see some of the attitudes and beliefs that we attributed to the cross-cultural impartial spectator as instead belonging only to our own cultural perspective, even as some attitudes and beliefs we encounter in other cultures will expand our conception of what that spectator would regard as decency or kindness. Accordingly, what we consider to be morally right—what we think the impartial spectator would demand of everyone— will change as we go along. We interpret cultures, humanity, and morality all at the same time; each bit of the process affects the other bits.

But we need not for that reason regard either the idea of a general human nature or the idea of cultural perspectives as a mere fiction. Rather, the

Smithian view of humanity we developed in chapter 2, as consisting in the having of distinctive perspectives, should incline us to think that the having of distinctive *cultural* perspectives is also fundamental to our nature, an extension of the imaginative activities that give rise to our individual perspectives. Cultural identity is no more a myth than is self-identity, even if cultures and selves must both be posited as part of an interpretive process, rather than picked out by empirical observation alone.

This model integrates Smithian and Herderian empathy. Smithian empathy will be essential to the construction of our general conceptions of human nature—of the impartial spectator perspective, whether in the individual or in the group case—but Herderian empathy is a necessary additional tool, irreducible to the Smithian kind, when interpreting perspectives shared by a group.

To compare cultures with individual human beings in this way fits in with a view of culture that goes back to its roots in Herder. Herder employed Leibniz's monads, which were supposed to represent individual perspectives, as his model for making sense of cultures, and his followers in later years followed him in this Leibnizian orientation, speaking of cultures as having "souls" that mirror God, each in a distinctive way.[27] The idea that cultures form holistic systems, like the minds of individual human beings, and that interpreting cultures is of a piece with interpreting other minds, is in any case a common one among theorists of the social sciences. There are many reasons why this idea may be appealing. One is our moral commitment to a shared humanity. That commitment, if I am interpreting it correctly, entails that our cultural as well as individual differences reflect our shared humanity rather than defying it.[28]

5

Empathy and Affectional Ties

1. I have argued that empathy, as Smith construes it, is a central vehicle for discovering and expressing our kinship with all human beings. But our empathetic concern notoriously goes out far more readily to members of limited social groups—our family, our religion, our nation—than to humanity at large. Is this not a reason to abandon it, and move to more principle-based moral thinking instead? I don't think so, in part because I think principle-based moral thinking tends also to be biased toward limited, local groups.[1] A better response to the problem is to *use* empathy against the characteristic pitfalls of empathy—to open out our local groups by way of empathy, so that they can expand their range of empathetic concern to human beings generally. A sketch of how we might do that, drawing once again on Smith, is the subject of this chapter.

2. Before we get to that sketch, a terminological note. I spoke of "empathetic concern" in the above paragraph, but it would have been simpler to speak of "sympathy." We have here an occasion on which the term "sympathy," in its full modern sense, captures better what Smith is talking about, and what I want to talk about, than does "empathy." We are about to discuss Smith's account of affection, and while that draws heavily on his account of empathy, it depends also on his assumption that empathy will lead us to care for others. When Smith says that affection is "nothing more than habitual sympathy" (*TMS* VI.ii.1.7, 220), he probably has in mind this aspect of the empathetic process: he probably means at least in good part that habitual *acts of caring* build up, or constitute, affection. I say "probably," because it is not unimaginable that having habits merely of projecting ourselves into another's situation, and of, thereby, sharing many of their feelings, can build affection. Indeed,

when Smith identifies family affection with the "confidential openness and ease . . . in the conversation of those who have lived long and familiarly with one another" (VI.ii.1.8, 221), he seems to see it as a product more of the way we share feelings with our family members than of ways in which we care for them. That seems even more the case when he speaks of affection as arising among neighbors because "we respect the face of a man whom we see every day, provided he has never offended us" (VI.ii.1.16). People who get in the habit of sharing one another's experiences and feelings, even if they never lift a finger to help one another, can, it seems, become fond of one another. But elsewhere in the same chapter, Smith assumes that this empathetic sharing will often spill over into "that mutual kindness, so necessary for [human] happiness" (VI.ii.1.19, 225): into beneficent *deeds* on behalf of one other. So this is an occasion on which we should take Smith to be talking about what we ordinarily call "sympathy" and not just empathy. Of course we should also bear in mind that the sympathy in question is supposed to be bred by and guided by empathy; it is *Smithian* sympathy, *empathetic* caring, and not a sympathy that might arise from instinct or duty. That said, it will generally be useful in this chapter to retain Smith's own term "sympathy," especially as it appears in the phrase "habitual sympathy," rather than translating it into "empathy."

3. Smith emphasizes the fact that our sympathies work outward in concentric circles.[2] We care most for ourselves and our immediate families; a little less for our friends, neighbors, and extended families; less still for anonymous others in our city or nation; and very weakly for humankind as a whole. Smith thinks that we can, do, and should care to some degree about the happiness of all human beings,[3] but that we will never be able to care about the more distant of them as strongly as we do for our families and friends. Nor should we try to equalize our caring in that way. Our role in life is to help those near us, not to help everyone. "The administration of the great system of the universe," the attempt to bring happiness to everyone, is "the business of God and not of man" (*TMS* VI.ii.3.6, 237).

This view follows readily from Smith's account of empathy: I share your joy or your sorrow if and only if I understand the situation that gives rise to it and can see myself as having similar feelings in that situation. The more fully I can do this, the more fully I can share your feelings. Recall that Smith says that I must "bring home to [myself] every little circumstance of distress which can possibly occur to the sufferer," must "adopt the whole case of [my] companion with all its minutest incidents," if I am to achieve a robust empathy with him (21). And even then I will never quite feel what he feels for himself.

It follows that I am most likely to empathize with people I know well, who live in circumstances similar to mine, and with whom I share space and activities.[4] I am certainly most likely to *care* about people like that; I am most likely to have *sympathy* for them. But what we call "affection," says Smith, "is in reality nothing but habitual sympathy" (*TMS* VI.ii.1.7, 220). Consequently, my affection and my care are most likely to go out to people who live in circumstances similar to mine, and with whom I interact regularly. So I will care most about my family and neighbors, less for my fellow citizens, still less for humanity as a whole. The circles of sympathy follow directly from the nature of sympathy, as Smith understands it.[5]

Smith gives us a rich and astute account of how these circles work. When we share every bit of someone else's happiness or misery, he says, and are constantly trying "to promote the one, and to prevent the other"—as we do if we share a household—we come to have feelings for that person that we don't have for people outside our home. This normally takes place in biological families, but the "real principle and foundation" (VI.ii.1.8, 221) of family affection is not biological. For Smith, not instinct nor heredity but habits of feeling and practice that arise from living together make for family affection. That affection may thus obtain between parents and adopted children, or among adopted siblings, and fail to obtain among biological kin (222, 224).

In similar ways, coworkers can come to "call one another brothers, and . . . feel towards one another as if they really were so." Even "the trifling circumstances of living in the same neighbourhood has some effect of [this] kind." Unless he has offended us, "we respect the face of a man whom we see every day," says Smith (VI.ii.1.16, 224). Smith adds pragmatic reasons why we are close to neighbors. "Neighbors can be very convenient, and they can be very troublesome, to one another," he says. We normally share concerns with them—a downed tree or a backed-up sewer—and need to work together to address those concerns. This gives us additional motivation to try to get along with our neighbors. It also means that human beings at large understand that, and why we help our neighbors "in preference to any other person who has no such connection" with us. Preferential help of this sort is a good thing even from the impartial or moral point of view.

Thus far, I think Smith captures the nature and importance of associational ties very well. He is less convincing when he tries to explain why we have special feelings for or duties to members of our country. Smith says that we come to love our country because it normally includes "all those whom we naturally love and revere the most"—our families, friends, neighbors, et cetera—and because it is "the greatest society . . . whose happiness or misery" our conduct can ordinarily affect. Love of country is for him an outgrowth of the habitual sympathies we have for more local groups, but also a reflection of the fact that our countries ordinarily delimit the boundaries of our effective care. But neither of these points is entirely true. To be sure, in Smith's day the family members, friends, and neighbors of most people were likely to be contained within a single country—the ties across long distances that we maintain today, via air travel and phones and the internet, were unimaginable. But even in Smith's day, many families and some friendships (Smith's own friendships in France, for instance) did spread across borders. And while it was and is easier to help fellow countrymen than humanity at large, this was not true for people who lived near a border, or in places where people of various nationalities meet. In addition, neither then nor now do we have face-to-face contact with most of our fellow countrymen, and it is unclear why our feelings for "those whom we naturally love and revere the most" should spill over to the many people in our country whom we do not naturally love or revere at all. Countries are very artificial entities, filled with human beings we don't know.

Nevertheless, we often have an outsize fondness for our countries: stronger than our love for our neighborhood, for instance, for which we are unlikely to sacrifice our lives. What accounts for this? Smith's friend Hume made the interesting suggestion that national character may be in part path-dependent: that the accident of having striking people dominate the early years of a country will have a deep impact on the beliefs and attitudes of subsequent generations. "Whatever it be that forms the manners of one generation," he says, "the next must imbibe a deeper tincture of the same dye; men being more susceptible of all impressions during infancy, and retaining those impressions as long as they remain in the world."[6] Perhaps national bonds are similarly path-dependent. Once they begin to arise, for whatever reason, they are deeply felt by the generation raised on them, and then get passed down to each subsequent generation.

We might also bring in Benedict Anderson's suggestion that modern national bonds are in part the product of the novel and the newspaper, which allowed people across large distances to become acquainted with the detailed circumstances of others who shared their language and geographical location.[7] This fits well with Smith's account of empathy. By learning the details of lives of distant others, we enter their emotions and come to feel a habitual empathy with them. And this habitual empathy breeds affection: indeed, an affection much like what we feel for our family. So the novel and the newspaper make our fellow citizens feel like family to us—like intimate others, for whom we can richly care.

Whatever the explanation, it seems true that we tend to care more deeply for fellow members of our country than for human beings in general. For all his astute analysis of tribalist feelings, Hume seems to have been more optimistic about our ability to overcome this tendency than Smith was. At least he seems to have thought that he had himself overcome it. Hume describes himself in a letter as "a Citizen of the World," saying that people hate him because he is not a Whig, not a Tory, not a Christian, not even a Scotsman or Englishman.[8] By contrast, Smith quotes the ancient Stoics as declaring that we *should* see ourselves as "citizens of the world" (literally, "cosmopolitans"), but then goes on to criticize this ideal as unsuited to our relations to family members (*TMS* III.3.10–14, 140–43). Stoic cosmopolitanism seems for Smith, unlike Hume, to be at best a remote *ideal*, not something we can normally expect to put into practice.[9] On rare and special occasions, perhaps, we can see ourselves as citizens of the world, but first of all and most of the time we are citizens of our families, our neighborhoods, and our nations, not of the world. We care for these groups more than for other people, and will fight for them against other people if necessary. And on this point I think Smith is right. We are, and for the foreseeable future will remain, beings with local ties rather than cosmopolitans, however attractive cosmopolitanism may seem in theory.

That is not to deny that our local ties are dangerous, or to suggest that Smith overlooks those dangers. On the contrary, he is very worried about faction (*TMS* VI.ii.2.12–14, 231–32), and says that "false notions of religion . . . can occasion . . . gross perversion[s] of our natural [moral] sentiments" (III.6.12, 176). He notes that in national conflicts we are surrounded by people who share our biases and lose sight of the impartial point of view: "The partial spectator is at hand: the impartial one at a great distance." In "war and negotiation" between nations, therefore, "the laws of justice are very seldom observed" (III.3.42, 154). This last effect of local bias is particularly unfortunate and irrational. Smith thinks that nations with an understanding of their true interest should rejoice in the prosperity of neighboring countries rather than resenting it—that the well-being of each nation is bound up with the well-being of all—but that "the mean principle of national prejudice" blocks us from recognizing this (VI.ii.2.3, 228–29).[10]

In addition, Smith does not deny that empathetic concern for any and every human being is possible in principle. In the last chapter of his excursus on the circles of sympathy, he says that "our good-will is circumscribed by no boundary, but may embrace the immensity of the universe." Indeed, he tells us that we can care about any *sentient* creature: "[We] cannot form the idea of any innocent and sensible being, whose happiness we should not desire, or to whose misery, when distinctly brought home to the imagination, we should not have some aversion" (VI.ii.3.1, 235). And God, he argues, must be regarded as caring for "the universal happiness of all rational and sensible beings." But he also argues that *only* God can actively care for all such beings—can "administ[er] the great system of the universe." It is not our "business" to try to do this: "To man is allotted a much humbler department, but one much more suitable to the weakness of his powers, and to the narrowness of his comprehension: the care of his own happiness, [and] of that of his family, his friends, his country" (VI.ii.3.6, 237; cf. III.5.7, 166).

I think the cosmopolitan attitudes described in this chapter are meant to represent not just the broadest of Smith's circles of sympathy, but the frame within which the others are painted. It is *because* we have "good will" for all rational and sensible beings that we understand that our active caring must be circumscribed, for the most part, to our local communities—to the people we can most effectively help. We might even say that built into our local sympathies is an aspiration for a broader, more cosmopolitan kind of caring, but that that aspiration needs to be kept in check, else it will interfere with the caring we can effectively accomplish. In some circumstances, of course, our capacity to have benevolent feelings for anyone may be translated into active caring. If we are thrown together in a difficult situation with distant others—marooned on the proverbial desert island, say—we may come to sympathize deeply with them. But in normal conditions we lack face-to-face contact and immediate interests with these others, so we should not expect to care for them.

Smith is surely right about most of these points. We are likely to develop common interests and habits of familiarity primarily with people immediately around us, rather than people distant from us. Our most basic interests—in the food, health care, and protection from danger that we need for survival—are likely to be satisfied only when they are satisfied for our proximate others. Modern science also supports Smith. Evolutionary biology tells us that human beings developed most of their distinctive traits when they lived in very small groups, where they needed to develop strong affectional ties to fellow group members rather than to outsiders. Outsiders indeed often posed a danger to the group. And modern psychology tells us that people need and tend to form especially strong bonds with the in-groups around them, and to display empathy more to members of those groups than to outsiders.[11]

4. *That* our sympathies tend to move out in concentric circles from a small, close group thus seems clear. *Should* they function in this way? Should we not instead resist these tendencies and aim to cultivate cosmopolitan affections (as John Stuart Mill, for one, argued)? After all, familial and tribal loyalties

EMPATHY AND AFFECTIONAL TIES 95

can lead to or maintain very immoral behavior, from feuds to ethnic hierarchies and interethnic violence.

This is an important challenge, but there are good responses to it. In the first place, if we are structured to favor our local communities, full cosmopolitanism may well be impossible for us, and morality should not aim for the impossible. In the second place, there are moral advantages to the centripetal structure of fellow feeling. Smith points some of these out. It makes sense that nature would structure us this way, he says, because we are most able to help those who live near us (*TMS* VI.ii.1–2, especially 219 and 227). We are also most likely to help these people effectively and appropriately, while we may make a mess of helping distant others.[12] A concern for all human beings may sound nice, but most of the time it is pointless: I can do very little, from where I am now, to help those who live thousands of miles from me. Such concern is also likely to be misdirected where I can employ it: I may mistake people's real needs, or run roughshod over their cultural sensibilities. The long, depressing history of ineffective humanitarian movements that wind up harming the people they try to help, or that attempt to impose Western culture on everyone, bears out Smith's concerns.[13] One might think that globalization and the internet have changed things, but if it is perhaps more true today than in the past that I can sit in Evanston, Illinois, and send money for food or health care to Nigeria, it remains just as true that the organizations collecting that money and transforming it into food and health care are often inefficient, insensitive, or oppressive.

We do well to recognize this fact, and to focus our caring on those we know how to help. Allowing our sympathy to flow out from us in concentric circles thus both expresses and fosters a useful cognitive humility about the limits on our ability to help others. It *expresses* humility insofar as it amounts to an acknowledgment that we are unlikely to be able to change our emotional nature sufficiently to care equally for all human beings. It *fosters* humility insofar as it reminds us of the many practical difficulties in the way of helping distant others, and of the cultural difficulties in figuring out what would best constitute help for someone in material and social surroundings very different from ours.

Feeling particularly close to small circles of others that are bound together by shared concerns and face-to-face contact also means that the moral correction we receive within these circles is likely to be more nuanced, and better suited to our particular personalities, than correction from any and every human being. The judgments made of me by my family and friends, and to a lesser extent by my coreligionists or fellow citizens, are likely to reflect an understanding of my intentions that people far beyond these circles will not have. I can also assume that these people, especially within the closest of my affectional circles, will generally have my best interests at heart, and will try to help me fit within a social group (theirs) that I want to belong to. Of course, there are occasions on which the moral judgments of complete outsiders to my local groups can be more useful than the judgment of an insider. An outsider may see through prejudices in my local groups, or may stand beyond the excessive fondness, anger, or envy that my family and friends feel toward me. A stranger, particularly one who lives far away, is also likely to have less of an interest in manipulating me. So I should not ignore or downplay moral judgments from distant others. But most of the time, I am likely to gain most from the guidance of local spectators. Giving and taking moral guidance primarily from local circles also expresses a sort of cognitive humility: this time about what sorts of people we are likely to understand well enough to correct fruitfully or take fruitful correction from.

5. So much for a defense of Smith's circles of sympathy. As Smith himself notes, the fact that our sympathies move through these circles can also breed grave moral problems. If I am likely not to care much about people in other countries, it is easier for me to support a war against them, and to refuse to listen to their grievances against my country. And I am unlikely to want to help them much, even when they undergo great suffering.

The same thing may happen with people who live in parts of my country far from my own, or who live in my neighborhood but have a different culture from mine. Gang warfare, NIMBY politics, hostility toward immigrants, and indifference to the poor all flow from ways in which our affectional ties pull us together into groups that ignore or oppose other segments of humanity. The weakness of sympathy, as it moves into more and more distant circles, makes it a poor tool for large social projects and a thin barrier against hatred.

It is for reasons of this sort that some social reformers have called for programs to broaden our sympathies. From Stoic cosmopolitanism, through John Stuart Mill's call for a "feeling of unity [with humankind] to be taught as a religion,"[14] to the efforts of Marxist movements to make their members feel solidarity with a worldwide proletariat, there have been many attempts to overcome local allegiances in favor of a commitment to humanity at large. This has been especially true during the last two centuries. In addition to the followers of Mill and Marx, think of the founding of religions like Ethical Culture, Ahmadi Islam, and Baha'i; of attempts to unite all religions, like the Parliament of World Religions; of the educational programs of John Dewey and Shinichi Suzuki; or of the hippie movement in the 1960s. The activists in all these movements hoped that feelings of solidarity across humanity would bring about world peace, end political oppression, and minimize other sources of violence and hatred.

I take it to be obvious that all of these programs, while doing many good things, have failed in their cosmopolitan aims, at least thus far. They indeed look rather naive from the vantage point of the early twenty-first century. In recent decades we have seen a fierce revival of national and religious hatreds, a rise in hostility to immigrants, and sharply increased political polarization. Smith's appraisal of our limited capacity for cosmopolitanism thus appears, if anything, more realistic than it may have appeared in his own day. That is especially so given that Smith is not a cynic about cosmopolitanism, nor an enthusiast for local ties. The mixture in his writings of low expectations for our ability to transcend our circles of sympathy with an acknowledgement that we have the capacity for good will toward anyone bespeaks a wise, realistic idealism.

6. If we accept a Smithian, restrained view of our capacity for cosmopolitanism, there are ways to handle the baleful effects of the limits on our sympathies. We may divide these baleful effects into two broad categories: those that arise from our inadequate concern for people outside our close circles, and those that arise from our excessive concern for people within those circles. The first is a matter of indifference to distant others, which leads us to fail in our duties of humanity to them. The second is a matter of bias, a tendency to favor our local circle that leads us to excuse their wrongdoings. These types of problem are intertwined. Our inadequate concern for distant others disables our local norms from properly incorporating a respect for humanity as such, and the inadequate humanism of our local norms contributes to our indifference toward distant others. But the two problems are not the same, and do not always accompany one another. A person unconcerned about distant others may yet be a good critic of her local norms, and a person who does not properly scrutinize her local norms may yet care richly about distant others.

The main Smithian solution to the first problem is to increase face-to-face contact among distant others. There is no substitute for the importance of this sort of contact, on Smith's views or in fact. Only by actually interacting with people on a day-to-day level do we gain a deep understanding of their circumstances and how those circumstances affect them. No one will learn by reading books alone what it means to be a Palestinian in Gaza, a homeless person in Bombay, or an Inuit trying to keep his culture alive. Some Smith scholars have suggested that we need simply to become aware of the *views* of people outside our local circles, and incorporate them into our process of moral judgment. "Impartial views may come from far or from within a community," says

Amartya Sen; "Smith argued that there is room for—and need for—both."[15] But Smith did not argue this,[16] and it does not suit his method of expanding our moral imaginations. For Smith, the stuff of our moral imaginations—what enables us to empathize properly with and thereby fairly judge other people—is detail about others' *circumstances*, not about the views they uphold. Moreover, for Smith it is *habitual* sympathy, modes of shared feeling that we build up over time, that creates affection. There is no way to develop these habits without actually encountering others and indeed living with them on terms of some intimacy.[17] So the real solution to local prejudice is to travel beyond our localities and live elsewhere for a while. That is why Smith, following Montesquieu, says that "Commerce . . . ought naturally to be, among nations, as among individuals, a bond of union and friendship" (*WN* IV.iii.c.9, 493). Trading relationships, and the diplomats and migrants that come along with such relationships, can create sympathies across borders.

Of course, not just any contact with outsiders will create such bonds. In the very passage I just cited, Smith notes that, whatever commerce "ought naturally" to be, it was in fact a "fertile source of discord and animosity" in the Europe of his day. To lead us to "union and friendship" instead, our commerce with others needs for one thing to be conducted under conditions of equality and mutual respect; it will not arise when one group dominates and exploits the other. That said, it is also unlikely to arise without face-to-face contact.[18] Smith says that we experience a "delicious sympathy," a "confidential openness and ease," with others only when we "have lived long and familiarly" with them (*TMS* VI.ii.1.8, 221). Clearly, such warm and open feelings are impossible unless we have lived with them on terms of equality and mutual respect. But even more clearly we must have *lived* with them—encountered them face-to-face, often, over an extended period of time.

We may be able to lower some barriers between groups without face-to-face contact. Again, I think it is a mistake on Sen's part to suppose that merely learning about the norms or moral philosophies of other cultures will help us much, but imaginative literature can go some way toward mitigating prejudice. Following Benedict Anderson, I have suggested that sharing novels and newspapers can build sufficient affective bonds among otherwise distant people to mold them into a shared culture or nation. Similarly, by reading the novels of *another* culture, and reading about members of that culture in our newspapers, we may be able to put ourselves in their shoes and feel as they do: to develop empathy for them, and some degree of sympathy. It has been widely argued that the novel, and other modern kinds of narrative, have enabled readers to project themselves into the situations of the underprivileged in their societies (see chapter 2, section 9, and chapter 3, section 3). So it is reasonable to suppose that such narratives can similarly help readers enter the perspectives of people in cultures distant from their own. A Westerner who reads Naguib Mahfouz and Chinua Achebe, or Janichiro Tanizaki and Anita Desai, often finds herself achieving a level of empathy with people in Egypt, Nigeria, Japan, or India that she has never experienced before. This is probably not enough to bring about any deep and long-lasting empathy for members of different cultures—the many particulars of everyday life, which we pick up almost unaware when we actually inhabit another's environment, can hardly be contained between the covers of any novel—and it cannot bring about the habitual and mutual sympathy that Smith identifies with affection. But imaginative literature can at least extend our moral imaginations, and mitigate the ill effects of the closed circles that sympathy normally creates.

7. Turning now to bias, the second of the problems with local circles of sympathy: a Smithian solution to this problem is to use the warm feelings our near and dear feel toward us as a framework in which we can effectively correct one another's biases. The very love and security we feel for those in our close circles makes us more likely to listen to moral correction that comes from these circles than we are to admonitions from outsiders. When a stranger admonishes us, we look for the interests of his own that his critique may serve, or we suspect that he takes pleasure in humiliating us. And even if he means well, we may assume that he doesn't understand us. Since he doesn't know our local norms and beliefs, doesn't share our habitual attitudes, and is not well acquainted with the details of our situation, we suppose that he misunderstands our actions or their intentions. We ask, "Who are you to judge us?" and expect that he would be similarly indignant if we presumed to judge him.

Of course, this is not always true. Sometimes an act so clearly and egregiously violates general human norms that we should not be surprised by criticism and can hardly object to it. Murder and rape obviously fall into this category, but so do certain kinds of rudeness or careless inattention. Strangers should not be, and are not, barred from moral criticism in such cases. Some strangers are also thoughtful enough, and attend sensitively enough to our circumstances, that their criticisms of more subtle wrongdoing should be heeded. On some occasions, moreover, a stranger's rebuke may be more disinterested and dispassionate than that of an intimate other. But on the whole, we expect better moral criticism from intimate others than from strangers, and rightly see this intimate criticism as more likely to come out of affection: to reflect a nuanced knowledge of and deep concern for us. Such criticism is therefore more likely to help us improve our lives than criticism from a stranger. The greater empathy and deeper, longer-lasting affection that we can expect from our intimate circles make for more useful moral guidance, as does the fact that we normally share interests and values with those circles. The degree to which we expect and give guidance of this sort tends to vary in direct proportion to the degree of intimacy we have with those we are addressing. We are far more likely to listen to someone who is a member of our "people" (however we define that term)[19] than to a stranger.

And the fact that we expect and give criticism of this sort to members of our intimate circles—the fact that this is indeed an intrinsic part of maintaining such circles—means that we are more able to change the norms current in those circles than to affect the norms of humanity as a whole. If we want to change moral norms anywhere, we do better to talk to our families or neighbors or fellow citizens than to humanity at large. Inter alia, then, if we want to open human beings at large to a greater concern for the rights and welfare of distant others, we do best to initiate our campaign by trying to open our intimate circles to that concern. To contribute to a movement of all human beings toward greater concern for human beings as a whole, we had best nudge our local groups to expand their moral reach, not try to turn everyone into a cosmopolitan. Ironically, perhaps, we can only achieve cosmopolitanism in a parochial way. We need to use the power of intimacy if we want to move people beyond intimacy.

This is especially true, although also especially difficult, when we are part of a people engaged in a struggle with another group. Groups that see a particular set of others as a threat to their lives or identity have a tendency to demonize those others, to block any leanings they find in themselves to sympathize with their opponents. Israelis and Palestinians, Hindus and Muslims in India, and Protestants and Catholics in Northern Ireland all offer striking demonstrations of these tendencies—even while invoking universal human rights in defense of their causes. How to discern and move toward the truly universal demands of humanity in such circumstances? Here, where reaching beyond one's local circles of sympathy is most important, it is also most difficult. But here, for that very reason, it is especially valuable to have voices loyal to each side calling for humanitarian concern for people on the other side. The partisans on each side are in a frame of mind in which they are unlikely to heed voices from outside their intimate circles, and are likely to move beyond that obstinate closedness only if urged to do so by voices they trust. Gandhi, fasting publicly to call for an end to Hindu violence against Muslims, provides a model of this sort of voice.

But voices of this sort are liable to being labeled traitors—as Gandhi was by, among others, the Hindu nationalist who assassinated him. "Traitor" is an interesting category. Why do we consider a traitor so much worse than any

EMPATHY AND AFFECTIONAL TIES

other enemy? The centripetal structure of empathy helps answer that question. If we are especially likely to trust the moral guidance of our intimate circles—of people who have habitual sympathy for us, and with whom we share interests and ideals—then an especially effective way for our enemies to manipulate us is to employ such trusted people for their purposes. This may happen by way of bribery, corrupting a member of our circle so that he displays apparent loyalty to us while he is really serving the enemy; or it may happen if a sincerely loyal member of our circle becomes convinced that something that would destroy us is actually in our interest. Either way, what such a person says and does can be extremely dangerous to his own group. Groups are therefore highly and rightly concerned to identify such people and shun or destroy them. It is very important, then, that a moral critic from within shows that he is not a traitor (that he show this to *himself*, sometimes, as well as to others). This can be difficult, and it is unsurprising that those who commit their lives to internal critique of their group often try, or are expected to try, to demonstrate their loyalty to that group. Where they succeed in this, they can be particularly effective agents of change. Where they fail, they may lose all respect within their home group—or pay for their efforts with their lives, as Gandhi did.

But it is essential to what such internal critics are trying to do that they make use of their affectional ties and work within their group to help it broaden the reach of its concern, rather than disparage those ties in favor of a cosmopolitan citizenship shared by all humanity. For the latter kind of citizenship, no matter how inspiring in principle, is irrelevant to our everyday moral lives. Our affections go out, for good reason, in especially strong degree to members of our intimate circles, and can be directed toward distant others only by way of norms and practices that those circles themselves uphold. A Jew is more likely to move fellow Jews out of a xenophobic stance if she can give them reason to see that stance as a betrayal of Jewish values. Americans appalled by their fellow Americans' anti-immigrant and anti-Muslim feelings are most effective if they can show such feelings to be "un-American." What we need to do is show our near and dear that caring about the far and not so dear is part of our local identity: that our local norms and practices implicitly entail a respect and concern for all humanity. To say instead that we should drop our local norms and practices in favor of a universalist way of being human is both naive and offensive. It is naive because it overlooks the depth of the human impulse to form local circles of affection. And it is offensive because it scorns that impulse. Kantian universalists can once again learn from Smith; humanism can and should embrace local ties while building cosmopolitan concern into those ties. Cosmopolitanism cannot be achieved directly.

6

Utilitarianism and the Limits of Empathy

1. We come now to a challenge to our entire emphasis on empathy. Paul Bloom and Jesse Prinz have both written recent articles entitled "Against Empathy"; Bloom has expanded his article into a much-discussed book.[1] I think they make important points, but they are not careful about distinguishing kinds of empathy: some of their criticisms miss their target if directed against *Smithian* empathy. Other criticisms strike me as misguided on any reading. I will take up a series of their objections to empathy in this chapter, responding to each from a Smithian point of view. The result should help locate the place of Smithian empathy within a wider moral system. I'll turn, then, in chapters 7 and 8 to the question of what sort of wider moral systems we should be seeking. Bloom and Prinz, along with such popular moral psychologists as Jonathan Haidt and Joshua Greene, urge us to eschew empathy in favor of utilitarian cost-benefit analysis as the main basis of our moral decision making. In chapter 7 I'll rehearse some of the many problems with utilitarianism—ignored, remarkably, in the writings of all these figures—and suggest that empathy is precisely the tool we need to overcome those problems.[2] Then, in chapter 8, I'll sketch what an approach to human ends based centrally on empathy might look like: what it might mean for empathy to play a foundational role in structuring our moral theories.

2. To begin with Bloom:

(a) Bloom stresses that empathetic distress—the pain of feeling other people's pains—can exhaust one, and put one in a position in which one finds it hard to do anything, including help the objects of one's empathy: "Experiencing others' pain is exhausting and leads to burnout."[3] The more empathetic we are, the less we are likely to care for others effectively.

UTILITARIANISM AND THE LIMITS OF EMPATHY

(b) Bloom also reports studies showing that empathetic people are more aggressive than others in their responses to people who cause suffering: degree of empathy correlates with degree of vindictiveness.[4] Empathy with the victims of crimes can lead people to a blind and indiscriminate anger, such that they want the criminal punished harshly, and may wish that his or her entire family or people be wiped out. Racists and anti-Semites, Bloom notes, have exploited this tendency for centuries.

(c) Empathy is narrow, says Bloom: "It connects us to particular individuals . . . but is insensitive to numerical differences and statistical data." He quotes Mother Teresa: "If I look at the mass I will never act. If I look at the one, I will." This sums up accurately how empathy works, Bloom maintains, but for that reason, "our public decisions will be fairer and more moral once we put empathy aside." We need in our public decision making to attend to the numbers of people affected by social and physical problems. To help everyone equally, and as many people as possible, we need to *override* our empathetic responses—"to draw on a reasoned, even counter-empathetic, analysis of moral obligations and likely consequences."[5]

(d) Bloom says that empathy is presentist; it gives us no reason to help future generations. It tells us not to prevent further climate change, for instance. Actions we take to prevent climate change will hurt many individuals who are here on earth now, and with whom we can therefore empathize. By contrast, "the millions or billions of people who at some unspecified future date will suffer the consequences of our current inaction are . . . pale statistical abstractions." Empathy can get no grip on them (*AEB* 126).

There is a fairly easy Smithian response to each of these points. In making the case for (a) and (b), Bloom takes "degree of empathy" to mean the degree of *intensity* with which we feel empathy. That's not the only way to give degrees to empathy, however. We might be concerned instead with the *precision* of empathy—the degree to which our feelings for another aptly fit the other's situation. Or we might consider the *scope* of empathy: the degree to which we empathize with all parties to a situation rather than just one. It is perfectly natural to describe Joe as more empathetic than Jane if he is better than she at feeling himself into what it might be like to be homeless in New York, or to live under occupation in the West Bank, regardless of how intense his feelings are on behalf of these people. It is equally natural to describe Jane as more empathetic than Joe if she tries harder than he to empathize with the passerby who is frightened by the homeless person as well as with the homeless person himself, or with the Israeli soldier in the West Bank who sees himself as protecting his family as well as with the Occupation's victims. Degree of empathy in either of these senses need not lead to emotional exhaustion—the level at which one feels the pain of others may be a mild one—and in the second case empathy is likely to work against blind vindictiveness rather than promote it. Both precision and scope are more important to Smithian empathy than intensity, however. Smith calls on us to empathize as precisely as possible with others, and with all parties to a conflict, but not to feel their pain with any particular degree of intensity. So Bloom's critique tells against just one dimension of empathy, and not the one of importance to Smith.

As for (c), the point that Bloom misses is that we can empathize with groups via representative individuals in them.[6] We in fact often do this. We see the picture of a single Syrian child washed up on a beach, and that is enough to give us a sense of the suffering that thousands of refugee families are undergoing. The large numbers may indeed matter to us, but they matter to us as a multiplication of *individuals* like this child and his family.

The same idea gives us an answer to (d). A pitch for action on climate change might ask you to imagine a child growing up in 2070 in unbearable heat and amid extreme water shortages and violent conflicts over water and food. Having come, via this imaginative projection, to appreciate the severity of the consequences of climate change, you are now in the position to appreciate its immensity and urgency. Statistics about the numbers of people likely to be affected, and the need for immediate action if the problem is to be avoided, now have a vivid impact on you. We care about the numbers because we care, via empathy, about representative individuals in those numbers— even if we need to imagine those individuals, since they do not yet exist.[7]

I'll return to representative individuals when I come to Prinz, who makes the same criticisms as Bloom about empathy and groups.

3. At the heart of the ways in which Bloom's critique fails to engage with Smith—whom he admires, and quotes effectively at times—lies a conceptual problem. Bloom defines empathy as feeling what you believe someone else is feeling: "coming to experience the world as you think someone else does." (*AEB* 16; see also 35, 39) He also says that this is Smith's definition of empathy (35, 39). But it is not. For Smith, empathy is a matter of feeling what you think *you would* feel if you were in someone else's circumstances, not what you think he or she actually feels. The differences between these two things are subtle but important.

Because Bloom misses the nuances of Smith's definition of empathy, he also misses the differences over empathy between Hume and Smith, generally lumping their accounts together (*AEB* 39, 165). He attributes to Smith the idea that empathy is a kind of "mirroring" of what others feel (150–51), for instance, a notion that suits Hume but not Smith. Bloom seems not to grasp the difference, or at any rate to vastly underestimate the difference, between contagion and projection.

Relatedly, Bloom overstates the degree of emotional identification that Smithian empathy entails. The mirroring he talks of requires that the truly empathetic person will feel just as agonized as you are when you smash your toe into a wall, just as angry as you are when a friend insults you, just as fearful as you are if you are a toddler who is scared of dogs or thunderstorms (*AEB* 43, 141). Perhaps that is true on a contagious account of empathy. The exercise of imaginative projection that Smith describes is likely, however, to result in a cool shadow of your feelings, as Smith himself stresses[8]—sometimes just a twinge of like feeling, sufficient for me to understand the emotion you are experiencing and what has brought that on in you. It is this relatively weak sharing of feelings that Smith regards as essential to our sense of human solidarity and our ability to help one another. He has no interest in the stronger mirroring, which might blind or incapacitate us, that Bloom identifies with empathy. I need some sense of how it feels to be sneered at for one's weight, and how that might differ from being sneered at for one's race, in order to understand what the humiliated person might need from me in these cases; I don't need to feel the same *degree* of humiliation. But in that case, empathy needn't be nearly as exhausting as Bloom suggests. Nor need it be as conducive to sharing the aggressive anger of one with whom we empathize—especially if we also try to empathize with the potential victim of that aggression, as Smith insists we should. Sharing a bit of the feelings of people on all sides of an issue should calm our inclinations to aggression, and mitigate the blindness that full-on identification with a single other might raise in us.

Now the idea that I need to share another person's feelings in order to understand her is something that Bloom rejects. He thinks Smith is wrong to see empathy as simultaneously an affective and a cognitive state. For Smith, we come to understand other people by trying to feel as they would in their circumstances. For Bloom, these are two very different things, and he wants to endorse the importance of the cognitive kind of empathy while siphoning it off from the emotional kind. I think Smith rather than Bloom is correct here. My understanding of others is severely limited if I have no sense of what they feel. If I know *that* you enjoy eating snails or seeing slasher movies, but have no idea of what it would feel like to enjoy those things myself, then I will not regard myself as really understanding your tastes. If I know that you feel humiliated in response to some remark that doesn't seem insulting to me, then I am likely to say, even to myself, "I know *that* she feels humiliated, but I don't understand why." In these and other ways, we generally take affective and cognitive empathy to be closely linked, just as Smith does, and it is only a concept of empathy with these links that can do the work of developing our identity and giving us moral guidance that Smithian empathy accomplishes.[9]

These features of Bloom's account have a number of consequences. The most obvious is that several things he writes off as having nothing to do with empathy will not be independent of empathy for Smith. Bloom says, for instance, that when I care for a child who is afraid of a barking dog, "there's no empathy there [since] I don't feel her fear" (43). But I probably *do* think something along the lines of, "If I were so little, and inexperienced with dogs, I would be afraid too"; and I may recall times when I had that fear, or was afraid of similar things. As a result, I probably do feel at least a twinge of her fear.

And I am unlikely to care sensitively for her otherwise. If I thought she was making a fuss over nothing—as I might well feel regarding other fears she expresses (of the spinach on her plate, perhaps)—I would probably dismiss her reaction impatiently, or offer her a perfunctory gesture meant more to distract than to comfort her. What makes the difference between a gesture like that and true comfort is precisely that I *understand* her fear: and that understanding seems very much to proceed via Smithian empathy, not via a cold awareness of how children work.

Finally, empathy for Smith is the central presupposition and locus of the reflections by which we work out our own and other people's identity, a point Bloom fails to recognize entirely. As we've seen in chapter 2, Smith hovers between urging us to imagine how I would feel *as myself* in your circumstances and how I would feel *as you* in those circumstances. And, on my reconstruction of his views at least, Smith's back-and-forth movement on this point reflects the fact that identity is a loose and ambiguous notion, bound up both with how we see ourselves in relation to others and what we take to be normal modes of human emotion and action in general. I interpret who I am in large part by figuring out my similarities and differences with you, and by understanding both of us in the light of my standard of what human beings in general are and should be like. At the same time, I work out who *you* are, and what my standards for human nature are, by way of my interpretations of myself. My identity, my relationships with others, and my morality are thus interwoven; and at the center of the weave lies empathy.

But if this is right, then empathy of the Smithian variety has an enormous impact on what we think we and other people need, and what we think we should be doing to help others get what they need. That is, what Bloom takes to be obvious—the needs of others that we are called on morally to help meet—is something that I take to be in many cases not obvious at all, and which it takes empathy to figure out. Bloom disguises this from himself by talking almost exclusively about situations in which we can help someone escape a premature death or a debilitating disease. It *is* obvious that none of us wants to die prematurely or suffer terrible illnesses, and that when we can prevent such things, we should. But many of our moral decisions, and most of our most difficult moral decisions, concern far less obvious goods and bads: small tokens of respect from others, or small insults and humiliations, along with a wide range of religious or cultural ends and taboos. To determine which of these things truly *are* goods and bads may well require entering into the perspective of other people. But if so, the cool utilitarianism that Bloom recommends in place of empathy will not be adequate to our moral needs.

4. Let's turn now to Prinz. I'll begin again simply by listing some of his points, this time responding to each one immediately after I describe it.

(a) Prinz thinks it is a mistake to suppose that empathy could possibly constitute moral approval, as—he believes—Hume and Smith suppose.[10] When I approve of your gratitude, I am not myself feeling grateful; when I admire your generosity, I am not myself feeling generous. (*AEP* 217) On the other hand, I may empathize with you while simultaneously disapproving of you. As an example, Prinz gives a recovering pedophile, sharing the feelings of another pedophile while nevertheless condemning those feelings. (218).

Prinz is undoubtedly right about the difference between empathy and approval, but he may not be right to attribute a conflation of the two to Hume.[11] Even if he is, that would not be the right way to read Smith. Smith distinguishes clearly between empathy and moral approval. For Smith, I empathize with you when I feel what I think I *would* feel in your circumstances, not what you actually feel, and I approve of what you actually feel only when it matches up with my empathetic feelings on your behalf. So if you are grateful, and I think I would be grateful in your circumstances, then I approve of your feelings—but my approval is not constituted by my empathetic gratitude, just by my awareness of the match between our feelings. Moreover, this process results in *moral* approval only when it is guided by the impartial spectator. I feel moral approval of your gratitude only if I think an impartial spectator would feel gratitude in your circumstances. If you are grateful that someone murdered your boss, I will not bestow moral approval on your gratitude—even if, having also hated your boss, I share your feelings. This disposes of Prinz's pedophile case. The recovering pedophile does not think that an impartial spectator would share another pedophile's inclinations. Hence he does not morally approve of them.

Relatedly, if we move from a Humean to a Smithean account of empathy, we can make sense of empathy with oneself, which Prinz dismisses as incoherent (*AEP* 219). As we saw in section 7 of chapter 1, I have Smithian empathy for myself when I think my feelings match those that a spectator would have for me. And I have Smithian moral empathy for myself when I think my feelings match those that an *impartial* spectator would have for me. This seems right. Indeed, empathy for oneself seems to be not only coherent but common.

(c) Prinz criticizes empathy for its partiality (*AEP* 223–24, 228–29) and its susceptibility to manipulation (227).[12] In its place, as sources of moral motivation, he recommends anger, disgust, contempt, guilt, and our conditioned negative responses to certain action types.[13] He acknowledges that these other emotions are also "prone to proximity effects," but says that empathy "seems to be *intrinsically* biased" (emphasis added) while the other emotions are not. "Empathy is not a suitable tool for morality," he says. "We can no more overcome its limits than we can ride a bicycle across the ocean; it is designed for local travel" (229).

I am baffled by these claims. Anger, contempt, disgust, and guilt are notoriously biased against out-groups, at least as much as empathy is, and they are probably yet more vulnerable to manipulation.[14] All our emotions are built, in the first instance, "for local travel." We are most angry at people and actions who harm or threaten our local community, and we are most contemptuous of and disgusted at behavior that offends against that community's norms. We feel guilt most intensely when we think of how our family and neighbors might regard our actions, and in response to what they consider wrong. And we get our conditioned negative responses from the local community that has socialized us—which normally leads us to be concerned above all with its welfare. In the environment in which most of our traits originally evolved, we needed all these local feelings to hold together the small groups in which we lived. As we have expanded our social reach, it has been difficult to stretch our emotions so that they concern other human beings at a great distance from ourselves. Why Prinz thinks otherwise is a mystery to me. It is equally a mystery why he thinks there is any greater problem in this regard with empathy than with our other emotions. Indeed, empathy—Smithian empathy, anyway—seems more open, not less, than anger and contempt and disgust to being extended beyond our local circles. We merely need to employ our imaginations more broadly than we are used to doing, to imagine ourselves into the situations of people distant from us.

(d) Prinz half recognizes this last point, but then pulls back from that recognition. "The great efforts that are made to cast [the] net [of empathy] wider [than a local community] have some positive impact, but too often land in the wrong place," he says. Like Bloom, he thinks that these efforts tend to lead us to empathize just with a distant individual here or there, which makes for further inequity:

UTILITARIANISM AND THE LIMITS OF EMPATHY 109

> When we empathize with a person awaiting an organ transplant, we let her jump to the front of the queue, elbowing out many who have been waiting longer. Likewise, an empathetic plea for hunger relief might cause us to send checks to one family rather than a village, or we might help one community, when others are in greater need (*AEP* 228).

There is undoubtedly something to this. It is a common moral mistake to be more concerned about a person whose picture we have seen, or story we have read, than about anonymous other people, let alone large groups of anonymous people. But Prinz misses a crucial feature of how attempts to cast "the net of empathy" more broadly work. The picture of a dead Syrian toddler, face down on a beach after every member of his family except his father had drowned at sea, did not stir up empathy across the world on behalf of *that* family; rather, the child and his father stood in for the masses of Syrian refugees, each one of which could be undergoing or about to undergo a similar tragedy. Novelists have aroused empathy on behalf of slaves or poor workers with fictional accounts of individuals or families, which readers transferred to groups of real people, seeing them in their mind's eye as if every individual in the group were subject to similar conditions. Smith, in passages of the *Wealth of Nations* that seem designed to arouse the reader's empathy for poor people, speaks of *a* mother who doesn't see her children live to maturity, or *a* carpenter who works to the point of exhaustion, without even naming these characters. They stand in for a mass of anonymous strangers, and enable us to empathize with that mass via representative individuals in it.[15] Psychologists have also shown that empathy with a single member of a stigmatized group can improve attitudes toward the entire group.[16] Prinz misses the exemplary role of individual stories in extending our empathetic reach. That exemplary role may misfire, to be sure, such that we care merely for the particular individual who serves as an example. But very often it does not. And it is only in this way that we can appreciate the humanity of members of large groups: we need to take these people one by one, not lump them together. Something similar goes for our anger on behalf of groups, and our contempt and disgust for them. We have contempt or disgust for bigots and drug dealers when we imagine them one by one, and we feel angry on behalf of a group when we feel that its representative individuals, however unknown to us, are deprived of their rights. Human beings en masse may form a lively or frightening feature of the landscape, which we avoid or run to depending on how we feel about crowds. But they do not in themselves call up moral responses.

4. I've given a series of responses to specific claims that Bloom and Prinz make, but the general tenor of their complaints about empathy has much to be said

for it, and their critiques serve as a healthy reminder that empathy alone makes for a poor guide to morality and politics. In saying this, I am not departing from Smith. For all the importance that Smith gives to empathy, he recognizes many of the same moral problems with it that Bloom and Prinz do, and he does not rest his moral and political system on it alone. We'll return in the next two chapters to the wholly unempathetic moral and political system that Bloom and Prinz recommend (Prinz calls for "the extirpation of empathy"),[17] and the deep failings in it from a Smithian point of view. But let's first consider the way Smith places empathy into a larger moral and political scheme.

To begin with, Smith notes several of the concerns about empathy that we have reviewed:

(a) We tend to feel greater empathy with successful and privileged people than with those lower down in the social order. Smith calls this "the great and most universal cause of the corruption of our moral sentiments" (*TMS* I.iii.3.1; 61), stressing that it follows from the nature of empathy as imaginative projection: it is much more pleasant to imagine a situation filled with opportunities for joy than one that conduces to sorrow. Consequently, the rich man rightly supposes that his wealth "naturally draw[s] upon him the attention of the world" while "the poor man goes out and comes in unheeded, and when in the midst of a crowd is in the same obscurity as if shut up in his own hovel." (I.iii.2.1; 51). Smith condemns this tendency in us: "Wealth and greatness," he says, "are often regarded with the respect and admiration which are due only to wisdom and virtue," while "the contempt, of which vice and folly are the only proper objects, is often most unjustly bestowed upon poverty and weakness" (I.iii.3.1, 61–62). But he doesn't think much can be done about it. He may, however, be trying to work against it in the *Wealth of Nations*. When he describes the circumstances of poor people in great detail, and shows how the feelings they have and choices they make are much like those of his well-off readers, his point may be precisely to raise greater empathy for them.[18] If so, his strategy suggests a belief that conscious exercises of empathy can compensate for some of the natural limitations of empathy.

(b) Smith is also aware that empathy tends to be partial, and skewed by prejudice. Like Hume, he stresses the fact that we tend to feel greater empathy for family and neighbors than for people distant from us (*TMS* VI.ii.1.1–8, 219–21). He also discusses the fact that political and religious "fanaticism" and factional rivalries can distort or block our empathy (III.6.12, 176–77; VI.ii.2.15, 232–33). Indeed, his insistence that empathy be filtered through the device of the impartial spectator is meant in part to correct for these distortions. He does not discuss systematic prejudice as we understand it today: standing, subconscious attitudes, widely shared across a culture and fostered by myth and class interests, that demean people because of their racial, sexual, or religious identity. But nothing he says gets in the way of a concern with this sort of prejudice, and his remarks on fanaticism, faction, and the need for impartiality provide a good starting point for an account of it.

(c) Finally, Smith seems well aware that we often need to think about the numbers of people affected by our decisions, and that empathy will not lead us to do that. "Upon some occasions," he says, "we both punish and approve of punishment, merely from a view to the general interest of society," even where no particular person has been harmed. He gives the example of a sentinel who is executed for falling asleep on his watch. The severity of this punishment, he says, "may, upon many occasions, appear necessary, and, for that reason, just and proper" (*TMS* II.ii.3.11, 90). This is a hesitant and much-hedged judgment—Smith seems very uncomfortable with it—but there is no doubt that it is his settled view. And later in the book, Smith says explicitly that the utility of a system of practice is one factor, if perhaps the least important—it comes "last of all" in a list of four—in our evaluation of actions (VII.iii.3.16, 326).

6. So Smith recognizes that empathy alone cannot supply us with adequate moral guidance. Instead, he embeds empathy in a wider moral theory in which it is shaped and checked by the judgments of an impartial spectator, the application of general rules, and a realistic, careful appreciation of the often utilitarian workings of large-scale social institutions. Indeed, Smith's *Lectures on Jurisprudence* and *Wealth of Nations* provide us with a superb model for how to supplement empathy with general moral and legal rules, and a detailed attention to institution building. The *Wealth of Nations* is nothing if not an exercise in the dispassionate analysis of social structures, which considers the costs and benefits of various policies in great detail. Yet empathy is not absent from this project. Smith's institutional proposals regarding the poor, especially, are deeply informed by empathy with their situation.

A few examples:

(a) Smith urges that homes be taxed by the number of their windows rather than the number of their hearths, because a tax gatherer needs to enter every room in a house to determine how many hearths it has, while the number of its windows can be counted from the outside (*WN* V.ii.e.16–17, 845–46). To see how important the difference is between these two things, we need to enter in imagination into the situation of the person who has to open his home to an unwelcome official, and share the feelings that such a visit is likely to bring on.

(b) In the course of a consideration of luxury taxes, Smith notes that a linen shirt "is, strictly speaking, not a necessary of life. . . . But in the present times, . . . a creditable day-labourer would be ashamed to appear in public without a linen shirt, the want of which, it is presumed, no body can well fall into without extreme bad conduct" (*WN* V.ii.k.3, 870). We are brought closely into the day laborer's situation here—down to the symbolic significance, for him, of the want of a shirt. The point, presumably, is for us to be led from this empathy to an empathetic caring, out of which we will oppose a tax on the shirts of laborers. This attention to the nuanced effects of social policies, by way of empathy with everyone who experiences those effects, helps make the policies fairer. Empathy thus operates as a valuable constraint on our thinking about large-scale social structures, even if it cannot alone tell us how to carry out that thinking. And the relevant kind of empathy is an attempt to enter the situation of *each* person affected by the policy in question, not—even if that were possible—to add up the policy's pleasurable and painful effects on everyone involved, and then weigh them against each other.[19]

(c) Smith opposes taxes on liquor in his *Lectures on Jurisprudence*,[20] saying that "man is an anxious animal and must have his care swept off by something that can exhilarate the spirits" (*LJ* [B] 231; 497); he also suggests that a good educational system will provide a poor child with "ideas with which he can amuse himself" instead of "betak[ing] himself to drunkenness" (*LJ* [B] 330; 540). Drunkenness among the poor was a long-standing concern in early modern Britain,[21] but most policy makers were concerned just about how to control it: how to prevent people from engaging in it, or how to punish them when they did. Smith thinks himself instead into the heads of poor people, and sees from that perspective why drink might be attractive to them. That leads him to proposals for helping them overcome alcoholism that they themselves might endorse—that do not treat them as mere *objects* of policy, but as fellow agents with their own legitimate needs and interests.

(d) Something similar goes for Smith's treatment of another long-standing complaint about the English poor: that they were lazy, unwilling to work more than four days a week. Smith says about this that "excessive application during four days of the week is frequently the cause of the idleness of the other three."[22] *Most* people, he says—which is to say most well-off people, as well as most poor people—will be exhausted by "great labour . . . continued for several days together," and will feel a desire to relax: a desire so strong that "if not restrained by force or by some strong necessity, [it] is almost irresistible." Masters who "listen to the dictates of reason and humanity" should therefore "moderate, rather than . . . animate the application of many of their workmen." Once again, Smith thinks himself into the position of poor laborers rather than viewing them from above or outside, as objects to be controlled.

And once again, that leads him to more humane proposals for how to handle social problems concerning them.

7. One thing that these uses of empathy in the *Wealth of Nations* should make clear is that there is rich continuity between Smith's two great treatises, not the gulf that some have seen between them. The fact that the *Theory of Moral Sentiments* is taught in moral philosophy classes while the *Wealth of Nations* is read in classes on political economy, along with the supposed "Adam Smith Problem" invented by scholarly commentators in the late nineteenth century, have given many the impression that the *Theory of Moral Sentiments* presents people as empathetic and benevolent while the *Wealth of Nations* assumes that people are driven exclusively by self-interest.[23] This is a mistake on many levels.[24] For one thing, Smith gives self-interest exactly the same role in the economic realm as did his teacher Frances Hutcheson, the greatest proponent of benevolence in the eighteenth century. For another, the capacity for projecting ourselves into the lives of others, as analyzed in the *Theory of Moral Sentiments*, appears both explicitly and implicitly in the *Wealth of Nations*. Its most explicit appearance comes during a discussion of why poor people in large cities tend to be drawn to moralistic religious sects (*WN* V.i.g.12; 795–96). The poor person, Smith says there, is constantly observed and "attended to" if he lives in the country, and is therefore likely to hold himself to high moral standards. But when he moves to a large city, "he is sunk in obscurity and darkness. His conduct is observed and attended to by nobody, and he is therefore very likely to neglect it himself." Only when he joins a small religious sect does he have people around him who watch what he does and care about it, thereby leading him to care about it himself. The empathetic interplay between spectator and agent central to the *Theory of Moral Sentiments* runs through this account, and it leads the agents in question to an empathetic interplay with themselves, and a consequent moral development, that also recalls the *Theory of Moral Sentiments*.

This empathetic interplay also underlies the passages from the *Wealth of Nations* about hearth taxes and linen shirts, quoted above. But the most important role that empathy plays in the *Wealth of Nations* is the implicit one of underwriting Smith's entire view of economic activity. Consider the famous passage in which Smith tells us that, when buying meat from our butcher or bread from our baker, "we address ourselves . . . to their self-love" (*WN* I.ii.2, 27). The point of this line, as Smith makes clear in the rest of the paragraph in which it appears, is that we know *how* to appeal to others' self-love, not that they or we are self-loving. It is the capacity for understanding other people's self-interest, not a tendency to pursue our own self-interest, that Smith thinks "is . . . to be found in no other race of animals" (I.ii.2, 26). Other animals also pursue their own interest; they just don't know how to share that pursuit with one another. And it is sharing interests, not being self-interested, that stands at the center of Smith's discussion of the butcher and the baker. The butcher and baker's customer may be buying food for her family, for a neighborhood party, or for a local soup kitchen; nothing about this passage suggests that she need be getting it for selfish purposes. Nor does the passage say that the butcher or baker himself is selfish: it assumes simply that he is unlikely to give meat or bread to his *customers* out of benevolence. Which is to say, the *context of economic transaction* is one in which we appeal to one another's self-love rather than one another's benevolence.[25] But even here, it is our capacity to *understand* one another's self-love, not to *be* self-loving, that enables us, unlike other animals, to engage in such transactions.[26]

Of course, the awareness that the butcher and his customer have of one another when exchanging meat for money can and often will involve a minimal, cold, perspective-taking rather than the robust imaginative and emotional interaction characteristic of Smithian empathy. Yet even this minimal perspective-taking requires some of the skills that go into the more robust kind of empathy. Moreover, in the sorts of relationships between shopkeepers and customers with which Smith was acquainted—in small-town neighborhoods, where most customers were "regulars" at one place or another—the exchange of goods for money was usually nested in more extensive friendly banter, which called on more robust sorts of empathy. ("And how are things with you, Mr. Smith? Still writing that long book?") That was even more true, and remains true today, of relationships between business partners, or representatives of firms that work with one another. A robust empathy, even in the economic realm, tends to be both necessary to long-term exchange relationships and a common result of such relationships. Certainly Smith thinks so. He says explicitly, as we saw in chapter 5, section 3, that "colleagues in office, partners in trade, call one another brothers; and frequently feel towards one another as if they really were so" (*TMS* Vi.ii.1.15, 224)—accounting for this feeling, as he does for family affection, by way of "habitual sympathy." So for Smith, empathy in a fairly full-bodied sense drives economic activity. And even in the butcher/baker paragraph of the *Wealth of Nations* it is empathy, not self-interest, that distinguishes and defines humanity. The *Wealth of Nations* and the *Theory of Moral Sentiments* are united on that point.[27]

That said, we have seen that Smith is also clear in the *Wealth of Nations* that empathy alone cannot guide policy; most of that book makes a broadly utilitarian case for various policies and institutions. Empathy comes into the

Wealth of Nations above all when Smith discusses the poor: a despised and neglected group, respect and concern for whom Smith needed to arouse in his mostly well-off readers.[28] This provides the core of a Smithian answer to Prinz and Bloom. Empathy alone may be an inadequate foundation for morality and politics. But it nevertheless contributes a crucial element to our moral and political thinking—crucial, in particular, to the humane treatment of people we might otherwise ignore or contemn. We'll explore this point in the next chapter.

7

Empathy and the Limits of Utilitarianism (I)

1. Bloom and Prinz want us to rely strictly on utilitarian calculations when designing policy. This is seriously wrongheaded, I believe. We can indeed best appreciate the role that empathy can play in moral and political theory by examining the failings of utilitarianism.

Consider what the object of moral assessment looks like for Prinz, once he has stripped empathy away. "What makes an action wrong in cases where empathy is invoked is the harm it causes," he says, "not our vicarious experience of that harm." And "what makes an action good is the pleasures it brings to beneficiaries of that action." (*AEP* 225) We should consider these harms and pleasures, we should do "cost-benefit analysis," and look for "the greatest long-term payoffs" of our actions, in order to figure out what to do (228).

This turn to a bald utilitarianism—as if the thoroughgoing critiques of utilitarianism by Bernard Williams, John Rawls, Alasdair MacIntyre, John McDowell, Charles Taylor, and many others had never been written—is breathtaking. Setting aside the many complaints one could launch against it, let's focus just on what is implied when Prinz draws our attention to the "harm" caused by an action, as opposed to our vicarious experience of that harm. He is right, of course, that our vicarious experience of harm does nothing to *make* an action wrong. But in his call for an "extirpation of empathy," (*AEP* 228) and a replacement of it by cost-benefit analysis, he wrongly indicates, also, that we can figure out what counts as harm perfectly well without feeling our way into other people's situations.

Of course in some cases we can do that. Cass Sunstein has argued that cost-benefit analysis is a superb tool for cutting through various cognitive errors and biases to which we are prone when assessing the facts relevant to policy decisions.[1] He is undoubtedly right about this. But it is no accident, I think, that all Sunstein's examples come from the realms of health and environmental regulation.[2] Regarding many other moral and political issues, we cannot so much as figure out what the relevant costs and benefits *are* without empathy. If we "extirpated" empathy, as Prinz wants us to do, would we even know what to count as a "harm" to minimize, or a "benefit" to maximize?

Prinz makes things worse for himself by crudely equating benefits with "pleasures." There are many things we regard as goods that bring more pain than pleasure (running a marathon, watching a great tragic play, attending the funeral of a loved one), and many others in which pleasure plays a negligible role. These are just some of the many problems that philosophers have pointed out, for decades now, with hedonic accounts of the human good like Prinz's.[3] And nonhedonic accounts of the good often give empathy a large role in helping us to recognize what is good. Martha Nussbaum, for instance, identifies the goods we seek with eudaimonia or "flourishing," and cashes that term out in terms of the things that "occasion a strong emotion in us" because they correspond to "what we have invested with importance in our thoughts, implicit or explicit, about what is important in life."[4] This is a much deeper and more plausible view than Prinz's, but perhaps it builds empathy too much into the very definition of a good to set it up against Prinz's view. It is obvious, after all, that for someone else to appreciate "what we have invested with importance," he or she will have to empathize with us. Is there a way of getting at "benefits" or "goods" that does not beg the question of whether we can recognize these things without empathy? Perhaps, but most accounts of which I am aware do tend either to suffer from the crudity of Prinz's hedonism or to call on empathy in the criteria they set for counting something as a good. Let's therefore set "goods" aside, and focus instead on harms, which we might think *must* be recognizable without empathy.

2. So what is a harm? In many cases, that seems easy to answer. Death, physical injury, hunger—these things are easy to determine by empirical observation alone. We all also know what's wrong with them, and that they are terrible for all human beings. We don't need empathy to know this; we just need experience, and very little of that.

But other harms are harder to determine without empathy. I remember once hearing about a scholarship to college for poor people that was set up in such a way that it could not go toward tuition or room and board. My first instinct was to think that this was a ridiculous constraint. What else does a poor college student need, if tuition and room and board are covered? Chocolate? Beer? A sweatshirt with the school logo? But the person explaining the point of the scholarship then mentioned a student who had dropped out of college because he didn't have money to do laundry regularly, and was ashamed to go to class in dirty clothes. That suddenly opened up for me a world of small details in the life of a poor person that can make for humiliation. And I could see these things *as* harms because—and, I think, *only* because—I could imagine myself into such a life and recognize how I would feel there. (Recall here how particularist Smithian empathy is: if goods and harms depend greatly on details of context, as they often do, then empathy of the Smithian kind is precisely the right organ to pick them up.)

Another example is the recent debate over whether transgender people should be able to use bathrooms reserved for people with the gender with which they identify. Sometimes the harm associated with a transgender woman's having to use a man's bathroom is ascribed to the danger of violence from men who hate transgender people, but often it is said to be an infringement of the person in question's dignity or sense of self. Exactly what that means, and why it is a serious harm, is very difficult to grasp without imagining oneself into the way that transgender people experience the world.

A slightly different situation arises if we consider the Bengali widows who described their health to the All-India Institute of Hygiene and Public Health in favorable terms far more often than local widowers did, even while objective measures showed them to be in far poorer health. A plausible explanation for this discrepancy is that the traditional culture in these areas discourages women from complaining—or even seeing their lives as worthy of complaint—while encouraging men to voice their unhappiness with things as much as they like.[5] Here there are certainly harms that we can appreciate without empathy. It's obvious enough that illness is a harm, and that keeping quiet about one's illnesses, let alone failing to recognize them, is likely to make them worse. But the *explanation* of why these women keep quiet about, or fail to recognize, their illnesses requires an understanding of their cultural milieu, which in turn depends on empathy. Only imagining oneself into a world in which attempts to stand up for one's own well-being are regarded as a betrayal of one's role can help one understand why these women put up with or internalize their oppressive situation.

3. Now consider another, more complicated example, from E. M. Forster's richly empathetic *Passage to India*. Dr. Aziz, the British-educated Indian doctor who aspires to the culture and habits of his imperial rulers, has just heard his new friend Fielding curse at having broken his last collar stud. Aziz offers to help, falsely assuring his friend that he has a spare stud, and stepping into the shadows so that he can remove the back stud from his own collar. Fielding doesn't notice the deception, and Aziz, delighted, is able to help build their

EMPATHY AND THE LIMITS OF UTILITARIANISM (I)

new friendship. A while later, Aziz and Fielding encounter Ronny Heaslop, one of the novel's stuffiest, most bigoted characters. Afterward, in the course of an irritated conversation with his fiancée, Heaslop notes that "Aziz [had been] exquisitely dressed, from tie-pin to spats, but he had forgotten his back collar-stud." This Heaslop considers exemplary of Indian culture as a whole: "There you have the Indian all over: inattention to detail; the fundamental slackness that reveals the race."[6] The possibility that anything *but* "slackness" could have explained Aziz's missing collar stud—forget generosity; perhaps *Aziz* had broken his last collar stud—does not even occur to Heaslop. And the reader instantly becomes aware of another kind of exemplarity: of how typical this incident must have been of the arrogant dismissal of Indians by the English, and of how difficult it was for even an Indian with a thorough British education, and a strong desire to get along with the British, to break through that arrogance. In this tiny vignette, the gross harm to human dignity inflicted by the British Empire as a whole on India is wonderfully encapsulated.

Several things to note about this example:

First, I pick this incident in the novel rather than the horrific one at its heart partly because in the latter case, the harm in question is easy to see—whether that be sexual assault or a false accusation of assault—while it is not easy to imagine how one could recognize Heaslop's dismissal of Aziz as a harm without empathy. Many English people in fact did not perceive casual bigotry like this as a harm to Indians until quite late in the history of the British Empire: in good part because they were fixated on cost-benefit analysis and pointed out (correctly) that they had brought modern infrastructure and schools to India, and helped develop its economy. Utilitarians notoriously offered justifications for the Empire (not least in the person of John Stuart Mill); in other places and times, utilitarians have justified other empires, the unconstrained expansion of Western capitalism, and the work of culturally insensitive nongovernmental organizations (NGOs). It was the efforts of writers like Forster (and Conrad and Orwell and Somerset Maugham) that most helped counter this utilitarian mindset regarding the Empire—just as Dickens earlier had helped counter it in regard to poor workers, in *Oliver Twist* and *Hard Times*.[7] It takes the detailed placing of oneself in the circumstances of others that only novelists and long-form journalists carry out to see what goes wrong with projects that involve subtle oppression. And writings of this sort succeed, when they do, if and only if they manage to get the reader to feel the humiliation or uprootedness of the people affected by these projects: to have Smithian empathy for them.[8]

Second, part of what is going on in the episode we are considering is that Aziz's act of generosity to Fielding was something that no self-respecting

Englishman at the time would have been likely to carry out. Growing up in England myself, forty years later, I was acculturated into a world in which norms of decorum were adhered to largely in the spirit of the admonition that airline staff give to their passengers about putting on oxygen masks: take care of yourself first, and then worry about anyone else who might need help. Even Fielding, the most morally attractive character in the novel, would never himself have disrupted the propriety of his own evening dress in order to help a friend. Aziz's concern for his friend thus shows his *failure* fully to grasp a norm of the English society he so much wants to enter. And the reader of the novel is supposed to grasp both this fact about Aziz and the sweet, misguided generosity that blocks him from grasping the norm—and thus to feel an especially sharp empathetic twinge of pain when the consequence of his generosity is to render him vulnerable to Heaslop's contempt.

Third, Heaslop's remark accurately represents the attitude that most Englishmen, and especially most English officials, had toward Indians at the time. It shows the complete failure of the British to come anywhere close to imagining the motivations actually at work among the people they ruled—of imagining, for example, that generosity might override a concern with propriety for them. So the remark is a gross failure of empathy on Heaslop's part. But the reader of the novel is supposed to be able, by way of Heaslop's lack of empathy, to widen his or her own empathetic horizon. Precisely because Heaslop's reaction is so familiar—something that an English reader should be able to understand very well—but at the same time so ill-suited to the actual facts of the situation, the reader is invited to explore what goes into his or her own generalizations about Indians, and wonder whether, when he has thought or acted like Heaslop, he has similarly failed to understand an Aziz.

Of course today, in the twenty-first century, readers of *A Passage to India* can congratulate themselves on not being anything like Heaslop, and on having known everything that Forster has to tell them long before they came across the book. But that is easy only because India's struggle for independence is long over, and attention to the subaltern point of view has become an intellectual fad. It was not easy in the 1920s; Forster was remarkably empathetic with Indians for his time, and remarkably good at evoking empathy for them in a population disinclined in that direction. Only when we recognize this can we understand the power of *Passage to India* in its time. Forster was one of the first to help his countrymen understand what sort of harm their nation was inflicting on another people: what sort of harm they were inflicting on those people's dignity, especially. He helped them see harms that were hitherto invisible to them—helped them come to a new understanding of what *counted* as a harm.[9]

EMPATHY AND THE LIMITS OF UTILITARIANISM (I)

It's not accidental that several of the examples I've given concern harm to dignity, something that is particularly hard to grasp without entering into how the person affected sees him or herself. But these are a significant subset of the harms we suffer, often looming larger for us than physical harms or material losses, when we look back on our lives.

4. I don't mean to deny that statistical data of various sorts might be useful even in connection with the sorts of harms I've just described. One might wonder, for instance, how widespread the laundry problem at college and similar small threats to dignity among poor students really are; survey data will be essential to answering that question. One might also wonder how deep the wound to dignity goes in the transgender case—how many transgender people actually worry about bathroom use, and how much of a problem they consider using the inapt bathroom to be. Survey data can again be useful here. Statistical information is also important to the very presentation of the gap between the actual health and the self-reported health among Bengali women.

Still, empathy gives us our first cue that there are problems to worry about in these cases; it helps us figure out what questions to put on our surveys. Empathy will often be needed as well, to interpret the data we collect. When we ask transgender people how much they mind using the wrong bathroom, some may say they don't really mind it much, out of discomfort with the question, or out of fear that they will look like a "whiner" if they express strong feelings about it. Others may, on the other hand, proclaim a greater anger than they really feel, out of a sense of solidarity with those who have made the issue an important cause. Interpreting the answers we get will therefore require an attempt to think ourselves into the position of the people we are surveying.

Something similar, probably stronger, goes for asking women who have been acculturated to not complain about illness whether they are repressing their feelings out of fear of what people will say. Depending on how deep the acculturation goes, we may simply prompt the factors that lead them to keep quiet about their illnesses in the first place. Or we may prompt or encourage a spirit of rebellion against their culture that leads them to exaggerate their repression. Further survey information and other objective data aimed at overcoming these limitations will often be open to the same ambiguities. I see no good way of interpreting the information we collect so as to approximate the impact of these women's perspectives on what they say without some degree of empathy.

5. This last point about survey data brings out the fact that relying on empathy to determine harm is not the same as relying on self-reporting or any other

direct expression of preferences. If I ask you, a transgender person or a traditional woman in a sexist culture, what serious harms you face, I may well *not* turn up some of the harms that empathy would reveal to me. Nor will I necessarily pick up those harms by looking at your choices as a consumer or voter. You may use the bathroom you'd rather not use because it's the most convenient one available to you, or because you fear the hassle of using one that will bring on other people's disapproval. You may not consult a doctor even when you should, because you feel pressed by other things you need to take care of, or because you have internalized an "I'm never sick" mentality. You may also vote for candidates who will do nothing to alleviate the things that harm you because there are other issues you care more about, or because you are uncertain what the candidates stand for—or, again, because you have internalized a view that makes it difficult for you to recognize the harms being done to you.[10]

In short, because people's choices reflect a multitude of preferences and it is never easy to determine which of them plays the primary role in a particular choice, because people are often misinformed about the options open to them or fail in various ways to understand the information they do have, and because people frequently accept views leading them to repress the fact that something harms them, or fail to recognize that it does, the empathetic understanding of an outsider may pick up harms that the person principally concerned does not recognize herself.[11]

6. We've seen that cases in which empathy is needed to recognize a harm prominently include harms to dignity, an elusive good that cannot be readily measured. We've also seen, in the example of the Bengali widows, that empathy can be valuable even as regards physical harm. Sometimes recognizing that such harm has occurred requires cutting through prejudice and self-deception.

A third category that empathy can help us recognize is harm that can be seen as such only through the importance of a cultural worldview. I'm not confident that drawings of Muhammad should count as a harm to Muslims. Many Muslims certainly feel *pain* when they hear about such things, but people feel pain in response to many things—the success of a rival, the sight of an interracial couple—not all of which count as harms. But those of us who are not Muslim have no hope of appreciating why such drawings *might* count as a harm except via an empathetic understanding of what a devout Muslim life is like, and how and why people are drawn to such a life. Objective facts about Islam—an account of what it teaches, and the reasons given for those teachings—will not be enough. With an account of this sort in hand, we might simply regard the religion, or the aspect of it that bans drawings of its prophet, as absurd. Only grasping how and why people come to love Islam, only seeing how we ourselves might do that, can give us insight into why they accept its teachings on blasphemy.

The same goes for understanding any harm (or good) that depends on a project we don't ourselves share. A devout Christian or Hindu, a convinced Cornish or Tamil nationalist, a person fervently committed to Italian opera or punk rock, will see certain things as great harms that appear trivial to others. Only empathy—understood, as always, in the Smithian manner—will give others so much as a glimmer of insight into why a person might care so much about the desecration of the host, the disappearance of the Cornish language, or the closing of a bel canto festival.

7. I've thus far mostly appealed to intuitions to suggest that we cannot understand certain harms without Smithian empathy. What exactly might it be about such empathy that helps us out in these cases?

Well, in the first place, Smithian empathy is particularist—we must enter into "the whole case of our companion with all its *minutest* incidents," Smith tells us—and that is precisely what is needed to grasp what is going on in the Aziz example: precisely why it takes a novelist (or a journalist or social scientist willing to play out cases with the detail of a novel) to bring out the situation in question. Smithian empathy focuses us on the details that differentiate each person's situation from other situations, or that differentiate that person from other people who live through similar situations. But we are highly differentiated creatures, attentive to the fine differences among things we experience and attached to the differences between us and other people. A dog might eat just anything; we don't. We care greatly about the particular sufferings and joys we have gone through, and the particular desires and aspirations we have as a result. So grasping the details of our characters and our situations is crucial to understanding what makes for our happiness or well-being.

Second, and relatedly, empathy enables us to appreciate and take seriously one another's cultural and historical placement. Among the factors that most importantly differentiate us are the cultural and historical conditions in which we have been formed. If we try honestly to enter one another's perspectives as fully as possible, we cannot but take note of and try to understand these cultural and historical factors (layering, here, Herderian empathy onto our Smithian empathy; see chapter 4, above). But we are cultural and historical creatures as much as we are particularistic ones—our cultures and histories do much to distinguish us and our various situations—so grasping these factors is again crucial to understanding what makes for happiness or well-being for each of us. As the Aziz incident illustrates, we cannot so much as figure out what others are doing, let alone what might count as a harm to their dignity, without this cultural and historical sensitivity.

Finally, only via empathy can we grasp how things appear as *good* to others, rather than just as pleasant or desirable. Only by entering others' perspectives can we see what they *approve* of and why, rather than just what they like or seek; only in this way can we see the interlacing of their bare favorable attitudes with their ethical outlook. But to cut people's feelings and preferences off from their ethical outlook is to strip them of all that makes their feelings and preferences *matter* to them—all that gives us reason to attribute ethical significance to those feelings and preferences. I may enjoy getting drunk, but feel ashamed of myself when I do; I may desire to be accepted by an "in-group" around me, but wish I didn't desire that. By the same token, I may wish I enjoyed art more, or could work up more enthusiasm for certain religious activities. It is the mesh between my pleasures and my evaluative perspective that determines what I regard as integral to my true happiness or well-being, just as it is the mesh between pain and my evaluative perspective that determines what I regard to be a serious insult or injury (think here of the transgender bathrooms, and drawings of Muhammad). Only empathy gives us a grasp of this mesh. Only empathy, then, can give us access to the well-being of a person, as that person conceives it.

8. Empathy can play an especially crucial moral role in leading us to respect the views and promote the well-being of others whom we regard as enemies, or as very alien to us. Acting on principle need not lead us to a true respect and concern for such people, nor will a purely theoretical belief in solidarity with the oppressed do that. Kant notoriously held sexist, racist, and anti-Semitic views despite his noble profession of the absolute and equal value of every human being; and principled but prejudiced Kantians have hardly been unknown since his day. Divine-command theorists are often equally blind to ways in which their principles are cruel and unfair to groups who don't share their conception of the divine, and Marxists have indulged in gross violence and cruelty to members of groups they consider privileged. What goes wrong in all these cases seems clearly to be a lack of empathetic concern for the members of certain groups—oppressed or privileged, as the case may be—not a failure of reasoning, or a weakness of the will. The problem is not even a lack of moral emotions; just a lack of the mode of *sharing* emotions that leads us to understand other people from within their own perspectives.

My own attitudes toward people very different from myself have changed most when I have read imaginative literature putting me into their shoes. I felt that I finally understood what is appealing to Christians about Christianity

EMPATHY AND THE LIMITS OF UTILITARIANISM (I)

when I read Dostoevsky's *The Idiot* and *Brothers Karamazov*, what draws Hindus to Hinduism when I read R. K. Narayan's *The English Teacher*, what is appealing to Muslims about Islam when I read Salman Rushdie's *The Satanic Verses* (ironically, since the book has been widely taken to be an attack on Islam; I think that is a mistake). It took Athol Fugard's *Master Harold . . . and the Boys* to make the horrific indignity of apartheid fully clear to me, and Sayed Kashua's *Second Person Singular* to bring home to me the humiliation and frustration of being an Israeli Arab. No theoretical description of other religions has ever been able to get me into the perspective of people who embrace them as deeply as fiction has, and no general invocation of the importance of human rights has enabled me really to understand the issues that affect oppressed people until I was brought into their perspectives via fiction. This fits in with the value of fiction for raising empathy, which we noted earlier.[12]

Correlatively, the people I've known who are kind to members of their own community while countenancing brutality to outsiders have seemed to be limited above all in their empathetic concern. They are by no means without principle, nor do they lack the ability to care for others. What they lack, regarding members of the groups they despise, is empathy. They either do not try to enter the situation of these others, or they front-load any such exercise with prejudices and ideological commitments that block them from properly imagining those situations. It is no accident that when they do soften their positions, it is because they have had an opportunity to listen closely to the stories of those others. Groups like Breaking the Silence and the Bereaved Parents' Circle testify to the value of this sort of exercise in connection with the Israel/Palestine conflict, as do reports of Palestinians who have visited Auschwitz.[13]

Of course, this motley of anecdotal evidence falls far short of a full case for the value of empathetic concern. I cannot supply such a case—I am not a psychologist or historian—but there are some general considerations that favor it. Above all, we are creatures driven by emotion more than reason (there are good evolutionary reasons why that should be so),[14] and emotions are aroused more by particular cases than by general concerns. When we do get caught up in reasoning from principle, the abstraction of our thinking tends to turn off or submerge the emotional responses that would enable us to recognize that we are implicitly weighing the needs of one person or one group of people differently from the needs of other people. So we should not be surprised if Kantians can uphold principles proclaiming the equality of all human beings while failing to notice that they are actually demonstrating sexism or racism, or if Marxists and devotees of one or another religious ideology can be uninterested in the fate of particular people, or blind to the baleful effects of their movements on whole groups of people. A dose of Smithian empathy, by way of novels or personal experience, can get at what these rationalist views do not reach. Books like *Uncle Tom's Cabin* and *A Passage to India* are said to have had a far greater impact on policy than any philosophical argument against slavery or colonialism.[15] I indicated in the previous chapter, and have argued elsewhere, that Smith's *Wealth of Nations* did something similar for attitudes and policies toward the poor: that in the *Wealth of Nations* Smith uses the techniques of arousing empathy he had described in the *Theory of Moral Sentiments* to put his well-off readers into the situation of poor people, and that these exercises in fact did a great deal to change commonly held pictures of poor people.[16] Whether or not this is true of the *Wealth of Nations*, it certainly seems to have been true of the novels of Dickens, Zola, and Steinbeck, which brought readers, in imagination, vividly into the lives of the poor.[17]

9. The points I've made in this chapter can be seen as having either small or large implications for the sort of utilitarian agenda favored by Prinz and Bloom. Even those who find these points persuasive, and think they show that we need empathy in order to recognize certain harms and benefits, may suppose that that requires but a small modification to the utilitarian program. Initially, we need to use empathy to recognize certain harms, they may say—we need to understand the seriousness of the offense to transgender people, say, if they have to use a bathroom of their birth gender—and then we can put on our maximization caps and calculate how best to prevent such harms. Something similar goes for the other cases. Empathy will give us initial access to a kind of harm we had hitherto not noticed, and we can then plug that harm into our utilitarian calculus.

A more robust challenge to utilitarianism arises if, as I tried to suggest by way of the episode from *Passage to India*, certain harms and benefits are so inextricably bound up with the context in which they arise that they will never fit into a utilitarian calculus. Jonathan Dancy has argued that reasoning is always indexed to context. Reason is holistic, he argues, and the relevance of a particular reason to a decision in one context depends on its relations to all the other reasons that arise in that context. So there cannot, even in principle, be a general formula to tell us how we should make our decisions.[18] I would not go this far, although I do think it is wrong to suppose that moral reasoning must take the form of a maximizing formula. And I think the goods and harms relevant to many moral judgments have such a particularist structure that nothing but Smithian empathy can give us access to them.[19] That is enough to suggest that the utilitarian approach to moral problems will often go wrong.

EMPATHY AND THE LIMITS OF UTILITARIANISM (I)

But there is a yet stronger challenge we can pose to utilitarianism, in the name of an ethical outlook rooted in empathy: we may ask whether there really is any single thing that all human beings want called "happiness," which we can hope even approximately to calculate, let alone to distribute such that as many people as possible achieve as much as possible of it. I'll explore that challenge in the next chapter. We'll then begin to see how empathy can thoroughly restructure our approach to moral theory.

8

Empathy and the Limits of Utilitarianism (II)

1. Utilitarianism has been subject to withering criticism over the past forty years or so. There is a Kantian line of critique, emphasizing the inability of utilitarianism "to take seriously the distinction between persons," as John Rawls put it.[1] There are virtue theorists—Alasdair MacIntyre, John McDowell, Rosalind Hursthouse—who have taken aim at the utilitarian account of decision making, at its emphasis on action rather than character, and at its conception of happiness. There are neo-Platonists, like Charles Taylor and Robert Adams, who similarly reject the utilitarian account of agency and its view of the good. There are intuitionists (Derek Parfit, Judith Jarvis Thomson) who think that utilitarianism at best tells only part of the story about what we value and how we make moral decisions. And at the beginning of this onslaught there was Bernard Williams's "Critique of Utilitarianism," which anticipated practically all of these lines of criticism.[2]

Yet utilitarianism has been making a comeback. Popular books by moral psychologists with some philosophical training, like Joshua Greene's *Moral Tribes* and Jonathan Haidt's *The Righteous Mind*, openly endorse utilitarianism.[3] We've seen that Paul Bloom and Jesse Prinz also argue for a return to utilitarianism. And Peter Singer, the radical utilitarian once regarded in the discipline of philosophy as a clever but curious leftover from a bygone age, has become perhaps the world's best known moral philosopher.[4]

Greene grounds his case for a return to utilitarianism on our need to find a "common currency" by which to commensurate the various goals and ideals we acquire when we are socialized into our "moral tribes."[5] A utilitarian calculation of the costs and benefits of our decisions is the only way for us to base our moral decisions on reason, he thinks; otherwise we will be guided just by immediate emotions and impulses. There is much to object to

EMPATHY AND THE LIMITS OF UTILITARIANISM (II) 129

in Greene's view of reasoning. He seems not to understand Kantian reasoning or the philosophical arguments for engaging in it,[6] and wholly unaware of the kind of reasoning that goes into virtue ethics.[7] That said, his call for a common moral currency has much to recommend it. Bentham's original turn to a hedonic calculus was in good part motivated by a similar search for such a currency,[8] and it is true that we need something, in making public policy at least, to bring together our disparate sources of moral judgment. But utilitarianism does not do a good job at providing us with that something. An approach that employs empathy can improve on it.

2. Before laying out what this alternative might look like, let's explore two problems with utilitarianism in more detail. One is its definition of happiness. The other is its elitism—its unsuitedness to policy debates in a liberal democracy.

To begin with the latter: Bernard Williams gestured at this problem by coining the phrase, redolent with empire, "Government House utilitarianism."[9] The coinage hit home, since the bureaucracy of the British Empire did in fact use utilitarian principles to justify its paternalistic attitudes toward the people it controlled. Williams may indeed have had John Stuart Mill in mind—an employee of the British East India Company for much of his life, and a prominent advocate of top-down policies for the British to use in India—but many other utilitarians also filled the administration of the British Empire. A particularly apt example of the kind of thing Williams was addressing comes out, however, in these lines from someone who was not an employee of the Crown—Mill's philosophical successor, Henry Sidgwick:

> It may be desirable that Common Sense should repudiate [those utilitarian] doctrines which it is expedient to confine to an enlightened few. And thus a Utilitarian may reasonably desire, on Utilitarian principles, that some of his conclusions should be rejected by mankind generally; or even that the vulgar should keep aloof from his system as a whole, in so far as the inevitable indefiniteness and complexity of its calculations render it likely to lead to bad results in their hands.[10]

The greatest happiness for the greatest number may be attainable, says Sidgwick, only if most of that number don't know what is being done on their behalf. This is clearly true if we need to commit acts of injustice or dishonesty in order to maximize happiness, but it may even be true for a utilitarian who accepts side constraints to rule out such acts. For as long as we mean by "happiness" something other than what the agents with whom we are concerned mean by it—as long as we translate some of their goals into pleasure if they don't do that themselves, and presume that they would be satisfied by different goals that gave them the same amount of pleasure—there will inevitably be cases in which we, the "enlightened few" who are strict utilitarians, will want to do things for other people that they would not choose themselves. And if we have the power to do these things, and can do them without arousing too much attention from the populace, then of course, on utilitarian grounds, we should do them.

In actual Government Houses, this approach led to policies of deposing local rulers of whom Europeans disapproved, building schools that taught European culture to Indians and Africans instead of their local traditions, and trying to end local practices that seemed barbaric to Europeans, from widow burning and unsanitary medical procedures to the recognition of *hijra* as a third gender. Some of these things brought about real improvements in well-being—the introduction of modern medicine clearly did that, as did the ban on widow burning—while others were arrogant impositions on the local culture. But the presupposition of this entire approach to policy was that governance should be carried out by an elite on behalf of unenlightened masses, rather than by those masses themselves.

That presupposition shows up again and again in political uses of utilitarianism. It is manifest in the mindset that led mid-twentieth-century public housing administrations in the United States to shove poor people into massive, ugly "projects," ripe for crime, like the Robert Taylor Homes or Cabrini-Green in Chicago, in the paternalism with which welfare agencies treat their clients to this day, in the insensitivity of many international NGOs to the cultural or societal complexities of the countries in which they work, and in the breathtaking confidence of experts and pundits in the superiority of their views on quality-of-life issues, the virtues of cosmopolitanism, and the foolishness of religion. It is not as manifest, but just as clearly present, in the touting of the virtues of cost-benefit analysis as a panacea for resolving human misery to be found in Prinz and Greene and Bloom. For the presupposition that there is some common measure for human goods and harms, ascertainable by theorists regardless of what people actually regard as good or bad for them, inevitably gives rise to the idea that policy should rely on that measure and those theorists, rather than on what the people affected themselves have to say. This approach to policy thus relies on an inherently undemocratic presupposition. It is unsuited to wide public debate to which people are invited to come as moral equals, with their different views on how to live. Perhaps there are problems with undiluted democracy of this sort—a spate of elections across the world, at the time of this writing, has brought out the degree to which democracy can empower closed-mindedness, xenophobia,

EMPATHY AND THE LIMITS OF UTILITARIANISM (II)

and racism—but an approach that is heavily skewed toward the opinions of academic elites does not seem the best response to those problems. What we need is a moral theory that can underwrite policies that respect all of us, and which can help us all in the pursuit of our varying conceptions of the good human life. Utilitarianism will not do that.

3. Setting these political issues aside for the moment, let's turn to the problems in defining happiness. In the previous chapter, we considered some difficulties in how to recognize various kinds of harms without empathy—how to distinguish true harms, we might say, from the mere pains that figure in utilitarian calculi. We could have done the same thing with the distinction between true goods and mere pleasures. Which brings us to a famous critique of utilitarianism, enunciated in particularly pungent terms by Bernard Williams: that utilitarianism is structurally unable to recognize how much more important our various projects and commitments are to us than any bald sum of pains and pleasures. That leaves the utilitarian caught between an implausible insistence that we are all hedonists at heart, which runs up against what most of us actually consider to be happiness, and a view of happiness that concedes so much to our actual projects and commitments that it comes to serve as a mere placeholder for whatever people aim at. Utilitarianism thus winds up either mistaken or empty.

To explain this point in detail: It seems initially obvious that all human beings aim at happiness. Consider any goal you have. Either it is a means to a further goal, or it is good in itself. If it's a means to an end, then it derives its value from the end it serves. If it seems to be good in itself, the question we need to ask is: Why is it good? Often we fumble for an answer when asked that question ("Why do you listen to music, run marathons, go to foreign movies?"), but something like "Because it makes me happy" will usually do. So it seems that everything comes down in the end to happiness, either for ourselves or for others.

One might add, with Greene and Bentham, that we need some common currency in which to commensurate our various goals. Otherwise we can never settle the moral disputes among us, never overcome the sometimes sharp differences among those who pursue incompatible ends (Christians and Hindus, communists and nationalists), let alone come together to work on projects that can benefit all of us. Many utilitarians have been social reformers first and foremost—Bentham was above all an advocate of legal and penal change—and they saw it as essential to reform that people have a shared way of talking about their goals. Translating the various things people pursue into happiness seems the most promising way of finding such a shared telic language, given the intuitive appeal that attaches in any case to the idea that our goals bottom out in happiness. This is Greene's and Haidt's main reason for endorsing utilitarianism, and it is not a bad one.

The problem is that "happiness" is a highly ambiguous term. Its meanings range from something we can pin down quite specifically, but cannot easily show to be the ultimate human end, to something we can show quite definitively to be that end, but only by way of a tautology. On the one hand, happiness can mean, as it did for Bentham, the achievement of more pleasure than pain, where both pleasure and pain are definite, temporal sensations that can in principle be measured. *This* sort of tingling in my taste buds, *that* orgasm, this or that moment of calm mental arousal in the presence of a wonderful play—these are pleasures. And the moments when the dentist's drill goes a bit too deep for the Novocaine to block it out, or my friend slaps me in front of people I was trying to impress—those are pains. We can now define "happiness," very simply, as a preponderance of pleasures over pains.

But once we define happiness in this way, it's far from obvious that we all pursue it. Many of us are deeply committed to goals that entail a lot of pain and very little pleasure—fighting for immigrants' rights, trying to advance a difficult area of science, overcoming our temptations to sin—and may indeed see certain great pleasures (say, the satisfaction of sinful temptations) as something to *avoid*. When we have commitments of this sort, we do not in any case regard pleasure or the avoidance of pain as our real goal. We may *get* pleasure from winning a battle for immigrants' rights or making a scientific discovery, but we regard that pleasure as a side effect of our achievements, not the thing itself that we are trying to achieve.[11] This comes out, for one thing, in the fact that the pleasures we experience in the course of pursuing these commitments are not fungible ones: we would not accept the idea that if we could get the same intensity and duration of pleasure by playing a video game instead of making our scientific discovery, that would be just as good.[12] In this sense, then, "happiness" will not work as the common moral currency that utilitarians seek. It is just not true that everyone pursues a balance of pleasure over pain, construed as the set of sensations that Bentham had in mind. Indeed, it is not clear that *anyone* pursues such a life, aiming at bare, momentary sensations rather than the fulfillment of long-term projects—not anyone in good mental health, at least, and with the means to develop long-term projects.

Accordingly, we can move to a notion of happiness less closely tied to pleasure and pain, and more reflective of people's commitments. We may, for instance, incorporate into happiness John Stuart Mill's "higher" or "active" pleasures, the pleasures of mental and moral cultivation that he argued were better in kind, not merely degree, than the satisfaction of our animal desires. Mill also added Stoic elements to happiness—he saw it as a sober refraining from the pursuit of vain or unrealistic pleasures as well as the indulgence of healthy ones. These considerations led him to the following summary of what we aim for: "not a life of rapture; but moments of such, in an existence made up of few and transitory pains, many and various pleasures, with a decided predominance of the active over the passive, and having as the foundation of the whole, not to expect more from life than it is capable of bestowing."[13]

But this eminently sensible version of happiness risks depriving utilitarianism of precisely the corrective and commensurating function that it prides itself on. For one thing, Mill's definition of happiness is very vague. It will be hard to have any clear idea of whether a life *does* contain "few" pains, and "many and various" pleasures, or is founded in properly realistic expectations about what goods can be attained—too hard for this definition to be of use as a way of settling most disputes between different cultural worldviews, or of determining, in most cases, which of several alternative policies is most likely to maximize happiness for all. For another thing, when Mill is not vague, he is contentious: he makes claims that are unlikely to be shared widely enough for his happiness to serve as a common moral currency. Mill's attempt to argue for higher pleasures, in particular—with its suggestion that art is superior to popular entertainment, and philosophy superior to a life spent watching sports—is widely considered a failure.[14] Certainly, the immediate intuitive appeal of saying "We all seek happiness" vanishes once happiness is construed in ways so heavily shaped by substantive (not to mention Western and elitist) ideals.

Finally, Mill's claim that we pursue the sort of happiness he describes is open to the objection that some people may pursue goals that have nothing to do with pleasure, that may indeed entail great suffering—and that they may do this without confusion or irrationality. "The human being does not strive for happiness," writes Nietzsche; "only the Englishman does that."[15] As so often with Nietzsche, his hyperbole seems both clearly wrong and clearly right. Clearly wrong, because human beings across cultures often do pursue happiness; one can even find parallels to utilitarianism in ancient Indian and Chinese thought. Clearly right, because Nietzsche brings out astutely how much Bentham's and Mill's utilitarianism is a culturally located project, not easily gaining traction in societies where struggle is valued, or where people are committed to resisting many pleasures or overcoming the drive for pleasure.

So we can move yet further from an equation between happiness and pleasure toward a definition of happiness by which it encompasses everything that human beings actually seek. Anything that a person sets as a goal for herself, we may say, will count as part of her happiness. Even a life of hardship and struggle, if that's what a person wants, will count as "happiness" for her. On this definition, it will certainly be true that everyone seeks happiness. But that proclamation will now also be trivial. "Happiness" now just means "whatever each of us seeks." So the statement "Everyone seeks happiness" means "Everyone seeks whatever he or she seeks." And that's certainly true, but it gives us no information about *what* each of us seeks, and can't possibly be used to correct our various pursuits, or to commensurate the goals of different people. The common currency of which Greene boasts has become a blank check. Or rather: utilitarianism construed this way can no longer provide us with any common currency. It can only record the prices we put on things in the currencies we already use.

In addition, happiness defined this way doesn't lend itself to maximization. Some of us seek to be good Christians, and to make others into good Christians; some pursue communism or Tamil nationalism. But what might it mean to "maximize" Christianity? Maximize the number of people who regard themselves as Christian? Maximize the number of times people take communion, or pray in Jesus's name? And how could that possibly go along with maximizing communism, or Tamil nationalism? Maximizing the *conditions* for people to pursue each of these projects might make some sense—but even then, only insofar as those conditions consist in countable and fungible resources like money. At the end of the day, maximizing these conditions would also give people just a good *chance* at achieving their goals, rather than enabling them, in fact, to achieve them.

A utilitarianism that adopted this third definition of happiness would therefore be unable to carry out any of the functions that utilitarianism claims for itself. It would instead, as Williams says, "have to vanish from making any distinctive mark in the world, being left only with [a] total assessment [of what's good] from the transcendental standpoint."[16] This is very far from its roots as a moral theory designed for social and legal reform, and wholly different from the provider of a common moral currency that Greene claims for it.

I've given three accounts of happiness with which utilitarianism might work, but there is really a spectrum running through them. At one end, happiness has a clear, concrete meaning in terms of pleasure and pain, and can readily carry out the corrective and commensurating functions of utilitarianism— but at the cost of great implausibility. At the other end, it is wholly plausible but also wholly empty, unable to carry out the tasks for which utilitarianism needs it. In between lies a potentially infinite variety of attempts to add in various qualifications to the types of pleasure that should count as part of happiness,

EMPATHY AND THE LIMITS OF UTILITARIANISM (II)

and types of pain that should be excluded from it, at the cost of weakening either the plausibility of the idea that happiness is the universal human end, or the ability of happiness to correct and commensurate our different ends. When we bear this spectrum in mind, the idea that "everyone seeks happiness" should begin to look highly equivocal—and to veer irremediably between the clearly false and the clearly empty.

4. How then might we find a common moral currency on which to base public policy? As I've indicated, I agree with Joshua Greene that we need such a thing, some way of assessing goods and evils that cuts across our various cultures and religions and ideologies.[17] In an increasingly globalized world, especially, we need some such currency even as individuals, in order to figure out how to negotiate with our culturally and religiously varied fellow citizens; where to devote our charitable energies and resources; what sides to support in international conflicts; and when and where, if ever, we should encourage our country to intervene in other countries' affairs. As a society—a liberal democratic society, especially—we have a yet greater need for such a currency: it is essential if we are to come to reasoned agreement about what we should do together. But as a liberal democratic society, we need a shared way of assessing goods and evils that lends itself to free, inclusive, and broad-ranging public discussion, not the top-down common currency that utilitarianism urges on us. As Rawls might say, we need an account of goods and harms that can be justified to our public political culture[18]—an account of goods and harms suitable for public proclamation and discussion, which is to say an account that speaks to the distinct concerns of distinct free and equal citizens.

One way of arriving at such an account of goods and harms is to appeal to one of Rawls's own proposals. Rawls urges us, when considering the public distribution of goods, to set aside the many different things that people consider good, and focus just on what he calls "primary goods." These are things that every rational person wants whatever else she wants,[19] all-purpose goods without which we cannot pursue any other goods. This enables us to avoid the besetting sin of utilitarianism, which Rawls identifies as ignoring "the distinction between persons": we can seek to provide each other just with the means necessary to pursue our own separate and often quite different ideas of how to live. Rawls includes basic freedoms, as well as wealth and "the social bases of self-respect," among his primary goods, and the list he comes up with seems a good summary of the sorts of things we need in order to pursue our separate ends.[20] Rawls rightly regards this emphasis on primary goods as an important step away from utilitarianism, since most primary goods are not the sort of thing that get added up across persons (your having greater freedom to speak does nothing to compensate for my not having that right). Famously, Rawls also argued for a principle of distribution that would aim to give as much wealth as possible to the lowest stratum of society, rather than maximizing it for the society as a whole. And he stressed that a principle like this, and a conception of public policy that rested on primary goods rather than happiness, would be eminently suited to public discussion, and would lead us away from the secretive and elitist policies that Sidgwick recommends. The publicity condition he lays down for political principles is indeed crucial to his defense of his account of justice, especially as against utilitarianism.[21]

But for all the merits of Rawls's move to primary goods, I don't see how it alone can solve the problems we discussed in the previous chapter: how it can alert us to harms like the indignity to transgender people of having to use the bathroom of their birth gender, or the pervasive slights and contempt that Indians had to put up with under the British Raj. To be sure, Rawls includes the social bases of self-respect among his primary goods, but to recognize *that* these sorts of things constitute a threat to self-respect, we first need Smithian empathy. Nor does a nod to the social bases of self-respect, on its own, give us any clue as to what sorts of setbacks to a religious or ideological project should count as true harms to the self-respect of the people enduring those setbacks; it cannot begin to tell us what projects of this sort are basic to their identity. The general point is that Rawls's emphasis on primary goods will help us pick out only goods and harms that are shared by all human beings. They tell us little or nothing about goods and harms that depend on the details of an individual's circumstances,[22] or of his or her ethical or spiritual perspective.

So the Rawlsian approach is only a first step in developing a public conception of goods and harms, of moving away from utilitarianism toward a common moral currency that adequately reflects our differences in circumstance and perspective.

5. Some philosophers have proposed alternatives to Rawls's primary goods in the form of lists of basic goods and harms that human beings across cultures seem to converge upon.[23] These accounts also improve on utilitarianism in many respects—they are thicker and more plausible goals than happiness, and do not presuppose that goods can be readily maximized across different individuals. But they also share some of the flaws of utilitarianism. For one thing, they are overly general, in the same way that Rawls's primary goods are. Nussbaum speaks of the importance, to each of us, of our ability to "play"— but it isn't clear what that capability amounts to in particular circumstances,

EMPATHY AND THE LIMITS OF UTILITARIANISM (II)   137

or what will properly fulfill it. Goods like knowledge, friendship, sexual satisfaction, and the appreciation of beauty, which appear on many of these lists, also have very different realizations in different places and times. And the subtle wrongs done to even comfortably-off Indians under the British Empire, or the harm to transgender people that comes of having to use their birth-gender bathroom, will not become evident by consulting any general list of this sort.

For another thing, these lists—even when sensitively crafted, as Nussbaum's is, with attention to the differences in how people from different cultures think about human life, and an openness to what those people say they are looking for[24]—are in the end still products of a theorist rather than the result of public discussion. So there remains something "top-down" about this way of coming at goods and harms—something elitist, which finesses the ethos of liberal democracy. That may not be the intention of the list maker, but lists of objective goods will inevitably have this elitist quality, unless they are constantly held open to challenge and revision by the citizenry.

6. One way to avoid the threat of elitism is to replace substantive accounts of goods and harms with a procedural approach to these things. Instead of the substantive common moral currency that Greene and other utilitarians recommend, we can try to build a *procedural* common currency—a *way* of thinking about goods and harms that we can share, for the purposes of public decision making. Proceduralism has seemed an attractive response to our differences over the good to many philosophers in recent years. T. M. Scanlon and Gerald Gaus both propose variations on the thought that morality should be defined by those principles that all reasonable people would accept (or not reject).[25] They go on to spell out some of the principles that they regard as meeting this counterfactual test without actually polling any reasonable people, but the very fact that their tests appeal to a procedure that we should all be able to agree to, rather than to a substantive conception of the human good, implicitly acknowledges our attachment to our different perspectives. And Jürgen Habermas and his followers explicitly acknowledge the importance of these distinctive attachments, developing moral philosophies that focus purely on the conditions for a fair and rational discussion of principles among people with different values, with the right principles for all of us to follow being whatever is required to set up such a discussion, along with what the participants in such a discussion would converge on, were it to continue until convergence was reached.

These procedural ways of achieving a common moral currency are every bit as rational as proposals that set out a single end for all human beings and then try to calculate how best to achieve it, and they promise to succeed precisely where utilitarianism fails: in reflecting the differences that even thoughtful and decent people have over what to pursue in life. They are therefore far better suited to a liberal democratic order than is utilitarianism.

7. I'll come back to proceduralism of a dialogical sort in a little while, incorporating a version of it into the approach to goods and harms that I recommend. But Habermasian dialogue is generally construed as a purely rational procedure, guided by general rules and aimed at producing principles of a Kantian sort. It's the thesis of this book that rationality needs supplementation by sentiment, that we identify ourselves as inhabiting perspectives that are shaped in considerable part by sentiment, and that we understand one another by entering one another's perspectives empathetically. So before returning to the importance of dialogue, let's consider how empathy might provide us with a procedural approach to human goods and harms.

To begin with, we might try to come to a shared account of goods and harms simply by coordinating the various things that each of us sees as good and bad from within our individual perspectives. This would be a perspectivalist procedure for arriving at a public philosophy of goods and harms, suited both to the view of our humanity that we've been exploring and to a liberal democratic order—showing respect, as it manifestly does, for the views of each and every citizen.

What might such a procedure look like? Well, in the first place, it would require us to try to figure out what we would regard as good if we occupied everyone else's perspective. As we've seen in chapters 2 and 4 of this book, that means that we need to imagine ourselves into the other's circumstances in great detail, factoring in her character, her social surroundings, her history, and her culture. Note that the result will not be quite the same as identifying her view of what is good (for herself and in general) with what she *says*, or even thinks, is good. She may be blinded by momentary passion, or she may be misinformed. Empathizing with her as spectators, we can bracket her momentary passions and supply her with information that she is missing.[26] And when we apply these correctives, what we come up with may improve on what she has come up with, even in her own eyes. We suggest to a friend that he really wants exercise rather than a snack, a quiet moment rather than a new activity, an apology from someone who insulted him rather than a chance to insult her back. He says, "Yes, that's what I really want; I was just too frantic (upset, angry) to realize that." And we may do the same with larger goods, helping one another see that what we really want, from within our own perspectives, is different from what we initially thought we wanted. We

EMPATHY AND THE LIMITS OF UTILITARIANISM (II)

can be given, or can give others, entire bodies of knowledge—of science or history—that change what we believe is possible, or how we regard certain groups or social arrangements, and consequently what we aspire to socially and politically. We can engage each other in imaginative exercises that undermine deep-seated prejudices, and thus similarly change our social and political projects. Empathy thus gives us the space from which to correct some aspects of one another's notions of what's good or harmful, even while working within their outlooks.

But empathy doesn't give us *much* space for these sorts of corrections. Suppose our friend is driven by neurotic obsessions, or biases so widely shared by her society that they are impervious to our imaginative exercises, or religious beliefs that depend (we think) on confused metaphysical arguments or wildly implausible empirical claims. We can try to bracket these, imagining how she might look at the world if she overcame her obsessions or biases, or dropped her confused beliefs. But many, if not all, of her obsessions and biases and dogmas will pervade anything we can plausibly identify as "her perspective." In that case, the more we bracket these things, the less we can say in good faith that we are really trying to see through her eyes. We will instead come more and more to construct the good *for* her on the basis of how we think human beings should think and feel. Empathy then becomes pleonastic in our approach to the good, a wheel that turns without moving anything else in our telic procedure.

So we might instead take what she actually thinks and feels as our data for what is good on her view—corrected just for momentary passion and obvious misinformation—and then try to cure her of her neuroses, or talk her out of her biases and implausible views. But we may not succeed, and would then seem forced to say that certain actions or practices are good, by her lights, that we are very disinclined to describe that way. We don't want to say that drug addiction or living with an abusive spouse is good for her, even if she seems firmly to think so. Nor do we want to say that abusing or humiliating other people is good, even if she is convinced that what we regard as abuse or humiliation actually does her victims good: if she sees slavery as good for her slaves, for instance.[27] We are likely to think instead that anyone who pursues self-destructive ends, or who refuses to recognize obvious harms to others *as* harms, must be making a mistake of some kind.

Is this enough to vitiate any perspectival/empathetic procedure for getting at goods and harms? Not necessarily, although it does indicate that we can't rely solely on empathy to generate the account we need. We'll need at least to supplement what we come up with in that way with some more objective standard for what people seek—if only to help us interpret the people with whom we are empathizing. Does X *really* think that being abused by her partner is a good thing? Does Y *really* think that slavery is good for her slaves? We may find these things hard to believe, and want to continue to try to persuade X or Y that her own perspective doesn't entail such views. And that is not unreasonable; most of us accept the idea, in principle at least, that we could be deluded about some of the features or consequences of our own perspectives. But if we are to have any hope of succeeding in these attempts at persuasion, we need a basis on which to show one another that some attitudes or beliefs either arise from outlooks that no human being should hold, or defeat ends that all human beings should have. We need to show one another, to use Smith's terms, that there are ways of thinking about ourselves or others that none of us could accept, were we to take up the standpoint of an empathetic but impartial spectator.

8. How might we find a basis for these efforts at persuasion? Well, we might at this point supplement our perspectival/empathetic approach with an appeal to primary goods. That would allow us to take account of certain general kinds of good that cut across perspectives without committing us to the utilitarian homogenization of human life. Or we could try to develop some minimal notion of the general shape that the human good takes for all of us, regardless of how specifically we fill it in. I'll call this last option "a thin theory of happiness." It is quite different from the robust—thick—theory of happiness that is supposed to serve as the utilitarian measure for all moral decisions, and it can be represented nicely by the way happiness figures in Smith's writings. Smith tells us that "the chief part of human happiness arises from the consciousness of being beloved" (*TMS* I.ii.5.1; 41). He asks, rhetorically, "What can be added to the happiness of the man who is in health, who is out of debt, and has a clear conscience?" (I.iii.1.7; 45). And he suggests that happiness consists in a balance between "tranquility and enjoyment," with the accent on tranquility (III.3.30; 149). He also often implies, without quite saying so explicitly, that being free of domination by others is a precondition for happiness:[28] that we don't like living under the control of other people, and want instead to shape our own characters and lives, as much as possible, on our own. (In any case, we can add this condition in for him, since valuing freedom in this sense is a presupposition of the emphasis we have put on seeing each person's life from within her own perspective.)

Finally, Smith refers throughout the policy section of his lectures on jurisprudence to three material goods as being essential to all of us: food, clothing, and lodging. He indeed mentioned this threesome often enough that a student taking notes on his lectures at one point refers to them simply as

EMPATHY AND THE LIMITS OF UTILITARIANISM (II)   141

"fcl."[29] Food, clothing, and lodging are items we all need in order to act from day to day, and to achieve a basic level of dignity in our societies. Smith is concerned with them for both of these reasons. As we've seen, at one point in the *Wealth of Nations* he says that linen shirts have become a necessity in most of Europe because "a creditable day-labourer would be ashamed to appear in publick" without one (*WN* V.ii.k.3; 870). For him, maintaining one's "creditability," one's honor in the eyes of others, is a human necessity. That's no surprise, since Smith's moral theory revolves around the way we look in one another's eyes. We cannot be happy, cannot achieve even the basic human good, without dignity. We also need dignity, need to be respected or at any rate not contemned by most of the people we meet, in order to have successful social and economic interactions with them.

Bringing these various points together, we can draw the following sketch of happiness: People want to have friends, to be healthy, to be free of domination, to have a "tranquil" rather than a constantly disrupted course of life, to live up to the basic standards of what they consider to be virtue (to "have a clear conscience"), and to have the basic material goods they need in order to act and to maintain their dignity. There may be more to happiness than this, but much of the rest will be contested while this much holds of all human beings, and has been recognized as such by practically everyone and every human group.

This widely shared picture of happiness could easily be put in different terms—the casual way in which Smith throws off the remarks I have quoted suggest that he *expects* us to be able to put them in different terms—and it belongs more to the maxims of common sense than to a philosophical theory. The vagueness and banality of Smith's remarks on happiness is also a point in their favor. We are looking for a thin, pretheoretical set of intuitions about what makes for good human lives everywhere and at all times. Given our emphasis on human diversity, however, if there are such intuitions, they can only be vague, expressible in many different ways, and embedded in the elements of common sense that are shared across cultures: the sort of thing that shows up in wisdom literature, for instance. If the full, rich content of what each of us takes to be a good or a harm must be given from within our varying perspectives, then only a vague and obvious common good, recognized by all societies and expressible in many different ways, can be found outside of those perspectives.

Suppose now that we define real or full happiness as consisting of these vague, general goods plus whatever it is we each aim for as a result of the beliefs and attitudes that make up our particular perspectives. Better, perhaps: happiness amounts to the way these vague, general goods are *filled in* by the particular things we each aim for—the particular things that bring us tranquility, the particular virtues we seek, the particular ways in which we make use of our independence. This seems to be how Smith regards happiness, and in this sense he does consider it to be the highest or most comprehensive human good; that is the grain of truth in the common view of him as a utilitarian. The common view is misleading, however, because Smith does not think we can pin down what happiness amounts to for each of us with any specificity, nor that it is the sort of thing that can be maximized—even for an individual, let alone across a society.[30] Accordingly, we cannot make decisions by considering whether an action conduces to or takes away from the greatest happiness for the largest number of people: that phrase, coined by Smith's teacher Frances Hutcheson, never appears in Smith's own writings. On the contrary, Smith tells us that "the administration of the great system of the universe, . . . the care of the universal happiness of all rational and sensible beings, is the business of God and not of man." Our job, he says, is instead the "much humbler" one, suited to the limitations of our knowledge and abilities, of caring for our "family, . . . friends, [and] country," (*TMS* VI.ii.3.6, 237). And this we carry out "by acting according to the dictates of our moral faculties" (III.5.7, 166): doing, in each set of circumstances, what we think an impartial spectator would call on us to do. When we act in this fashion, we may indeed "be said, in some sense, to co-operate with the Deity" in bringing about the happiness of humankind.[31] But the qualification "in some sense" reminds us, once again, that we do not do this *directly*, by aiming straight at universal happiness and trying to maximize it.

I think the role of Smith's remarks on happiness in his moral system is best conceived as a constraint on how we understand others empathetically: on the sorts of things we should assume they really seek, avoid, and are comforted or disturbed by, even when they do not explicitly acknowledge them from within their own perspectives. A sketch of happiness like this can help us interpret the perspectives we enter empathetically, and criticize or correct them. If it seems to us, upon entering a person's perspective, that she values being sick, or is perfectly happy despite being sick, then we should wonder whether we could possibly have understood her aright—or, if we have understood her, whether she is in her right mind, or under the grip of deep prejudices. The same goes for someone who seems to be satisfied with a life in slavery. And when a person claims that *other* people are happy when they fall short of Smith's thin theory of happiness—when someone claims, say, that his slaves, or his sick and desperately poor workers, are perfectly satisfied with their lot—we should be even more skeptical. Were you to encounter someone who made these sorts of claims, you might remind him of the thin theory of

EMPATHY AND THE LIMITS OF UTILITARIANISM (II)

happiness (contained, I have suggested, in the common sense of most cultures), stressing its components of independence and health. You should not expect him immediately to change his mind, but you may lead him at least to engage or re-engage in the empathetic process. The thin theory of happiness can thus serve at least as a conversation opener, something that prompts us to bring the results of our attempts at empathy into discussion with others and open them to correction and enrichment. It can also serve as a reference point in conversation with those whose perspectives, we think, are clouded by self-delusion or prejudice or misinformation: a basis on which to try to persuade them to recognize these errors and revise their outlook accordingly.

9. Now conversation itself, when carried out honestly and openly, is itself an empathetic process.[32] And an approach to human goods and harms by way of empathy, if it is to correct for the errors and prejudices that can skew our empathetic exercises, will have to have a conversational component. We need to hear *from* the people to whom we are attributing goods and harms, not merely attribute goods and harms to them from afar. What others say about what they feel and believe is a crucial element of how we learn about their perspectives, even if it is not dispositive. A truly empathetic approach to the good of others requires us in any case to ask them what they think, since that is what we would want them to do to us, if they claimed to be interpreting what we seek. Asking such questions, and taking the answers seriously, is an essential part of respecting others as equals and honoring their independence, their dignity.[33]

What people say about their own good is especially important when claims are made by others, on their behalf, about what counts for them as a good or a harm. Thus, we need to ask slaves themselves whether they see slavery as good for them, and we need to ask Bengali women encouraged to ignore their poor health what they really think of the symptoms from which they suffer. We also need to make sure that we hear their answers in conditions in which they know their own minds and can speak their minds—in which they have adequate information about alternatives to the lives they are leading, and need not fear retaliation for what they say. Under these conditions, it is of course very unlikely that anyone *will* value slavery or ill health.

What if people do say some such thing? If we really want empathy, rather than a top-down theory, to deliver an account of goods and harms to us, we need to allow that from some perspectives slavery and illness, or something that comes along with them, might appear to a person as good. But we may also surmise that any perspective of this sort would very likely be corrected by further discussion: that no one who had properly thought the matter through could value slavery or illness, and that a sufficiently long and wide-ranging discussion would disabuse anyone of such a view.

Discussion of this sort might also correct for the problems in views of the human good that arise from wildly incorrect empirical claims or highly implausible metaphysical assumptions. Empathy alone will not unsettle such views; reasoning of various kinds must come in as well. Bringing our various perspectives, and our empathetic attempts to enter one another's perspectives, into rational discussion should lead us more readily to agreement about goods and harms, and to a more thoughtful agreement about them, than empathy alone could do.

So we might best adopt a position in which what really counts as a good or a harm for each person is what would result from a free and open discussion of the things that seem good and bad from within her perspective, as interpreted in accordance with an account of primary goods or the thin theory of happiness.[34] This would allow us to connect our perspectival/empathetic approach to goods and harms with the Habermasian view, mentioned earlier, by which truly universal human norms and ideals are those that would arise from an open-ended discussion among all human beings, carried out under conditions that allow each of us to shape its agenda and honestly represent our views. Amending Habermas slightly, we might say that we need fair, rational, *and empathetic* discussion to achieve an account of the good, rather than fair and rational discussion alone.

10. We now have a picture in which we can correct our empathetic grasp of one another's good by way of some general ideas about the human good— Rawlsian primary goods and Smith's thin theory of happiness—along with a dialogical procedure by which we can talk out some of our factual and metaphysical differences with one another. It seems likely that our empathetic exercises and dialogue with one another will also nuance our account of Rawlsian primary goods and our thin theory of happiness. I suggested in prior chapters that we come to appreciate what self-respect or dignity means in good part by way of empathetic projections; that was the point of the Aziz example and the case of transgender bathrooms. We may also realize that people need a different amount or kind of food, clothing, and lodging than we had at first supposed, upon projecting ourselves into the perspectives of, say, a poor person in an inner city who gets an adequate but unhealthy calorie intake from hamburgers, or who lives in a high-rise that meets health and safety codes but is drab and anonymous.

In these and other ways, the general standard we use to guide our empathetic understanding of others can be enriched or altered in the course of that understanding. When we empathize with others, and when we develop our theories of primary goods and of the minimal ("thin") elements of happiness, we draw on what we know empirically about human nature, as well as our intuitions into what makes for a free and happy life. This suggests a picture of how we might arrive at notions of good and harm not unlike the triangulating picture of empathy I proposed in chapter 2. We figure out what is good and bad for others by projecting ourselves into what they think is good and bad while correcting those projections in accordance with both what *we* think is good and bad, for everyone and for people with their particular outlook and circumstances, and what we think a general "anyone"—an impartial spectator—would take to be good and bad, for everyone and for people with their particular outlook and circumstances.[35] The specific things we consider to be good and bad for people will then always be in flux, changing in accordance with new empathetic exercises, conversations, and theoretical refinements. But the general procedure by which we reflect on such matters will be something we can hold fixed, and hold up for everyone to use. What we each regard as good and bad may differ, on this view; but we share the procedure of empathetic reflection by which we come to our views of what is good and bad, and adjust those views to one another.

This is a common moral currency, and one that is at least as capable of bridging moral differences and providing a widely acceptable basis for public policy as the conception of happiness to which Greene and Haidt and Bloom and Prinz appeal. This procedural common currency also has the advantages, for liberal democratic purposes, that it calls explicitly for open, egalitarian discussion and that it incorporates into its results what each person herself regards as good. In addition, it is flexible enough to yield different results for different kinds of cases. If I want a conception of goods and harms to guide my contribution to a neighborhood project, I may want to limit the empathetic exercises I engage in to the people in my neighborhood, and people directly affected by what my neighborhood does. If I want a conception of goods and harms to guide my charitable giving, I may need to engage in a much wider set of empathetic exercises, and try to enter the perspectives of people geographically and culturally distant from me. And if I am a politician or bureaucrat seeking a conception of goods and harms to guide the policies of an entire city or state, I should probably seek a conception of goods and harms formed by rational and empathetic public discussions among all the people I serve. What I regard as good and bad for human beings will thus differ in accordance with the purposes for which I use that conception. But that is as it should be, and it helps keep us from the hubris of utilitarianism and other one-size-fits-all ways of conceiving the good.

11. Let us take stock. On the view of goods and harms we have developed, our initial take on what is good or bad for another comes from what seems good or bad to us when we enter her perspective empathetically. But we correct this empathetic exercise in accordance with a thin theory of human happiness and the results of conversations with her about her aims and beliefs. What is *truly* good and bad for her may be defined as what all human beings would agree is good and bad for everyone, and in particular for her, if they engaged in an open and fair and rational and empathetic conversation long enough to reach agreement on that subject.[36] Whatever account of her good that we come up with at any particular moment may then be regarded as just a provisional *approximation* of that absolute good, to be further corrected in the course of further empathy, information, and fair, rational, and empathetic conversation. These approximations of the good, however, are enough for our everyday actions—what else do we have to go on?—and we can use them when we try to protect others we meet from danger, to show them kindness or respect, or to support political projects and the work of NGOs. The very idea that we are always acting on approximations to what is truly good or harmful for people also keeps us open to correction, blocks the hubris by which we might otherwise think we know all that there is to know on this subject.

Simplicity is a virtue in theories, and by that metric utilitarianism seems vastly superior to my perspectival/empathetic approach to determining goods and harms. But simplicity is only a virtue when a theory does justice to the phenomena it needs to cover. A theory in physics that posits only one force when the phenomena it aims to explain require the posit of more than one force cannot claim simplicity in its favor. Utilitarianism is simple because it is simplistic: it skirts the problem of what really constitutes happiness, allowing that idea to flail between a crude reduction of what we want to pleasurable stimuli, and an empty rubric for whatever ends human beings actually seek. The perspectival/empathetic approach, complicated as it is, can by contrast respect each of us as an independent source of values, clear away ends that reflect misinformation and bigotry, and bring our various ends into a whole that over time can be jointly protected and pursued by all.[37] That is, I submit, what we need from a theory of goods and harms. Any theory that ignores these factors is inadequate to the phenomena it is trying to explain.

The approach I have described is also not nearly as complicated in practice as it sounds in theory. In the simple cases on which utilitarianism likes to focus—threats to life or health—it delivers the same results as utilitarianism. Clean air and water, food security, basic medical care, and freedom from violence and manipulation are primary goods, central elements of any thin theory of happiness, and things we almost always find people wanting when we enter their perspectives empathetically. In more difficult cases, utilitarianism tells us little, and the empathetic approach is very much what well-meaning people tend to employ instead. I hear that you feel harmed by the fact that you must live as a minority in Sri Lanka and India, rather than having a Tamil state for your own people. I listen to what you say and try to enter your way of life empathetically, seeing whether I, if I shared that way of life, might feel the same way. If I encounter a severe mismatch between what you say and my empathetic attempts to enter your perspective—you know little about Tamil culture yourself, and your concern for Tamil independence seems weak and self-serving—I discount what you say heavily, and I do so as well if your views seem to reflect misinformation or illusion. When, on the contrary, what you say seems bound up with central elements of your identity, and is clear-headed and well-informed, then I come, at least provisionally, to see the value in your aspirations.

If the ends you are pursuing nonetheless worry me, I may question you about whether you have empathetically entered the perspective of those who may be harmed by Tamil nationalism (non-Tamils living in the area where your state would be established, or Tamils who prefer to live in a multicultural society) or who have thought about what I take to be the dangers of nationalism more generally. I may also alert you to facts about these harms and dangers that you didn't know, or propose imaginative exercises that I hope will bring the nature of those harms and dangers out to you. If we both take our search for commonality seriously, we will discuss these things for a while, each trying to appreciate what is reasonable in the other's objections, and to enter into the perspectives of everyone else affected by what we are discussing. A refusal to do that on your part will be a mark, to me, of something dogmatic or dehumanizing in your view. And a refusal to do that, on my part, will be a mark to you of my having abandoned the effort to come honestly to a view of your good.

In the end, one of three things will happen. I will persuade you that you should have different ends, you will persuade me that your end is in fact a good one, or I will continue to disapprove of your end without having persuaded you to abandon it. If I am a caring and empathetic person, I will feel a certain unease in the last of these scenarios, worrying about the gap between what I see when I empathize with you and what I see when I turn to the external constraints on my view of anyone's good. If I am a thoughtful person, however, I will probably also feel some unease in the first two scenarios, wondering whether I have either talked you over too easily or been too easily swayed by you: whether further information or a clearer analysis of the pros and cons of nationalism would have led us to different conclusions. The unease signals that my considered judgment of what is good for you, even under the best of circumstances, is always provisional, open to further correction in the light of greater empathy or further information or analysis. That does not stop me from helping you, when I (provisionally) think your goals are good ones, or from opposing you when I (provisionally) think your goals are bad ones.

So the approach to goods and harms I have outlined, for all its layers and complexity, is just a formalization of what we actually do to figure out when and how to help others—at least if we start from the presumption that they have a right to develop and pursue their own conceptions of the good. That presumption inclines us to favor empathy, although it does not tell us to rely on empathy alone. Accordingly, the approach I have described builds in various routes by which we may challenge another person's perspective and try to find ways by which conflicts over the good between us and her, or her and other people, can be resolved. What is crucial to this approach is that it rejects the confidence, often spilling over into arrogance, of theorists who come up with an account of goods and harms wholly on their own, without so much as trying to see whether their account is shared by the people to whom they apply it. The price in simplicity that the perspectival/empathetic approach pays vis-à-vis these alternatives is, I think, well worth its gains in humility—and in the likelihood that policies based on it will actually win the endorsement of those to whom they apply.

This is the deepest sense in which empathy can provide an attractive foundation for moral theory, improving not only on utilitarianism but on all theories that favor monologue over dialogue in the way they arrive at a view of the human good. If our humanity consists above all in our having and living out distinct perspectives, this is also the deepest sense in which empathy makes for humanistic moral theories. Empathy and humanism go together. Only an empathetic view of how to benefit others and protect them from harm respects each person as an independent source of reasons, an inhabitant of a view of the world different from our own but just as precious.

9

Empathy and Demonization

1. We'll conclude our investigation of empathy by exploring one of its antonyms: demonization.

It is hardly news that there's something wrong with demonizing people. What *exactly* is wrong with that, and what exactly demonization amounts to, is not so clear, however. Sometimes we say, "You're demonizing him" when we mean just that you are attributing unnecessarily bad motives to him. You think he's driven by spite; in fact, he's acting from fear. But people *are* sometimes driven by spite, so it cannot always be a mistake—it cannot make them out to be "demons"—to attribute such motives to them. A demon is not human. Attributing common human motives to someone cannot, therefore, amount to demonizing him. Demonization would seem to be a mode of interpreting people that we should never employ. The interesting question would then be why we are ever tempted to employ it—why we might so much as imagine that it is appropriate to understand another as if he were inhumanly evil.

Demonization is one of two main ways by which we deny the humanity of others. We can find models for both forms of denial already in Aristotle. Human beings are social animals, he said; those who do not fit into society are either beasts or gods.[1] Beasts cannot fit into society, cannot achieve the virtues, the self-direction especially, needed to live with the rest of us. Gods don't need society, and are beyond the social codes that enable us to live together: beyond good and evil.

I think we can reasonably say that Aristotle's "god" here is for all practical purposes is what we would now call a "demon": an intelligent and self-directed being *capable* of moral virtue but uninterested in it. Such a being would of course be extremely dangerous, liable to use her intelligence and strength to manipulate us. That fits both the way that demons have standardly been conceived, and the profile of many Greek gods. It also enables us to map Aristotle's two nonsocial possibilities nicely onto the two main ways by which human beings have written one another out of humanity: bestialization and demonization. Taking a cue again from Aristotle, who said that there were types of people "intended by nature" to have masters, since they were incapable of mastering themselves,[2] many societies in the West have treated nonwhite people and women as more beast than human—as, literally, subhuman. Jews in Christian Europe, along with "witches" and heretics, were on the other hand often regarded as literally the spawn of the devil—clever and eminently capable of achieving their ends, but void of conscience, and likely to use their cleverness to harm true human beings.

Today we no longer have open systems of slavery, and treating Jews and heretics as children of the devil is largely a thing of the past. But bestialization and demonization remain the two main paradigms for dehumanizing others. We regard certain others as beneath us, possessed of no more judgment than a dog or a cow, and we try to run their lives for them. Or we regard others as an inhuman force, bent on evil and needing to be eliminated. It's hard to say which is worse. Millions have died, millions have been tortured and abused, and millions have had their dignity destroyed as a result of bestialization. Millions have also suffered in all these ways from demonization. The profiles of the two forms of dehumanization are different, and they have different characteristic outcomes (slavery goes more readily with bestialization, genocide with demonization). But both are terrible, and both are ways of writing fellow human beings out of our shared moral universe—the gravest possible threat to a humanistic ethic.

Both pathologies also involve a denial of Smithian empathy to their victims. One could hardly see fellow human beings as beasts or demons if one imagined oneself in their place. The way empathy gets denied differs in the two cases, however. If I see you as a beast, devoid of the properties that distinguish human beings from other animals, I can still enter into some of your desires and passions. I simply imagine into you the purely animal side of myself—the uncontrolled lusts and fears and angers that I myself experience on occasion, and which predominated in me when I was a small child. I can continue to see you as capable of some sort of empathy for me, moreover, in the same way that I see animals as capable of doing that.[3] But I won't see you as channeling your empathy into any kind of controlled caring for others. So I am likely to think that you need to be controlled by other people, just as I would need to be were I to lack self-governance.[4] Hence the tendency of bestialization to go along with a vindication of slavery, or of racial or class hierarchies.

But in demonizing you, I refuse *all* empathy with you, and expect no empathy from you. I regard you as driven by a love of evil for its own sake, which is something that, as we'll see shortly, I have trouble making sense of in myself. I see nothing of myself in your motivational structure, and can therefore attribute to you horrific aims that have no connection with the way my fellow human beings operate. Hence the tendency of demonization to go along with a vindication of genocide. Demons cannot be controlled and are implacable enemies of humanity. So there is no betrayal of humanity involved in destroying them.

Demonizing people is thus the antithesis of empathizing with them. That's one reason why I focus on demonization in this final chapter.[5] Another reason for that focus is that demonization is a great and growing plague in public life today. The inhumanly cruel but clever profile once reserved for Jews is widely applied by people on the right to liberal intellectuals and journalists, and by people on the left to capitalists. A whole array of other groups of people are also seen by their political opponents as the enemy of any decent social order. The Enlightenment faith that we can differ deeply without demonizing one another is increasingly treated with contempt. I shall argue here that refusing to demonize anyone—even the Nazis and white nationalists who themselves make a fetish of demonizing others—is essential to a humanistic outlook. I will also argue that Smith's conception of empathy gives us a powerful tool for recognizing this point, and for working against our demonizing tendencies.

I will turn to Kant, however, not to Smith, for materials from which to build a theory of demonization. Smith does not discuss the topic. Indeed, the word "demon" hardly ever appears in his writings,[6] and "devil" and "diabolical" never do. The simplest explanation for this is that Smith wrote little about religion. (The words "devil" and "diabolical" appear in his friend Hume's work only when he is discussing religion: in his *Dialogues concerning Natural Religion* and in the sections of his *History of England* to which religion is relevant.) But we may also infer that Smith's mind did not much run to irremediably evil forces. Indeed, at one point he explicitly denies the existence of such forces: "Nature . . . does not seem to have dealt so unkindly with us, as to have endowed us with any principle which is wholly and in every respect evil, or which, in no degree and in no direction, can be the proper object of praise and approbation" (*TMS* II.i.6.8; 77). And throughout his two great treatises, as well as his lectures on law, he seeks explanations of human phenomena in terms of tendencies that can also further the good.

Accordingly, he is frustrated by both his British countrymen's hatred of the French and the hatred of the French for the British (*TMS* VI.ii.2.4, 229); he counters stereotypes of his time against Native Americans and Africans

(V.2.9, 204–6); and he tries to explain actions that repulsed his contemporaries in terms designed to help them see how they themselves, in different circumstances, might behave in similar fashion. Thus he explains the riots of poor people as an understandable response to their desperate circumstances (*WN* I.viii.13, 84–85), and gives a plausible account of how infanticide may originally have been necessitated by poverty (*TMS* V.2.15, 210). He also takes pains to note, after his bitter attack on the East India Company in the *Wealth of Nations*, that he "mean[s] not . . . to throw any odious imputation upon the general character of the servants of the East India company," let alone particular people among them:

> It is the system of government, the situation in which [these people] are placed, that I mean to censure; not the character of those who have acted in it. They acted as their situation naturally directed, and they who have clamoured the loudest against them would, probably, not have acted better themselves (*WN* IV.vii.c.107; 641).

This generous note is of a piece with Smith's general approach, in the *Wealth of Nations*, even to the worst actors he describes. Merchants are pressed by their circumstances into the manipulative stances they take; foolish aristocrats barter their wealth away out of tendencies to vanity that we all share; the cruelty and injustice of slaveholders and feudal lords arise from tendencies deeply rooted in human nature.[7] Smith's way of explaining human action is consistently nondemonizing. He helps us see even the worst actors among us as like ourselves, and ourselves as capable, in other circumstances, of acting like them. In this, Smith provides us with a model for both social science and political polemic. His nondemonizing practice is something we could use more of in our political debates today, and it follows directly from his commitment to universal empathy.

But, as I have said, this nondemonizing practice goes along with an absence of any direct discussion of demons or demonization. That is not so for Kant, Smith's contemporary and admirer across the water in Germany,[8] who draws an interesting contrast between the human and the demonic in a late book he wrote on religion. Kant helps make clear why we should never explain any human action as demonic. Expanding on what he says, I'll argue that demonization is an ever-present temptation in our understanding of other human beings, which we need constantly to resist. These same Kantian themes will help us arrive at a more precise definition of "demonization"—which turns out, in that light, to be a process that undermines our ability to see even ourselves as part of a shared humanity. But, as I have done throughout this book, I'll understand humanity in Smithian rather than Kantian

EMPATHY AND DEMONIZATION

153

terms: as consisting less in a capacity for rationality than in a capacity for entering empathetically into the perspectives of others, in such a way that we can experience fellow feeling with them while still appreciating their differences from us. So we demonize people when we give up on the effort to empathize with them—when we give up on the effort to extend our sense of common humanity to them.[9] Both what demonization is and what is wrong with it should become clearer when we draw out these links with empathy.

2. Kant begins his *Religion within the Boundaries of Mere Reason* with an account of radical evil—"original sin," more or less. Radical evil, he says, consists in reversing the proper order in which our self-love and our moral drive should stand to one another. We are radically evil when we subordinate our moral drive to our self-love, rather than subordinating our self-love to morality: when we are disposed to be good only when that serves our selfish ends, rather than pursuing self-love only when that is permitted by the moral law.[10] This disposition is "radical" because it goes to the "root" of all our maxims (*RWR* 6:37). Changing it would seem impossible since we will do so, if we are constituted this way, only for selfish reasons: because we are persuaded that it is in our self-interest to reverse the disposition. But then we would fail to change after all. It is to solve this problem that Kant proposes a version of Christian faith. In reversing the order of our fundamental incentives so that we are self-loving only when we ought to be, rather than doing what we ought only when that furthers our self-love, we "die" to our old, evil selves and are "resurrected" as new, good selves (6:73–74): in repentance, we are Christ to ourselves. And by thus turning the central Christian narrative into a template for moral change, Kant is able to endorse it and hold it up as a model for rational religion.

What I want to stress in this stretch of Kant's thought is that his radical evil is not really so radical. Despite the clever gloss Kant provides on the word "radical," so as to shoehorn his radical evil into the traditional Christian concept of original sin, he is effectively changing that concept rather than adopting it. For he insists that there is no such thing as evil for its own sake. The ground of radical evil cannot be found in our sensuous nature alone, says Kant.[11] If it were, we would not be responsible for it (*RWR* 6:35)—we can be responsible only for something we choose. But our free agency, which is to say our reason, can also not be evil, for it makes no sense "to think of oneself as a freely acting being yet as exempted from" the moral law that defines our freedom (6:35). We cannot be thought of as having "an *evil reason*," he says; that would be suitable to "a *teuflischen* [demonic] being," not a human being 6:35). The point, and the word, appear again a few pages later: We cannot be

thought of as "incorporat[ing] evil *qua evil* for incentive into [our] maxim[s],"
says Kant, "since this is demonic [*teuflisch*]" (6:37). A bit earlier (6:27), Kant
describes the vices arising from our competitive tendencies—envy, ingrati-
tude, *Schadenfreude*—as *teuflisch*. In their "extreme degree of malignancy," he
says, they represent "the idea of a maximum of evil that surpasses humanity"
(6:27). These are vices that people actually have, so we might be tempted to
think that Kant here allows for the possibility that a human being could be
"teuflisch." But when we look closely, we see that he calls these vices demonic
only insofar as they represent an "idea . . . that *surpasses* humanity"; no human being can instantiate that idea.[12] Moreover, even at their demonic worst,
these vices amount to a corruption of self-love, not an inclination to commit
evil for its own sake. Nothing like the traditional Christian devil is anywhere
in view—even as an "idea" (Kant's term for a representation that transcends
all empirical conditions).

Kant thus gives us an anemic version of the traditional Christian notion of
radical evil. He indeed signals that that is what he is doing by describing radical evil as "incorporating . . . the (occasional) deviation from" the moral law
into our maxims (*RWR* 6:32). Nothing like an enthusiastic service to Satan,
or a defiant flouting of God's will, seems involved in this "occasional" moral
lapse. That is presumably why it seems possible to Kant that we can also be
Christ to ourselves, overcoming our evil tendencies without a vicarious re-
deemer (6:74. 81–84). Neither Kant's evil nor his solution to evil fits main-
stream Christianity very well; Jews, Muslims, and Hindus should be able to
adapt Kant's religion to their own traditions without trouble. Kant's account
of radical evil was for a long time dismissed as shallow or disingenuous by
Christian theologians, and his rational version of Christianity was regarded
as glaringly inadequate. More recently, there have been attempts to bring him
into the Christian fold. I suspect that the first view is more appropriate from
a traditionally Christian standpoint. But that is not my concern here.

What I want to explore is why exactly Kant refuses to countenance human
demonism. If we look simply at the texts in which he uses the word *teuflisch*,
it seems at first glance that he thinks human beings just *happen* not to be demonic. To reduce us to our sensuous nature would make us out to be mere
animals, Kant says, and to attribute an absolutely evil will to us would make
us out to be demonic. But "neither of these two is . . . applicable to the human
being" (*RWR* 6:35). On a straightforward reading of the text, Kant seems to
be saying that we could be demons but happen not to be, just as we could be
(mere) animals but happen not to be. It is an empirical fact about us that we
are not demonic, that our worst evil comes of excessive self-love rather than
a hatred of the good.

EMPATHY AND DEMONIZATION

On closer scrutiny, however, this reading doesn't make much sense. Kant's reason for ruling out demonic action, after all, is that we can't conceive of "a freely acting being" that doesn't follow the moral law, since freedom just *is* acting out of the moral law. A freely acting being that pursues evil for its own sake is therefore inconceivable. No other species, no race of aliens, not even a supernatural creature could freely choose evil for its own sake. Not even God could make a demon. We *could* be animals, but we cannot be demons. The anemic interpretation of radical evil that Kant adopts is forced on him by his conception of freedom; no more direct choice of evil is possible, on his account. Demonism is a thought experiment, a notional form of choice that, when pressed, delimits what choice cannot be.

3. Is Kant right? Can we really not be demons? Well, it is far from obvious that the very idea of rational choice makes evil for its own sake impossible: we certainly seem able to tell a coherent story about rational demons, as the large body of fiction featuring Satan attests. But this is just one of many reasons to suspect that Kant may be wrong about the nature of freedom, as many think he is. I do not in any case want my defense of his "no demons" thesis to rest on his controversial view of freedom as entailing the moral law.[13]

We could alternatively support the "no demons" thesis with a doctrine that goes back at least to Plato and dominates medieval Christian thinking about virtue: the so-called guise-of-the-good doctrine, according to which we never desire anything unless we see it as good. To be an end, on this view, is to be seen as good, and evil consists in attempts to destroy ends, or to obstruct someone's ability to reach an end. So there cannot be a coherent program of action with the aim *just* of being evil. Any program of action, even one aimed at destruction, must itself have an end—must represent itself to itself as aiming at some good. The attempt to realize pure evil would undermine itself.[14]

The guise-of-the-good doctrine remains controversial to this day,[15] though it has many defenders. It also does not go very far toward establishing the impossibility of demonic behavior. For what if the "good" of an agent—the end the agent sees as worth pursuing—is the needless suffering of others? Would that not be enough of an end to satisfy the guise-of-the-good doctrine while still allowing for utterly horrific behavior? The guise-of-the-good doctrine sets a very formal constraint on action. It may rule out pursuing evil qua evil, but it does not obviously rule out pursuing ends that are in *fact* gravely evil.

I suspect that we can draw a more substantive claim from the guise-of-the-good doctrine, by which we can rationally pursue only ends that are reasonably colorable as good: ends for which we can make a plausible *case* that they are good. That claim may well have the implication that no one rationally pursues the suffering of others unless she thinks that that suffering is *not* needless. And this version of the thesis may rule out demonic action. But understood this way, the thesis is likely to be very controversial—far more so than its formalistic counterpart. Defending it would require a long chain of highly debatable presumptions about the nature of action, and of the good. I shall therefore not pursue that defense here.

A less controversial way of defending Kant's view of evil might start by appealing to empirical fact, as Kant at first blush seems to do. *Do* people set out to commit evil for its own sake? Certainly they don't normally do so; it is unreasonable to suppose that most people, most of the time, aim at evil for its own sake. But there are cases that seem to fit that description. One might mention Hitler, or Pol Pot, or any of a long list of horrific torturers and killers such as Charles Manson or Jeffrey Dahmer. These people seem to have committed evil for the sake of evil—to have relished cruelty and the destruction of everything valued by and valuable about other human beings. Their actions seem eminently worthy of the adjective "demonic."

But it is notable that in many cases of this sort, we do not see the agents as demonic. We hypothesize that the cruel torturer or killer was himself beaten and tortured as a child—that, by way of his victims, he was playing out scenarios that eased his own pain and humiliation.[16] Or we suppose that a genuine if irrational fear of Jews motivated the Nazis, and that a bizarre but sincerely held vision of the good society motivated the Khmer Rouge. Perhaps we also put the actions of these people down to greed and lust for power. All these explanations make the agent out to be acting on misguided and excessive self-love, however, or even a misguided set of ideals, rather than a desire to commit evil for its own sake. Even the cruelest destroyer of another's life will on this sort of explanation be acting for his own good rather than the other's harm. Harming the other will only be a means to achieving that good.

When we have trouble finding explanations of this sort for a person's behavior, we tend to put that behavior down to madness: to uncontrollable passions or urges, rooted in neurological abnormalities. We cease, that is, to regard the person as a responsible agent at all. And there is often ample independent evidence for this hypothesis. We discover traits and conditions in a mass murderer's childhood that are highly correlated with madness, or find that he has strange tics and quirks of behavior which we would regard as signs of psychosis in a good person as well. So we do not have to regard what he does as *either* misguided self-love *or* evil for the sake of evil. "What he does" is more like what a deranged animal does, and should not be counted as action in the proper sense—willed behavior—at all.

4. Now we cannot assume that these modes of explanation will cover all cases. It is the nature of empirical explanations not to hold necessarily, and it is perfectly possible that we could encounter an agent whose cruelty and dishonesty would not have a ready explanation in childhood trauma or ideological fanaticism or insanity—for whom we at least had no good independent evidence that any of these things was the case. Of course we could *stipulate* that anyone who seems to commit evil for evil's sake is insane, but that would be to substitute stipulation for argument, and give us no further ground for the "no demons" thesis. Alternatively, we could back up our empirical observations with the guise-of-the-good doctrine, or with Kant's argument that the free choice of evil is incoherent. But to appeal to either of these formal doctrines would plunge us back into the mire of metaphysical controversy.

We may, however, be able to offer *ethical* reasons for sticking to the "no demons" thesis even where we find no clear empirical evidence for it: we may be able to argue that we need that thesis to make sense of our moral practices. This is an approach to the thesis that fits very well with Kant's project in the *Religion*. Kant held that our motives are ultimately unavailable to us—that we can never be sure, empirically, of the state of our wills. He remarks in the *Groundwork* that "it is absolutely impossible by means of experience to make out with complete certainty" that we ever act on purely moral grounds. Even when a commitment to morality seems far and away the best explanation of something we have done, "it cannot be inferred with certainty that no covert impulse of self-love, under the mere pretense of [morality], was not actually the real determining cause of the will."[17] This is not merely an empirical generalization on Kant's part. In the first *Critique* he argues strenuously that our true selves are not empirically available to us. Drawing on Hume's critique of personal identity,[18] he nevertheless insists that we must posit a transcendental self, unifying all our reasoning and experience, if we want to make sense of empirical evidence at all. But the transcendental self is, by hypothesis, unavailable to us empirically. So, to the extent that we can reasonably believe ourselves to have an enduring self to which we might, among other things, attribute our actions, that self is not something we can determine empirically.

With this in mind, I think we can see Kant's account of human nature in the *Religion* as a set of templates for how, in the light of his moral theory, we can *interpret* our "true" selves. The whole of the *Religion* is in essence an essay in hermeneutics, laying out models for how the basic texts, ritual actions, and communal structure of Christianity can be interpreted in the light of Kant's moral theory. And before Kant gets around to these interpretations of Christianity, he shows us how we can interpret *ourselves*: he gives us a theory, from the moral point of view, for making sense of human nature. On this theory, we can attribute to ourselves predispositions to animal desires, to amour propre,[19] and to morality. The first two of these predispositions can, moreover, be corrupted, while the third cannot. Kant's account of radical evil and its cure then builds on this theory: evil consists in our tendency to give our amour propre priority over our moral drive, and it can be reversed if we commit ourselves to giving our moral drive priority over our amour propre. But at no point does Kant make any attempt to *prove*—whether empirically or transcendentally—that we either have the initial tendency or can overcome it with the latter commitment. Instead, he shows us that and how we can reasonably *interpret* ourselves as, on the one hand, naturally inclined to favor our amour propre over moral demands and, on the other hand, capable of reversing this natural inclination and acting on the call of morality. Throughout, then, we are given tools for interpreting ourselves. And we need these tools if we are to retain a faith—a hope—that we can radically reform ourselves: that we can bring ourselves to the moral law no matter how deeply we seem to be driven by selfishness. Maintaining this moral faith or hope is exactly what religion is for, on Kant's view.[20] He accordingly understands Christianity as giving us stories that model that faith, and a community and rituals that reinforce it.

The "no demons" thesis is best understood, then, as one element among others in a hermeneutical tool kit—one element of a morally useful way of interpreting religion. It is not merely an empirical hypothesis, but its a priori underpinnings are substantive moral ones pertaining to how we need to interpret ourselves for moral purposes, not formal claims about the nature of rational agency.

5. On this reading, Kant's "no demons" thesis can make good sense even to non-Kantians. In the first place, we all have good reason to say, with Kant, that we can never know anyone's motives with certainty, even our own. Motives are not bald empirical facts, after all; we attribute them to people only when we take up what Daniel Dennett calls "the intentional stance."[21] We are never forced by empirical evidence alone to take up that stance, however, or to insist that it cannot be reduced to a physicalist mode of explanation. And when we do take it up, and treat it as an irreducible mode of explanation, we are always triangulating, as Donald Davidson might have said, among beliefs, motives, and choices;[22] we can always attribute a rather different motive to a person if we change what we take their beliefs to be. So we always have a choice as to how to interpret a person. We can, therefore, avoid ever attributing

"demonic" motives to him. The question is, why should we *want* to avoid that attribution? And the answer to that question is a moral one.

Or rather, a host of moral ones. Most obviously, when we demonize someone, we give ourselves an excuse for subjecting him to any and every kind of ill treatment. A demon is absolutely evil: beyond rehabilitation, and without any value that deserves respect or preservation. He is not really human, so the norms of shared humanity do not apply to him; even the concern we have for animals does not extend to him. In the name of all we value, including the members of "real" humanity, we need to do whatever we can to protect ourselves against him. So if brutally torturing him is the best way to do that, there is nothing wrong with such torture. By designating someone a demon, we lift all moral barriers against inhumane ways of treating him. And if we are wrong, then we have licensed ourselves to commit the greatest of evils: to become ourselves as close as human beings can to being demons.

In addition, by demonizing another, we relieve ourselves of the responsibility to figure out what explicable and potentially remediable causes may have led to his behavior. Possibly he has a neurological condition that can be cured, or suffers from a childhood trauma in ways that can be controlled. Possibly extreme poverty or the brutality and injustice of others have led him to commit terrible acts. Discovering causes like these for his dispositions may mean we can help him overcome those dispositions. And even if he is beyond help, such a diagnosis may enable us to prevent others from developing similar dispositions. When we demonize people, we cut ourselves off from these humane responses to evil.

We also cut ourselves off from examining our own conduct and seeing how we may have contributed to the evil of others. Demonization is most likely to occur in conflict situations—between groups or individuals embroiled in a feud; engaging in it relieves each side of considering their own responsibility for that conflict. Of course, responsibility for a conflict does not always belong equally to both sides, and we may rightly see our opponents as having committed grave moral wrongs. But by demonizing them, we remove the need even to consider how we may have harmed them. That is conducive to arrogant self-congratulation on our part. We are unlikely, in any case, to take steps that might alleviate the conflict between us.

All the moral dangers of demonization that I've just listed also constitute its temptations. We *want* to clear ourselves of all responsibility for conflicts. We *want* to see ourselves, and present ourselves to others, as upright innocents against whom our enemies have perpetrated unwarranted aggression. And we want to see our enemies as objects, which can be dealt with as we see fit. To take responsibility for wrongdoings on our own part means we may have to compromise interests we hold dear, and that we will in any case have to change course rather than continue what we are doing. Treating our enemies as demons is thus convenient as well as psychologically comforting. Both the convenience and the comfort are, however, temptations to evil; they are ways of serving the overweening self-love that Kant rightly describes as the real source of radical evil. By demonizing others, we cut ourselves off from seeing our responsibility for our relationship to them, and we close off our ability to relate to them in the future under the rubric of shared humanity. That is always a grave wrong. We need instead to see every evildoer, even a Hitler or a Charles Manson, as someone we ourselves could be if we lived in other circumstances. Only a commitment to seeing myself in every other human being, and seeing every other human being in myself, enables me to work together with all humanity in the effort to prevent and heal evil, in others as well as in myself. The humanist slogan declares, "Nothing human is alien to me." That goes for the bad as well as the good. No human wrongdoing, no human cruelty, no human blindness or self-deception or fanatic hatred is alien to me, any more than are the great goods by which individuals or societies can sometimes overcome these evils.[23]

6. But if seeing the evil others do as a possibility for ourselves is bound up with seeing the good they do as a possibility for ourselves, then demonization would also seem to obstruct our capacities for goodness. And indeed, one consequence of demonizing others is that it limits our own capacity for shared humanity, and our ability to perceive and pursue the human good. Let me elaborate this point a little.

For Kant and those who follow him, all moral norms flow from our humanity, where that term designates our rationality. Our being human is the necessary and sufficient condition for our making moral demands of ourselves and others. I'd like to weaken these conditions in two respects: by making the accordance of a norm with our humanity a necessary but not sufficient condition for its being moral, and by drawing on a conception of humanity, rooted in Smith rather than Kant, that brings our affective attitudes into play rather than just our rationality. The first of these modifications allows for a degree of cultural pluralism in moral norms. Norms about sexuality, child-rearing, interpersonal respect, and many other things may vary significantly from culture to culture, on this view, but all count equally as moral so long as they accord with the basic needs and rights of human beings. The second modification allows for a more intuitively plausible conception of humanity than Kant's. What is essential to human beings for Smith, I have argued, is

EMPATHY AND DEMONIZATION

that we have a distinctive perspective—a set of emotional dispositions, attitudes, and beliefs shaped by our distinctive experiences and amounting to a distinctive "take" on those experiences. Other human beings can enter this perspective imaginatively, recognizing that they could share it though in fact they do not. Our perspectives are shaped by rationality but not limited to it and they are richer than the thin subjectivity Thomas Nagel attributed to a bat:[24] we may need a novel to play them out properly. The fact that we have such perspectives lies behind our saying things like, "You don't know what it's like to be me," or affirming that you do seem to know that. I think we can fairly say that "what it's like" to be each of us, in this sense, is both definitive of who we are and something we regard as peculiarly human, something unavailable to nonrational, unreflective creatures.

But the curious paradox about the distinctiveness of our perspectives is that we become aware of it only insofar as we are capable of sharing other people's perspectives—of empathizing with them. Empathy is the key to recognizing both how we differ from one another, and that we all share the capacities that go into having a perspective. Your distinctive perspective is what most makes you human, and I understand your distinctiveness only when and insofar as I recognize our shared humanity. But that means that I recognize how your dispositions and attitudes amount to more or less appropriate responses to *your* experience, just as mine constitute more or less appropriate responses to *my* experience. I see, in empathizing with you, how I could have been you even as I also see how and why I am not you. Moreover, what I appreciate in you, and in me, is in good part the *fact* that we are able to differentiate ourselves from one another: our ability to be distinctive individuals is crucial to what I value in our shared humanity. And this point—that I experience and value shared humanity only insofar as I empathize with others—is, I have argued, one of Smith's core insights.

Now if this is right, then demonization is the refusal to empathize with another: the refusal to acknowledge that I could have been him, and he could have been me.[25] We cut off shared humanity with people we demonize. We do not see ourselves as driven and shaped by the same sorts of responses to experience; we refuse to acknowledge that we could ever have arrived at their perspectives. This not only writes *them* out of the human community, however; it also threatens our own membership in it. For what assurance do I have that I am truly human except by way of my empathy with others? On the Smithian view, my rationality is not enough for humanity; with that alone, I could be just a robot. I know that I am human only through fellow feeling: only when I participate in the *affective* community of human beings. But finding that I cannot empathize with another should therefore lead me to wonder *which* of us truly falls outside the human community: which of us is the true demon. Were the medieval Christians who brutalized and murdered Jews on the ground that Jews embodied the devil not *closer* to the demonic than the Jews they regarded as such?[26] Are the ISIS fighters who murder and enslave Yazidis, whom they accuse of devil worship,[27] not *more* like demons than their victims? Of course, the murderers and brutalizers in cases like these rarely themselves harbor any doubts about their humanity. They are confident that it is their victims, not themselves, who belong outside the human community. But their actions give rise to doubts about their humanity in their spectators: if anyone looks demonic in the interaction between them and their victims, it is them, not the victims. It is certainly hard for outside observers to see how the brutalizers' norms can count as humanistic ones. And members of the brutalizing group may well come to incorporate this outside view into their own consciousness, becoming willing (as are many ISIS fighters, and as were many Nazis) to commit a wide variety of further crimes, even against fellow members of their group. (One might say they come to demonize *themselves*.) The refusal to empathize, to see how we ourselves could be another, leaves us morally adrift.

Indeed, the refusal to empathize may undermine our grip on moral norms generally, not just in relation to those we demonize. Even if we accept the weak, non-Kantian connection between humanity and moral norms that I have just sketched, a norm that we cannot see as shareable by all other human beings will not be a moral one. The minimal humanistic test I proposed for morality in chapter 8 is one by which a norm will promote the good if and only if it could be endorsed from within the perspective of every human being—if it is something on which an empathetic conversation among all human beings could converge.[28] But if we cut ourselves off from the empathy that allows us to enter the perspectives of some human beings, then we block ourselves from being able, even in principle, to carry out this sort of test. This means that we run the danger not only of guiding our conduct toward the people we have demonized by immoral norms, but of losing access to the grounds on which we can regard our own norms as moral ones. Without the broad and open empathetic conversation by which we can share our moral views with every other human being, we have reason to doubt whether our norms about sexuality, religious practice, and justice are humanistic ones—are, indeed, anything more than arbitrary. Once we refuse to employ the tools that enable us to understand what all human beings share, we lose our grip on morality.[29]

7. It is rare to come across people in the modern world who describe others as *literally* demons—incarnations or spawn of the devil.[30] That sort of language belongs with religious worldviews that have by now largely faded from public

EMPATHY AND DEMONIZATION

discourse. But if demonization is in essence the refusal to empathize with other human beings, we engage in it to some degree whenever we attribute other people's actions to evil desires we don't think we ourselves could possibly have. That is what we commonly mean by "demonization." This process takes place along a spectrum—we describe people as *more or less* demonic—rather than having the binary character that goes with calling a person literally "teuflisch."[31] But it is driven by all the baleful temptations and has all the baleful consequences that I attributed to demonizing modes of interpretation above (section 5). It leads us to treat the people we regard in this way with disregard for their lives and dignity; it prevents us from understanding, and thereby being able to mitigate or change, the sources of whatever wrongs those people may be committing; and it enables us to clear ourselves of responsibility for any conflict we have with those people. All three factors ironically lead us to approximate demonic behavior ourselves, in our relationships with them.

In this sense, demonization is not at all uncommon. One obvious source for examples is the polemics in various Middle East conflicts. There is the Iranian leadership's use of the terms "the Great Satan," to refer to the United States, and "the little Satan," to refer to Israel, and its interpretation of the behavior of these societies, accordingly, as being driven by pure evil. There is the insistence on the part of Israel's prime minister, Bibi Netanyahu, that Iran is so bent on destroying Israel that it would use nuclear weapons to do so at the cost of its own destruction. Elsewhere, we find Steven Salaita saying that Zionists take a "sexual pleasure" in killing,[32] and Pamela Geller maintaining that when Muslims "pray five times a day, they're cursing Christians and Jews five times a day."[33] In all these cases, people attribute a motive to others that they do not think they themselves would ever act on, and which it is hard to imagine any human being acting on—any sane human being, at least, and the typical human being in any large society.[34] There are of course some individuals who are or seem to be willing to destroy others even at the cost of their own destruction, as well as individuals who seem to take a delight in killing, or whose religious worship stems from hate alone. But in attributing such motives to someone, we normally feel obliged to explain how her psyche might be severely damaged, or how her society has been thoroughly corrupted by civil war or a horrific dictatorship. We should in any case not *reach* for such attributions; and if we make them, we should realize that we are taking on a heavy burden of psychological or sociological explanation. Which is to say that we have good reason to suspect that the facts are not as Khamenei or Netanyahu or Salaita or Geller describe them—to view their factual claims with skepticism unless very strong evidence is given for them.

To assert such claims baldly, without explanation or any awareness that they require explanation, is demonization.

Of course, neither the demonization of Israelis by Muslims and Arabs nor the demonization of Muslims and Arabs by Israelis is intelligible without taking into account the violent conflict involving these groups in Israel/Palestine. In other conflict situations—Catholics and Protestants in Northern Ireland, Serbs and Croats in the former Yugoslavia, Muslims and Hindus in India—a similar tendency to demonize is common. Demonization can slip into more ordinary political debates as well: when anticapitalists portray corporate leaders as welcoming the death of workers, for instance, or when conservatives portray liberals as out to destroy morality. The rule of thumb in avoiding demonization is that we attribute evil actions as much as possible to motives we could see ourselves sharing. We need to avoid attributing motivations to others—especially standing or reflected-upon motivations—that we cannot imagine having ourselves: which place those others outside the empathic horizon of humanity. At worst, as Kant suggests, we should see human beings as acting out of perversions of self-love—killing or inflicting suffering on others because they don't care about those others, or because they care more about the benefit they get out of it—rather than because they enjoy murder or torture for its own sake.

I call this a "rule of thumb" because there are, of course, people who seem to take pleasure in murder or torture for its own sake—whether out of sadism, an ideology that valorizes cruelty, or a motive like envy or revenge. We considered such cases earlier, and it does the "no demons" thesis no favors to rule them out as a priori impossible. I would just reiterate that we should seek psychological and sociological explanations of such cases that show them to be pathological: which seek to show how a perverse upbringing or set of social conditions may have brought them about. Which is to say that we should seek even in cases like these to understand the perpetrators as fellow human beings. We may not be able to imagine, directly, sharing the satisfaction that Nazi commanders took in gassing Jews, but we should be able to imagine at least how in certain circumstances we could come to have a similarly distorted mind or be similarly blinded by ideology. At the same time, we should recognize the role that demonization itself can play in leading people into evil. A Nazi could kill his victims with indifference *because* he did not regard them as human. The same goes for a medieval Christian raping and killing Jews, or an ISIS soldier killing infidels. These people see the objects of their attack as embodiments of evil, not as fellow human beings, and they can therefore carry out their actions under the guise of the good.[35] That state of mind is, or should be, a readily imaginable possibility for all of us; the "no demons" thesis does not entail a no-demon*izers* thesis. No human being is a demon, but plenty of human beings are demonizers. That is indeed an ever-present danger we all need to acknowledge. But it is also a danger we have the resources to resist: even when it comes to understanding and responding to Nazis, and certainly in other, milder cases, where wrongdoing is susceptible of explanation by motives we can easily imagine holding—and can therefore imagine overcoming, and helping others to overcome.[36]

That last possibility—that we can work together with all other human beings to overcome the temptations to evil that we all experience—is the one most closed off by demonization. Keeping it open is, by contrast, an imperative of humanism. We keep our shared humanity alive, and fend off a grave threat to it, by never understanding a fellow human being as a demon, and rebuking others who do, whatever moral or religious or political reasons they may think they have for such a view. Demonization is an implacable enemy of humanism. Only by fending it off can we maintain a commitment to seeing every human being as worthy of our empathy—and worthy, therefore, of our respect and concern.

Acknowledgments

I began working on this book in response to an invitation from Ruth Boeker to give a paper at the Centre for the History of the Emotions at the University of Melbourne. That paper became chapter 2 of this book; Ruth also arranged for me to give a draft of the final chapter to the Philosophy Department at Melbourne. Ruth was a wonderful host, making my stay in Melbourne something of which I have very fond memories. She was also a great philosophical interlocutor; I have learned a lot from her.

I also want to express my warm thanks to Sherry Glied, Karolina Hübner, Allen Dalton, Steve Ziliak, Leonidas Montes, Li Qiang, Sasha Newton, Susan Bencomo, Yiftah Elazar, and Rachel Zuckert for invitations that have enabled me to give versions of various chapters of this book at their universities, or at conferences they organized. Audience members at these talks also helped me tremendously, by way of their rich questions and challenges.

Rich and extremely helpful questions and challenges came as well from Myisha Cherry, who worked through the manuscript with me in an independent study on empathy at the University of Illinois–Chicago, and from the graduate students in the seminar I gave there on empathy. Thanks very much to Kyoung Min Cho, Tony Hernandez, Jun Young Kim, Maria Meija, Hashem Morvarid, Bertin Polito, Robert Plizga, Bailey Szustak, Niranjana Warrier, and Joshua Williams. I owe a special debt to Tony, who spent many hours with me in my office, incisively probing positions I had taken in class.

I also received valuable input on this project from Olivia Bailey, Remy Debes, Zac Harmon, Nir Ben Moshe, Fania Oz-Salzberger, Hanan Schlesinger, Stephen Setman, Noam Zion, and several readers for the University of Chicago Press. One of those readers gave me the most useful set of comments I have ever received on a manuscript.

My thanks to the Berggruen Fellowship for underwriting a year of scholarly leave in 2016–17. Sherry Glied helped make that leave enjoyable by inviting me to join the lively scholarly community at NYU's Wagner School of Public Service.

My greatest thanks, as always, go to my dear wife, Amy Reichert, whose encouragement and support keeps me going through this and every other project.

Notes

I use authors and short titles to identify books and articles in these notes; full bibliographical information can be found in the bibliography.

Chapter One

1. Mencius, *The Book of Mencius*, Book 2, part 1, chapter 6, sections 1–3.

2. They are combined into one (just called "sympathy") in the writings of David Hume and Adam Smith, from whom I take my start in this book. For simplicity, I shall on the whole avoid the word "sympathy," using "empathy" instead for the sharing of feelings that Hume and Smith were talking about. See further discussion below.

3. See Rae Greiner, "1909: The Introduction of the Word 'Empathy' into English"; and Remy Debes, "From *Einfühlung* to Empathy."

4. See, especially, Michael Forster, *After Herder*; and Gregory Currie, "Empathy for Objects." I have yet to find quite that word in Herder's work, however. Currie (83n) cites Herder's *On the Cognition and Sensation of the Human Soul*, but the word does not appear on the pages Currie cites. A few pages earlier in *Cognition and Sensation*, we do get this: *Der Empfindende Mensch fühlt sich in Alles* (*Herder Werke*, vol. 4, 330). But the word *Einfühlung* does not appear here either, and the passage has nothing to do with understanding people in different cultures or historical periods. Closer is a passage Forster cites (introduction to Herder, *Philosophical Writings*, xvii) from *This Too a Philosophy of History*: *Um diese mitzufühlen, antworte nicht aus dem Worte, sondern gehe in das Zeitalter, in die Himmelsgegend die ganze Geschichte, fühle dich in alles hinein* (*Herder Werke*, 33). But even here, the word is *Hineinfühlung* rather than *Einfühlung*. And no form of the word appears in the German of the other passage that Forster indexes as containing it: letter 116 of the *Letters for the Advancement of Humanity* (*Herder Werke*, vol. 7, 701–2).

5. Many writers have noted that what Hume and Smith call "sympathy" is what we today call "empathy." See, for instance, Darwall, "Empathy, Sympathy, Care," 262; Coplan, introduction to Coplan and Goldie 2011, x–xi; Jesse Prinz, "Is Empathy Necessary for Morality?" 212; and Paul Bloom, *Against Empathy*, 16 and 39.

6. Batson, *Altruism in Humans*, 11–20.

7. Coplan, "Understanding Empathy: Its Features and Effects," in Coplan and Goldie 2011, 4.

8. See, for instance, Lori Gruen, *Entangled Empathy*, 47–48, 60–62.

9. Kant, *Groundwork for the Metaphysics of Morals*, 11–12 (Ak 4:398–9).

10. See Elias Canetti, *Crowds and Power*, 15–27, for beautiful accounts of this phenomenon.

11. "Something very like contagion can arise when, for example, we pick up the cheerful atmosphere in a pub or in someone's living room without the presence of another person."—Peter Goldie, *The Emotions*, 191.

12. Adam Smith, *Theory of Moral Sentiments* (hereafter *TMS*), I.i.1.5; p.21. The very awareness that we are engaging in an imaginative exercise in order to experience the other's feelings, Smith notes, will dampen the feelings we have on his or her behalf.

13. In addition to the other authors mentioned in this paragraph, see Joseph Cropsey, *Polity and Society*, 14, 17–19; Alvin Goldman, *Simulating Minds*, 17 and 299; David Raynor, "Adam Smith and the Virtues," 240; and my discussion of these figures in Fleischacker, "Sympathy in Hume and Smith," 277–80.

14. Miller, *Friends and Other Strangers*, 113.

15. "Against Empathy," *Boston Review*. Bloom falls into this confusion even in his initial, Smithian definition of empathy here. "To empathize with someone is to put yourself in her shoes, to feel her pain," he says. But putting oneself in another's shoes is not the same as feeling her pain—even if the one often leads to the other.

16. Prinz, "Is Empathy . . . ," 212.

17. Jamison, *The Empathy Exams*. The first essay in this collection presents a richly Smithian view of empathy richly, but in a later essay, Jamison writes, "Empathy is contagion" (*Empathy Exams*, p. 158). Yet even here she actually seems to have projective empathy in mind. She has just quoted a lyrical passage from James Agee, attempting to get his readers into the mind of a woman working in the cotton fields, and she wants to convey that Agee's empathy for this woman is contagious to us, the people reading Agee: his words "stay in us . . . ; catch as splinters." There is no hint here of Agee having simply "caught," without projection, the feelings of the field workers he was observing.

18. Hoffman, *Empathy and Moral Development*, 30.

19. "Several scholars contrast . . . two forms of empathy . . . : a basic form where perceivers . . . detect and decode cues such as facial expressions to understand another's emotions and a more advanced form that requires complex cognitive abilities to understand another's behavior, thought processes, or intentions. Recent research from our lab suggests that these basic and advanced empathic abilities may be separate abilities, orthogonal to one another. Across two studies . . . participants were given a simple nonverbal task . . . that required them to observe and label facial expressions as happy, sad, angry, or fearful. Participants also completed a more complex empathy task in which they inferred the thoughts and feelings of a target person discussing a personal experience. . . . For this second task, coders then rated the accuracy of these inferences by comparing them to the thoughts and feelings the target actually reported experiencing. Unexpectedly, the correlation between accuracy for decoding facial expression and accuracy for inferring thoughts was very low and nonsignificant in both studies. Our explanation for the surprising lack of correlation between these two types of empathy may be that they draw on different skill sets."—Lewis and Hodges, "Empathy is Not Always as Personal as You May Think," 73–74.

20. David Hume, *Treatise of Human Nature* (hereafter *T*), 317.

21. Hume also twice describes other people's emotions as "diffus[ing their] influence over" us (*T* 386, 592), and in the first of these passages he compares the workings of sympathetic emotions to a system of "pipes" in which no more can flow than what is put in from "the fountain."

NOTES TO PAGES 10–19

It's worth stressing that I am here exploring Hume's account just of what he calls *sympathy* (empathy), not of moral judgment. For Hume, there are several steps between our various sympathies with other people and our willingness to call them or their actions "virtuous" or "vicious." In the first place, sympathy is simply a tool for figuring out which traits or actions are useful and/or "agreeable" to other people. In the second place, we need to correct our inclinations to approve or disapprove of others for a variety of biases (toward our family, our ethnicity, or those who are proximal to us in time and place) if we are ever to "converse together on reasonable terms" about morality (*T* 581). So for Hume, thoughts about the consequences of actions are necessary to moral judgment, as is an appeal to a shared moral language (see *T* III.iii.i; and Hume's *Enquiry Concerning the Principles of Morals*, section V, part ii, and section IX, part i). They are not necessary to sympathy, which he construes strictly as a nonreflective transaction shaped by biological and social forces that we are barely aware of and cannot control.

22. See *T* 322–23, 359–62; and Hume, "Of National Characters," 202–6.

23. Coplan stresses the fact that in contagious empathy "the transmission of emotion occurs via unconscious processes and is involuntary," (8) while projective empathy "is a motivated and controlled process, which is neither automatic nor involuntary and demands that the observer attend to relevant differences between self and other" (14).

24. But see note 17 above.

25. Jamison, *The Empathy Exams*, 5.

26. I'll talk more about using empathy to bridge cultural gaps in chapters 4 and 5. Chapter 6 will touch on Smith's own use of empathy to bridge class differences.

27. For other indications of Smith's particularism, see *TMS* III.4.7–8 (159–60), which gives particular cases priority over general rules; *TMS* III.5.1 (162), which says that a friend and a wife whose loyalty is rule-governed "will fail in many nice and delicate regards, and miss many opportunities of obliging, which they could never have overlooked if they had possessed the sentiment that is proper to their situation," (162); and *TMS* VI.ii.1.22 (227): "If we place ourselves completely in [the impartial spectator's] situation, . . . we shall stand in need of no casuistical rules to direct our conduct. These it is often impossible to accommodate to all the different shades and gradations of circumstances, character, and situation, to differences and distinctions which, though not imperceptible, are, by their nicety and delicacy often altogether undefinable."

28. "The poets and romance writers, who best paint the refinements and delicacies of love and friendship, and of all other private and domestic affections, Racine and Voltaire; Richardson, Maurivaux, and Riccoboni; are much better instructors than Zeno, Chrysippus, or Epictetus[, regarding the development and expression of our kind affections]." (*TMS* III.3.14; 143). See also VI.ii.1.22 (227).

29. This notion has also been richly developed in the psychoanalytic tradition. See Nancy Sherman, "Empathy and Imagination," 93–96.

30. I elaborate this point in "Sympathy in Hume and Smith." Some of what follows, and the beginning of the next chapter, draw on this paper.

31. See again my "Sympathy in Hume and Smith," where I argue that Hume's account of the mind may be more easily prised from the private access model than Smith's. Indeed, Hume's very talk of emotions as "contagious" suggests an immediate availability of the contents of my mind to other people. That's precisely what Smith thinks is wrong with it, of course.

32. Wittgenstein, *Philosophical Investigations*, section 293.

33. On the role of paradigm scenarios in the formation of our emotions and our language for emotions, see Ronald de Sousa, *The Rationality of Emotion*.

172   NOTES TO PAGES 20–24

34. Compare Allan Gibbard, *Wise Feelings, Apt Choices*, 71–75, and Darwall, "Empathy, Sympathy, Care," 270: "Projective empathy [is] central to the formation of normative communities—like-minded groups who can agree on norms of feeling. (Think here of post-seventies talk taking the form: 'I was like . . . , and he was like . . . and I was like . . . , etc.' Or: 'He goes [some act displayed or described] and I go [some feeling displayed or described] . . .' We might see these attempts to elicit projective empathy in interlocutors as ur-versions of fully articulate normative discussion about how to feel.)"

35. Frans de Waal, *The Age of Empathy*, 98–100.

36. De Waal, *Age of Empathy*, 96–100, 51–52.

Chapter Two

1. I discuss this debate in "Sympathy in Hume and Smith."

2. "Simulation" may actually be a better word than "projection," but it smacks too much of contemporary "simulation theory." Hume and Smith cannot be aligned neatly with the contemporary debate between "theory theorists" and "simulation theorists"; see my "Sympathy in Hume and Smith" and below, chapter 3, section 2.

3. "Upon some occasions sympathy may seem to arise merely from the view of a certain emotion in another person. The passions, upon some occasions, may seem to be transfused from one man to another, instantaneously, and antecedent to any knowledge of what excited them in the person principally concerned" (*TMS* I.i.1.6, 11).

4. On the basis of this line, I read Smith as entirely rejecting Hume's contagion view—acknowledging merely that it *seems* correct in such cases, but reading even those cases as, in fact, a matter of projection. Most scholars see him instead as a projection theorist who accepts the contagion view as being true on occasion. This difference will not matter much for my argument here.

5. Hume calls cases like these—in which we sympathize without actually sharing the other person's feelings—"a pretty remarkable phaenomenon of this passion" (*T* 370). They are explicable only by appealing to general rules, he says. In this particular case, a general rule that foolish behavior leads people to feel ashamed of themselves has sway over us even when we see no sign of shame in the particular case. We see a person playing the fool; we apply the general rule "Most people who act this way will feel ashamed of themselves," and that leads us to think that this person must feel ashamed of himself too, even though he clearly doesn't. But a central teaching of the *Treatise* is that we need to be wary of general rules. They are an important source of distortion in our thinking (*T* 146–50, 293, 598), even if they are also essential to it. (For a nuanced account of Hume on rules, see Michael Gill, *The British Moralists*, chapter 17). So a sympathy produced by general rules is at best an anomalous kind of sympathy. And that's what Hume seems to think. He says that such sympathy "views its objects only on one side, without considering the other": as if it were in part *mistaken*.

This is a tortuous way of getting to a conclusion that, on Smith's projection theory, is straightforward. Smith alludes directly to Hume's example: "We blush for the impudence and rudeness of another, though he himself appears to have no sense of the impropriety of his own behavior" (I.i.1.10; 12). But for Smith, the explanation of our embarrassment is simple. We blush for such a person "because we cannot help feeling with what confusion we ourselves should be covered, had we behaved in so absurd a manner."

One might say that Hume recognizes projective sympathy, just as Smith does, and Smith recognizes contagious sympathy, just as Hume does: they simply put the emphasis in different

NOTES TO PAGES 25–28

places. Hume takes contagion to be the normal or paradigm case of sympathy, while Smith takes projection to be that normal or paradigm case. I think this understates the difference between the two, but it doesn't matter much to my purposes here whether I am right about that. For further discussion, see my "Sympathy in Hume and Smith."

6. Kahneman and Tversky, "The Simulation Heuristic," 203.

7. As Peter Goldie puts it, we are not given a "characterization" of Crane or Tees (Goldie, *The Emotions*, 198–202; see also Darwall, "Empathy, Sympathy, Care," 269). For Goldie, this means that the exercise involves neither empathy nor in-his-shoes imagining. "What the process consists of, rather, is centrally imagining *oneself* . . . enacting . . . two distinct narratives" (Goldie 200). As I'll make clear later in this chapter, I agree entirely that the process involves imagining ourselves into two distinct narratives—but I consider that to be *part* of Smithian empathy, rather than an alternative to it. Smithian empathy, on my view, constitutes a spectrum that includes both what Goldie calls "empathy" and what he calls "in-his-shoes imagining."

8. Darwall, "Empathy, Sympathy, Care," 270–71.

9. Hume, letter to Smith of July 28, 1759, in *Correspondence of Adam Smith.*

10. See for instance *TMS* I.2.2, 14: "Sympathy . . . enlivens joy and alleviates grief. It enlivens joy by presenting another source of satisfaction; and it alleviates grief by insinuating into the heart almost the only agreeable sensation which it is a that time capable of receiving." Compare also I.i.4.9, 22–23.

It's worth noting that in these passages the awareness of shared feeling is *mutual*: not only do I share your feelings, and know that I do, but *you* know that I do and I know that you know. All of these things are needed if I am to comfort you, which seems to be what Smith has in mind by "alleviating grief." But there are other cases where I share your grief or anger or joy but you don't know that, or you know that I share your feelings but I am unaware that you know that (you see me nodding my head when you speak up in righteous indignation, but I don't realize that you saw that). Is the shared feeling here also pleasurable, for Smith? I think so, since it clearly amounts to approbation. And the account I offer below of the pleasure in approbation—as a pleasure in human solidarity—will fit these cases well. But they are not the cases Smith generally has in mind. When he talks of our attempt to reach a "unison" in feeling with others, mutual awareness of one another's feelings seems clearly to be his paradigm. So there is a further distinction he could have drawn. Since it doesn't affect his main line of argument, however, I leave it aside in what follows.

11. David Raynor, "Adam Smith and the Virtues." See my response to Raynor in the same issue of the *Adam Smith Review*.

12. Which is not to deny that this "agreeable and delightful" feeling may be faint, and overridden by the painful first-order feelings to which it responds. This is presumably what happens at funerals. We take some pleasure in our mutual harmony of feelings, but that pleasure is overridden by our mourning.

13. To be sure, this modicum of pleasure in the concord of our feelings may be overridden by the anger or grief with which we feel that concord. But that is just what Smith himself says (sympathy "alleviates" grief, but does not remove it), and he goes on to stress that we much prefer to sympathize with joy than with grief. Hence, among other things, our baleful tendency to sympathize with the rich than the poor (*TMS* I.iii.3; 61–66).

14. John Steinbeck writes: "We are lonesome animals. We spend all life trying to be less lonesome. One of our ancient methods is to tell a story begging the listener to say—and to feel—'Yes, that's the way it is, or at least that's the way I feel it. You're not as alone as you thought.'" Quoted in George Plimpton, *Writers at Work*, 183.

If this is not obvious, put yourself in the place of a loner who always feels out of synch with the people around him. Imagine a lonely child cowering in the corner of a playground to avoid the attention of other children, or an adult who stays in the house for long days at a time, never venturing out into social situations for fear that he will say or do the wrong thing. You might also think of a loudmouth or bully who sounds like he owns the world around him, but internally feels like an outsider. For such people, finding that others share their feelings can be an intense joy, taken precisely in the sense that one belongs to the rest of humanity after all, in a sense richer than the possession of human DNA. And while these are extreme cases, practically everyone can bring a version of it home to themselves. We all feel like the lonely child some of the time, or fear being like that, especially when we have reactions that are not easily shared (anger, for instance); and we are all accordingly relieved to find that our reactions are in fact shared. But relief is a pleasure, and the pleasure we experience is one of discovering that we belong emotionally to the rest of humankind, even where we feared we did not.

There, are of course, darker versions of this desire for solidarity, in which we want to dominate others or conform to the will of others who want to dominate us. John McHugh discusses these kinds of cases incisively in his "Ways of Desiring Mutual Sympathy," arguing that for Smith the ideal is to desire mutual sympathy as "agreement-in-which-I-[and]-you-happen-to be-one-of-the-agreeing-parties" rather than "agreement-with-me" or "agreement-with-you" per se (624–27, 631). I am grateful to an anonymous reviewer for flagging this issue to me and pointing me to McHugh's marvelous essay.

15. Smith does not explicitly say that the reason empathy is always pleasurable is that in it we experience our shared humanity: I am reconstructing Smith's view here, rather than simply reporting it. See below, section 9, on my interpretive strategy in this chapter.

16. I am grateful to a questioner at the University of Toronto who pressed me on this issue.

17. It is not true, interestingly, of Molière's misanthrope: Alceste merely thinks that everyone is *insincere* in their expressions of shared feeling.

18. In my *Third Concept of Liberty*, I suggest that Smith's conception of empathy influenced Kant's conception of reflective judgment in the third *Critique*, and that there is a kind of "self of judgment" in Kant's writings of the 1790s that bears a strong resemblance to the empirically-shaped self of Smith. Even here, Kant avoids construing the self as dependent on *sentiment*, exactly, but he does speak of a feeling of common humanity—*sensus communis*—that unites us with others, and one of the guiding principles he gives to judgment ("think in the place of others") can readily be construed as a kind of Smithian empathy. So there may be elements of Kant that echo the themes I am attributing to Smith. But they are not the best-known elements of Kant, and they are certainly not to be found in the thoroughly rationalist, a priori self of the *Groundwork*.

19. Not coincidentally, this is a view of what we value in common humanity that conduces to liberal individualism—the political orientation with which Smith is generally identified. And indeed I think Smith's liberalism rests on his concern for each individual to be able to live out her life as she sees fit, *not* on a belief that we all are or should be self-interested. See again my *Third Concept of Liberty*.

20. Remy Debes proposes a notion of "affective perspectives" with many affinities to the one I develop here (including the idea that they are crucial to our agency and our dignity): Debes, "The Authority of Empathy," 185–89.

21. "A passion is an original existence, or, if you will, modification of existence, and contains not any representative quality, which renders it a copy of any other existence or modification.

NOTES TO PAGES 32–35

When I am angry, I am actually possest with the passion, and in that emotion have no more a reference to any other object, than when I am thirsty, or sick, or more than five foot high." (*T* 415). Compare "Of the Standard of Taste": "All sentiment is right; because sentiment has a reference to nothing beyond itself, and is always real, wherever a man is conscious of it. . . . No sentiment represents what is really in the object" (Hume, *Essays: Moral, Political, and Literary*, 230).

22. As did Hume, when talking about sympathy: *T* 320–21.

23. Cavell, *Must We Mean What We Say?* 52. See also Miranda Fricker, *Epistemic Injustice*, chapter 3, on the epistemic role of sensibilities and capacities that precede formal belief.

24. Importantly, this is in good part how we take on or uproot prejudices: both racism and antiracism depend on the way in which explicit beliefs are embedded in pre-doxastic attitudes and practices. See further discussion below, in chapter 3, section 13, especially note 74 and the text thereto.

25. Not accidentally, religious beliefs, so construed, will be beliefs we might hold out of a Kantian moral faith: an argument that they are needed to make sense of a way of living to which we are committed. I defend this sort of moral faith in my *Divine Teaching and the Way of the World*, 148–63, and my *The Good and the Good Book*, chapter 5.

26. It's worth noting that a perspectivalism of this sort is very different from the rationalistic one that may be found in Nicholas of Cusa, Johannes Kepler, and Leibniz. Leibniz's monads constitute distinctive finite subsets of God's infinite knowledge; Cusa and Kepler, before him, developed perceptual forms of perspectivalism, but were similarly concerned with the impact of perspective on what we know. Smith points us to an affectional and attitudinal perspectivalism, which has far greater relevance to our ethical than to our epistemic lives. On Cusa, see Karsten Harries, *Infinity and Perspective*, chapter 3; on Kepler, see Aviva Rothman, *The Pursuit of Harmony: Kepler on Cosmos, Confession and Community*, conclusion. On Leibniz, see Henry Allison, *Lessing and the Enlightenment*, chapter 1, and my *Ethics of Culture*, chapter 5.

27. Smith makes clear that our patterns of feeling and acting are not wholly determined by external factors in his description of the "wise and virtuous man," who carefully structures his character according to an internal design (*TMS* 247–48). The ambitious "poor man's son" of *TMS* IV.i also shapes his character on an internal model: this time the image of the idle rich, whom the poor boy wrongly takes to have achieved perfect happiness. One of these models is morally appealing, the other not; but both function to shape experience.

28. "Centrally imagining the narrative . . . of another person," as Goldie says (Goldie, *The Emotions*, 195).

29. See also Bence Nanay, "Adam Smith's Concept of Sympathy." Charles Griswold, relying on a similar distinction, accuses Smith of inconsistency, since in Part I of *TMS* he talks of imagining ourselves into the situation of others, while in Part VII he talks of imagining what it would be like to be *them* in their situations: Griswold, "Smith and Rousseau in Dialogue." Contra Griswold, I think this is not incoherence on Smith's part: I think Smith instead recognizes, rightly, that empathy must consist in both of these things. See further discussion below in section 9.

30. Coplan, "Understanding Empathy," 9–10.

31. See also Nanay, 91: "A crucial question to ask about Smith's account of sympathy is what we should mean by 'X's situation' when talking about imagining oneself in someone else's situation." Understanding how X might feel when attacked, for instance, will require us to consider such factors as whether "X knows something about the attacker that could be a means of defending herself (say, by blackmailing)." So "X's situation" will include "psychological [and] epistemic" factors as well as physical ones.

176　　　　　　　　　　　　　　　　　　　　　　　　　　　　　　　　　NOTES TO PAGE 35

Although Nanay does not stress this, "X's situation" will also include *affective* factors. If X, long steeled by military combat, takes physical attacks in stride, she will react very differently than if she has been sheltered from danger all her life. Her situation will also include cultural factors. An X raised in a culture that valorizes physical combat and pours shame on anyone who flinches in the face of danger will react very differently to an attack than an X raised on the motto "Discretion is the better part of valor."

32. An example that Goldie himself uses: "Centrally imagining *myself* (as an irritable person, I will correctly assume) missing the plane leaves the narrator very cross and frustrated. Successfully empathizing with, say, Mother Theresa . . . leaves the narrator serene" (201).

33. Goldie, following Max Scheler, thinks otherwise. In "emotional identification," he says, "one's sense of one's own identity to some extent *merges* with one's sense of the identity of the other, so that there is a sort of draining away of the boundaries of cognitive and sensory identity." He acknowledges that "it is not easy to say just what emotional identification consists of," but he mentions "identification with a totem or with one's ancestors, ecstatic religious experience, . . . a mother's identification with her child," and the coming together couples experience in "truly loving sexual intercourse" as examples of it (Goldie 193–94).

It is certainly true that people often say that they "merge" with others, "lose" their self, etc., in such experiences. But I see no reason to take that language as more than a hyperbolic way of describing a certain kind of unself-conscious joy or attention—in many cases also of an *illusory* sense that one has really "become" a different person (one's ancestor or one's lover: the latter illusion is not infrequently shattered moments after even "truly loving" sexual intercourse). In any case, there is no good literal sense to be made of this imagery: one of the stubborn facts about human consciousness is that it comes in discrete packages, and that we never merge with the minds of others the way two chemical substances can merge to form a new one. Of course there are science fiction scenarios in which minds do merge or "meld": but these scenarios may just falsely give us the *impression* that we can merge with another person. There may indeed be logical and not merely physical difficulties with these scenarios.

A careful analysis of phenomena described as "self-other merging" can be found in Batson, *Altruism in Humans*, 145–60. Batson concludes that "our self-concept is constrained both by our personal history and by our body," and that phrases like "including the other in the self," "oneness," and "self-other merging" should be taken metaphorically rather than literally (159). Coplan and Gruen both argue—one from an epistemological and one from a moral standpoint—that maintaining a clear self-other distinction is essential to empathy (Coplan 15–18, Gruen 59–60). Such a distinction is quite compatible with the dialectical process of self-identification I describe below, but not with any idea that different people can merge into one.

34. Goldie, again, seems to disagree, saying that ideally I should not introduce any "aspects of myself" into the imaginative process that constitutes empathy: that I should abandon my own perspective ("characterization," in Goldie's terms) as much as possible (Goldie, 202). But if I leave myself behind entirely, I will not be able to enter the other's perspective at all. Even if, to use one of Goldie's own examples, I—a solidly nonheroic middle-class person who has never experienced battle—want to think myself into the perspective of Tolstoy's Prince Andrei at the battle of Schön Graben, I will need to call on the moments in which I have felt a flicker of courage or aristocratic grace. I will not otherwise be able to recognize why Prince Andrei's graceful calm is so well-suited to his character: I will not be able to *feel* the rightness of this moment in the novel. Goldie compares empathy to acting in the style promoted by the Stanislavski school (Goldie 178), but the Stanislavski school famously urges actors to find something in themselves by which they can approximate the feelings and traits of their characters.

NOTES TO PAGES 35–38

On my view, what Goldie calls "empathy" and what Goldie calls "in-his-shoes-imagining" belong on a spectrum, rather than being sharply opposed to one another. I leave *more* of my perspective ("characterization") behind, and take on more of your perspective, in empathy, and I leave less of my perspective behind, and take on less of your perspective, in "in-his-shoes-imagining." But they are not different in kind, and we move fluidly along this spectrum in understanding both others and ourselves. That is why Smithian empathy, as I understand it, embraces the spectrum as a whole, rather than one or the other end of it.

35. Sometimes, of course, we react with such raw passion that we don't consider what others might think. But often we do factor in that consideration, and our *modes* of reaction, our emotional *dispositions*, are very much shaped by this sort of interaction. That includes, at least to some degree, our disposition to burst out in passion. Tolstoy illustrates this acutely. "I wanted to run after him," says the madly jealous Pòzdnyshev, about the musician with whom his wife has been breakfasting, "but remembered that it is ridiculous to run after one's wife's lover in one's socks; and I did not wish to be ridiculous but terrible. In spite of the fearful frenzy I was in, I was all the time aware of the impression I might produce on others, and was even partly guided by that impression."—Tolstoy, "The Kreutzer Sonata," 318.

36. "When we projectively mirror other's feelings, we not only show them how they feel, we also show them that we agree with them about how *to* feel. We show we understand their feelings and signal our willingness to participate with them in a common emotional life" (Darwall, 270).

37. It can certainly lead to a failure of Smithian empathy: what X most wants out of fellow feeling with me may well be cues as to how she should react to her situation, and if I simply take on her actual reactions, without any sense that other human beings (most human beings? the normal human being? virtuous human beings?) might react differently, I fail to give her that. But even if that is not the case, and I don't know X, or X doesn't need or want any cues about how to react, I misconstrue X if I take her to be incapable of adopting whatever reaction I think I might have to her situation, or that I think an impartial spectator would have.

38. I am in close agreement here, I think, with Karsten Stueber: The natural processes making for empathy "should be understood not only as allowing me to recognize others to be 'like me' but also as allowing me to recognize myself as being 'like you.' More pointedly and in more traditional terminology, one could say that within nature I understand my subjectivity as a moment of interpersonal intersubjectivity. Nature, one might say, *does not solve* the problem of other minds. . . . [Rather,] nature *does not have* the problem of other minds."—Stueber, *Rediscovering Empathy*, 143.

39. Compare Olivia Bailey: "It is not clear to me that there is a critical distinction to be made at the point at which imagining being me tips over into imagining being you" (Bailey, "The Ethics and Epistemology of Empathy," 25). Nancy Sherman also remarks that "just when we are moving from . . . seeing [an experience] as [the other] would, rather than as I would, has no firm criteria."—Sherman, "Empathy and Imagination," 102.

40. Compare Griswold: "For Smith, sympathy is constitutive of being a self . . . ; absent the 'mirror' in which one sees oneself, there is no self" (Griswold, "Smith and Rousseau in Dialogue," 63).

41. I don't mean to say that the self, for these philosophers, is *nothing but* a process of self-reflection. That would be viciously circular—and Locke's view of the self has indeed been accused by some commentators of such circularity. I suspect that the accusation is unfair even when applied to Locke. But in any case, for Smith there is certainly more to the self than its capacity for self-reflection: there are, for starters, all the first-order ideas and feelings *on* which

we reflect. It is just that these first-order sorts of awareness will not constitute a self unless and until the being that has them becomes aware that it has them, and begins to reflect on them. Self-consciousness is thus a necessary but not sufficient condition for selfhood, for Smith.

As regards Locke, one way of answering the charge of vicious circularity is to argue that he does not define the self in terms of reflection at all. Udo Thiel, in a masterful and thorough study, makes this case, maintaining that Locke instead defines the self in terms of consciousness, and consciousness in terms of a first-order awareness of things that need not include a second-order "reflection upon" that awareness: see Thiel, *The Early Modern Subject*, chapter 3. If Thiel is right, that would of course put in doubt my claim that early modern philosophers in general define the self as essentially self-reflective. But even Thiel acknowledges that Locke has commonly been read as identifying consciousness with reflection: for instance, by Leibniz, "who simply assumes that 'consciousness' is the same as 'reflection' in Locke" (112). If even such an astute reader of Locke as Leibniz understood him this way, however, then Smith is very likely to have understood him in the same way—and, if he were loosely associating himself with the Lockean tradition, as I take him to have been doing, to have defined the self in a similarly reflective way.

I am grateful to Ruth Boeker for directing me to Thiel's work, and to an anonymous reviewer of my paper on Smith and self-deceit, for the *Adam Smith Review* (vol. 6), for urging me to respond to the charge of circularity against Smith's account of the self, on my reading of it.

42. Donald Ainslie has made the richest and most careful argument for this point of which I am aware. See his "Skepticism about Persons in Book II of Hume's *Treatise*" and "Sympathy and the Unity of Hume's Idea of Self."

43. "In like manner it may be said without breach of the propriety of language, that such a church, which was formerly of brick, fell to ruin, and that the parish rebuilt the same church of free-stone, and according to modern architecture. Here neither the form nor materials are the same, nor is there any thing common to the two objects, but their relation to the inhabitants of the parish; and yet this alone is sufficient to make us denominate them the same" (*T* 258). Presumably, the sorts of reasons we have for saying that the rebuilt church is "the same church" as the one that preceded it carry over to personal identity. A human being who maintains the same relationships to others in his society—the same job, marriage, club memberships, etc.—will for these reasons remain the same "person," whatever the changes in his consciousness and feelings.

44. I may have some of the *materials* that go into a self, however: see note 41 above.

45. I thus disagree with Griswold's claim that Smith presents an incoherent account of empathy in *TMS*. Griswold quotes the bit of *TMS* about my condoling you for the loss of your son as if "I was really you," and changing not only circumstances but "persons and characters" with you, but stresses that Smith repeatedly says in Part I of *TMS* that we "conceive what *we ourselves* should feel in the . . . situation" of others, or that we imaginatively change "places"—*not* persons and characters—with others when we sympathize with them. These are two quite different pictures of sympathy, he says, and Smith never tells us how we are supposed to put them together. Smith indeed fails to provide any argument that the second, more "altruistic" or transformative kind of sympathy is so much as possible, says Griswold: "Smith is pounding the table [in Part VII] and insisting, with the help of his two examples, that this is what is "supposed" to go on when I sympathize with the sufferer" (67). He concludes that there is no such thing as "the" spectatorial perspective on the other's situation and experience, no "imaginary change of situations" that gets the impartial spectator inside the agent or the agent's situations in the way Smithian sympathy requires. What there is instead, in all of the interesting cases, is "an interpretive process expressed in part through . . . narratives, whose competing claims must themselves be adjudicated somehow" (Griswold 2010,71).

NOTES TO PAGES 39-44

On my reading, Smith sees us *precisely* as constructing ourselves and the selves of others by way of "an interpretive process expressed in part through . . . narratives, whose competing claims must themselves be adjudicated"—and the sympathy of *TMS* Part I and the sympathy of *TMS* Part VII are just different ways of viewing this process, or different elements of it. See further discussion in section 9 below.

It's worth noting that Griswold presented a view of Smithian sympathy (empathy) much closer to the one I defend here in his earlier work on Smith, speaking explicitly at one point of a "spectrum of sympathy" in *TMS*. See Griswold, *Adam Smith and the Virtues of Enlightenment*, 83–96; quoted phrase on 87.

46. Compare McHugh: "When one pursues mutual sympathy with [the impartial spectator], one is, almost by definition, seeking neither *agreement-with-me* nor *agreement-with-you*. According to Smith, this figure just *is* the representative of a perspective with which *anyone* can sympathize—that is, that of a 'man in general,' as opposed to any particular 'me,' 'you,' or 'you's" (*TMS* III.2.31, note on 129).

47. Compare Goldie: "Circumstances are not impersonally given, free of interpretation, to the interpreter. . . . If you are the interpreter, *your* perception of the circumstances, the way *you* see things, could be affected by *your* mood, emotion, and character, so this too has to be treated as an element of this 'hermeneutic circle' " (186).

48. See Korsgaard, *The Sources of Normativity*, and especially *Self-Constitution*. The fact that my reading of Smith brings him close to the Kantian tradition is an advantage of it, in my eyes; see my "Philosophy in Moral Practice: Kant and Adam Smith."

49. Griswold, "Smith and Rousseau in Dialogue," 71.

50. Ibid, 67–68.

51. Ibid, 71.

52. It's worth noting that Smith says, "I become in some measure the same person" with the target of my empathy on the very first page of *TMS*. So the other-oriented empathy of Part VII is present to some degree even in Part I.

53. Hans Kögler, "Empathy, Dialogical Self, and Reflexive Interpretation."

54. Consider also *TMS* III.1.6: "When I endeavour to examine my own conduct, when I endeavour to pass sentence upon it, and either to approve or condemn it, . . . I divide myself, as it were, into two persons; and that I, the examiner and judge, represent a different character from that other I, the person whose conduct is examined into and judged of" (113).

55. Smith opens *TMS* by insisting that we do not properly empathize even with another's grief or joy, which best fit the Humean contagion paradigm of empathy, before we ask "What has befallen you?" (*TMS* 11). Elsewhere in *TMS*, we are said to be "anxious to communicate" our feelings to our friends (15) or to be "told" about a stranger's loss (17), and are described as seeking empathy when we tell jokes or read books or poems to others (14), or as learning about empathetic relationships from plays or novels (143). Smith's empathy is thickly embedded in language, even while it also suffuses our linguistic exchanges with others.

Kögler attempts to make the stronger point that empathy is a *product* or *consequence* of language, but his argument for this claim strikes me as baffling. He writes:

> Linguistic meaning in its original mode is never oriented at itself but always discloses something, which is nonetheless thus experienced in a certain manner. Accordingly, [the] fact that four- to six-year-olds can take the perspective of the other . . . can be accounted for by the communicatively acquired capacity to move between different, linguistically disclosed perspectives (Kögler, 209).

180   NOTES TO PAGES 44–48

I confess that I don't fully understand this passage. As best I can make it out, however, Kögler seems to be arguing that language is objective, oriented toward a reality outside of itself, while also presenting that reality within its own framework. But these points do not show that language presupposes, or gives rise to, the idea of multiple perspectives among speakers.

Nor does the Maxi experiment support a reduction of empathy to features of language. As Kögler himself notes, it is *conversational* competence, not a command of language, that requires and fosters perspective-taking. Two- to four-year-olds often have considerable language mastery long before they are able to carry on a proper conversation—and that competence consists in a way of relating to other *speakers*, not in a relationship to language. Participating in conversation is, however, an essential feature of all cultures, so this relationship to other speakers must be a cultural universal.

It would follow that Smithian empathy, or something like it, is necessary for entry into the discursive worlds we inhabit even if discourse is also necessary for the deployment of Smithian empathy. Hermeneutics—discursive and cultural interpretation—will then depend on empathy, even as empathy also depends on hermeneutics: the two will be equiprimordial, and intertwined with one another. I think that this is in fact correct.

56. Kögler has such premises, I think, in the form of the view, to be found in the tradition that runs from Hamann and Herder to Heidegger and Gadamer, that specific features of language "disclose" the world to us. There is no close parallel to this thought in Smith.

57. Laqueur, "Bodies, Details, and the Humanitarian Narrative," 176–77.

58. Fleischacker, "Bringing Home the Case of the Poor: The Rhetorical Achievement of Adam Smith's *Wealth of Nations*."

59. Hunt, 39.

60. Hunt, 82–92.

61. Hunt, 54–55.

62. See, among other sources, Benedict Anderson's *Imagined Communities*, which brings out the way in which these sentimental identifications gave rise to modern nationalism.

63. Many attribute the idea that we each have a distinctive and holistic perspective to Leibniz rather than to Smith. Leibniz lived just a couple of generations before Smith, and it would not much disturb my story about the eighteenth-century invention of perspectivalism to anoint him the founder of the idea rather than Smith. Furthermore, Leibniz's monadology certainly does represent a kind of perspectivalism: each monad has a holistic view that differs essentially from that of the others. Along with other scholars, I have in fact argued myself that Leibniz's perspectivalism deeply shaped the cultural pluralism of Herder, who in turn was the major philosophical influence on the founders of both nationalism and cultural anthropology (see my *Ethics of Culture*, chapter 5). But Leibniz's monads are notoriously "windowless." None of them can enter the perspective of the others. Each of us, for Leibniz, knows *that* others represent distinctive perspectives by rational deduction from the nature of God—an all-perfect Being would have no reason to create identical monads—but we know nothing about the content of those alternative perspectives. Herder had to betray or ignore part of Leibniz's legacy when he said that each culture represents a distinct "circle of conceptions," but that outsiders could nevertheless enter that circle. Had he relied on Smith rather than Leibniz, there would have been no betrayal. Smith, we may say, gives us monads with windows. But that is because Smith's perspectives are not purely rational entities. They are empirical entities, if subjective ones, and are constituted as much by sentiment as by reason.

64. Kant, *Groundwork*, Ak 4:457.

65. We'll explore the implications of this point in chapters 7 and 8.

66. John Rawls, *Theory of Justice*, 27.

NOTES TO PAGES 50–53

Chapter Three

1. For an excellent introduction to the issues in this debate, see Tony Stone and Martin Davies, "The Mental Simulation Debate: A Progress Report."

2. Willard van Orman Quine, *Word and Object*, 92; quoted as a foundational source for simulation theory in Martin Davies, "The Mental Simulation Debate," 190.

3. Bence Nanay makes a similar observation, though for different reasons, in "Smith's Concept of Sympathy."

4. See, for instance, the essays by Charles Taylor, Robin Horton, and Steven Lukes in *Rationality and Relativism*, ed. M. Hollis and S. Lukes.

5. The point is most clearly made, I think, in Charles Taylor's "Interpretation and the Sciences of Man" and chapter 3 of Alasdair MacIntyre's *After Virtue*. But their arguments are anticipated in Max Horkheimer and Theodor Adorno's *Dialectic of Enlightenment*, Hans-Georg Gadamer's *Truth and Method*, (see especially 5–10, 23, and 322), and throughout the work of Michel Foucault (but see especially "Truth and Power," in *Power/Knowledge*).

It's worth stressing that the idea in all of these authors that prediction and control drives modern science does not entail that individual scientists pursue it for that reason: a particular simulation theorist, for instance, may have no interest in controlling her neighbors. The point instead is that the enterprise *as a whole* is governed by such purposes, and its methods and results will be judged in part by whether they contribute to our ability to control our environment. An individual scientist who doesn't see herself as being interested in controlling her neighbors will therefore be inclined, nevertheless, to favor one theory or method over another on the basis of how well it makes for prediction and control over some domain of objects. She will also be judged by her peers—get published, receive tenure, etc.—in accordance with whether she favors such theories and methods. But if this is true, simulation theory will be favored over theory theory, or vice versa, in accordance with its conduciveness to control over our fellow human beings (prediction *and* control: but in this context control is the measure of good prediction).

6. Goldie, *The Emotions*, 202.

7. It was only after deciding to illustrate the point about negotiation with this story that it occurred to me how uncannily the story fits with Smith's famous description of the "man of system": "He seems to imagine that he can arrange the different members of a great society with as much ease as the hand arranges the different pieces upon a chess-board. He does not consider that the pieces upon the chess-board have no other principle of motion besides that which the hand impresses upon them; but that, in the great chess-board of human society, every single piece has a principle of motion of its own" (*TMS* VI.ii.2.17, 233–34).

8. See Michael Hanne, *The Power of the Story*. Suzanne Keen adds other examples: "Richard Henry Dana's autobiographical *Two Years before the Mast: A Personal Narrative of Life at Sea* (1840) brought the abuse of sailors to public attention and may have influenced congressional debate over the following decades. . . . T. S. Arthur's temperance novel *Ten Nights in a Bar-Room and What I Saw There* (1854) rivaled even *Uncle Tom's Cabin* for popularity in its time and may have assisted in the spread of temperance sentiment."—Keen, *Empathy and the Novel*, p. 186n2. See also Wayne Booth, *The Company We Keep*, 278–79, for a long list of individual testimonies to novels that changed people's views of others. (Note, however, that in one of Booth's examples, the reader thanks Ayn Rand for leading him to stop donating money to charities.)

9. See Keen, *Empathy and the Novel*, and Batson et al., "Empathy, Attitudes, and Action," for evidence that fiction may help arouse empathy.

10. Shankar Vedantam, "Does Reading Harry Potter Have an Effect on Your Behavior?"

182   NOTES TO PAGES 54–62

11. Keen, *Empathy and the Novel*, chapter 3; especially 89–93.

12. Keen, 88.

13. Goldie, 195–98.

14. Sherman, "Empathy and Imagination," 90.

15. For a critical look at the philosophical significance of the literature on mirror neurons, see Remy Debes, "Which Empathy?"

16. See de Waal, *Age of Empathy*, 51–52.

17. Preston and de Waal, "Empathy: Its Ultimate and Proximate Causes."

18. Gruen, 109, note 29.

19. De Waal, *Age of Empathy*, 96, emphasis added.

20. Gruen, 94. See also Martha Nussbaum's nuanced discussion of what she calls the "roots of compassion and altruism" that we share with nonhuman animals, in her *Political Emotions*, chapter 6.

21. De Waal, *Age of Empathy*, 107.

22. Korsgaard, "Reflections on the Evolution of Morality," p. 3. See also 17–18, 22–23. I am grateful to an anonymous reviewer for pointing out the relevance of this essay to my argument.

23. Of course, what I say about seeing can be extended to sensing more generally.

24. See Kögler, "Empathy, Dialogical Self, and Reflexive Interpretation," discussed above in chapter 2, section 10.

25. See Donald Davidson, "Thought and Talk."

26. For a powerful case that practically all animals have a perspective and some capacity for empathy, and that they deserve our moral concern on that basis, see Christine Korsgaard, *Fellow Creatures*, 20–22, 27–35, 136–37. Korsgaard stresses that nonhuman animals do not have a capacity for what I call Smithian or projective empathy, however: *Fellow Creatures*, 50–51.

27. I owe this example to Richard Norman, "Ethics and the Sacred," 18–19.

28. Compare Nussbaum's discussion of the moral differences between us and other animals in *Political Emotions*, chapter 6. For a rich and deep critique of simplistic assimilations of human beings to other animals, along with a proposal for how moral fellowship with animals can be construed, see also Cora Diamond, "Eating Meat and Eating People," *Philosophy* 53 (1978).

29. Thus far, at least. It's not out of the question that one day other animals will speak, and if so, that will radically change our ethical relationship to those animals.

30. This is widely noted by contemporary writers on empathy: see, for instance, Nussbaum, *Political Emotions*, 146; Bloom, *Against Empathy*, 37–38, 200; and Darwall, 261, 272. Darwall writes: "Someone in the grip of resentment, envy, or the desire for revenge may take delight in the vivid appreciation of another's plight he gets from imagining what another's situation must be like for her" (272). Compare also Goldie: "[Empathy and in-his-shoes imagining] are consistent with a response which is the *opposite* of sympathetic, involving *rejoicing* in the other's suffering, or even, like the subtle and imaginative inquisitor, exploiting your sensitivity of the other's feelings to help you exacerbate his suffering" (215).

31. Martha Nussbaum brings the actor case: *Political Emotions*, 146.

32. Goldie describes this as having "an intellectual grasp of all [of another person's] thoughts and feelings" while lacking "the empathetic ability to have those thoughts and feelings *with the special sort of emotionally laden content* which gave them the power they had" (211, my emphasis).

33. Batson, *Altruism in Humans*, 11.

34. Batson, *Altruism in Humans*, 17, 18. Batson cites Smith in connection with these phenomena.

NOTES TO PAGES 62–69

35. Batson now says himself that "in the flow of everyday life, perspective taking lies a little downstream from valuing the other's welfare" (44).

36. Darwall, whose use of "empathy" is closer to Smith's than to Batson's, notes this as well (273).

37. Batson, *Altruism in Humans*, 163–64. See also John Dovidio, Judith Allen, and David Schroeder, "Specificity of Empathy-Induced Helping."

38. Slote, "Saucers of Mud," 14.

39. Jonathan Glover, *Humanity*, 379–80.

40. Gruen, *Entangled Empathy*, 52. Note that Gruen says "cognitive empathy *is thought* to generate an altruistic emotion"; she does not present this view as her own.

41. See also Bailey, *The Ethics and Epistemology of Empathy*, chapter 2, which raises similar questions to the ones I have just surveyed about the idea that empathy inevitably leads to altruism.

42. Bailey, "Empathy, Concern, and Understanding in *The Theory of Moral Sentiments*," 269. Compare Bloom, *Against Empathy*, 76: "It's not that empathy itself automatically leads to kindness. Rather, empathy has to connect to kindness that already exists. Empathy makes good people better, then, because kind people don't like suffering, and empathy makes this suffering salient."

43. As Smith himself supposed they were: *TMS* VII.iii.1.4, 317.

44. Where "hatred and resentment" are concerned, Smith says, our empathy "is divided between the person who feels them, and the person who is the object of them. The interests of the these two are directly opposite. What our sympathy with the person who feels them would prompt us to wish for, our fellow-feeling with the other would lead us to fear. As they are both men, we are concerned for both, and our fear for what the one may suffer, damps our resentment for what the other has suffered" (*TMS* I.ii.3.1; 34).

45. Goldie, *The Emotions*, 181, 213, 218.

46. See, especially, Carol Gilligan, *In a Different Voice*; Nel Noddings, *Caring*; Stephen Darwall, *Welfare and Rational Care*; Virginia Held, *The Ethics of Care*; and Michael Slote, *The Ethics of Care and Empathy*.

47. See Daniel Klein, ed., "My Understanding of Adam Smith's Impartial Spectator."

48. I've argued elsewhere that this is a major point of Smith's *Wealth of Nations*. See my *On Adam Smith's Wealth of Nations*, 205–9, and *A Short History of Distributive Justice*, 62–68.

49. Geoffrey Sayre-McCord develops an iterative (but non-Hegelian) account of Smith's impartial spectator along these lines. See his "Sentiments and Spectators: Adam Smith's Theory of Moral Judgment," and "Hume and Smith on Sympathy, Approbation, and Moral Judgment."

50. See Charles Mills, *The Racial Contract*.

51. I discuss his particularist leanings in "Adam Smith's Moral and Political Philosophy."

52. Dancy, *Ethics Without Principles*. See also John McDowell, "Virtue and Reason"; and Martha Nussbaum, *The Fragility of Goodness* and *Love's Knowledge*.

53. On the proto-Kantian aspects of Smith, see Fleischacker, "Philosophy in Moral Practice"; Ernst Tugendhat, "Universally Approved Intersubjective Attitudes: Adam Smith"; Leon Montes, *Adam Smith in Context*, chapter 4; Maria Alejandra Carrasco, "Adam Smith's Reconstruction of Practical Reason"; and Carrasco, "Adam Smith: Self-Command, Practical Reason, and Deontological Insights."

54. This account also comes in two parts. In Part I of *TMS*, Smith stresses our empathy with the motives of the person carrying out an action, while in Part II he looks at our empathy with those who benefit or are harmed by that action.

184 NOTES TO PAGES 69–71

55. I've changed the order in which he presents these things. Virtues enter in Part VI (most explicitly, at least: they are mentioned throughout the earlier parts), custom is discussed in Part V, and utility in Part IV. But I think the order I've given makes more sense logically.

56. There is even a passage in which Smith more or less announces that this is what he is doing:

> When we approve of any character or action, the sentiments which we feel, are, according to the foregoing system, derived from four sources, which are in some respects different from one another. First, we sympathize with the motives of the agent; secondly, we enter into the gratitude of those who receive the benefit of his actions; thirdly, we observe that his conduct has been agreeable to the general rules by which those two sympathies generally act; and, last of all, when we consider such actions as making a part of a system of behaviour which tends to promote the happiness either of the individual or of the society, they appear to derive a beauty from this utility, not unlike that which we ascribe to any well-contrived machine (*TMS* VII.iii.3.16, 326).

57. See my "Adam Smith's Moral and Political Philosophy."

58. Mill called himself an eclectic for a while, as had Cicero. Williams noted in his last book that "our ethical ideas are a complex deposit of many different traditions and social forces" (*Truth and Truthfulness*, 20), and devoted much of his work before then to delineating aspects of these traditions (Kantian, utilitarian, Aristotelian, and Homeric, as well as insights gleaned from such wide-ranging sources as British pornography law and a Czech opera), while denying that any of them could alone capture everything we want or need out of ethical reflection. For a fuller defense of my own moral eclecticism, see my *Divine Teaching and the Way of the World*, part 2, chapter 2, and *The Good and the Good Book*, 36–39.

59. See Gilligan, *In a Different Voice*; and Noddings, *Caring*. Noddings "contrasts . . . masculine and feminine approaches to ethics" throughout her book, but describes her ultimate goal as a "transcendence of the masculine and feminine in moral matters" (6).

60. Compare Lori Gruen: "An ethics of care sometimes was associated with 'feminine' characteristics and an ethics of justice [with] 'masculine' ones. This association was unfortunate because it further entrenched stereotypical gender roles and seemed to preclude the idea that men are caring. It also lead people to dismiss an ethics of care as a 'woman's ethic.' . . . [An ethics of care] is a theory for all people. . . . That the theory was developed by women as an alternative to what look like detached, alienating theories, in a social context in which gender is assumed to be binary, may have lent a certain insight to the theory. Nonetheless, it isn't a 'feminine' theory or a 'woman's ethic'" (Gruen 32).

61. Which is not to say that Smith himself was immune to the sexism of his time. He is apt, for instance, to identify women with fearfulness (*TMS* I.ii.3.5, 37), and to call a tendency to cry "effeminacy" (*TMS* I.iii.1.9, 46). There is rather less of this sort of thing in Smith than in other writers, and his admirers included some prominent protofeminists (Sophie de Grouchy, Mary Wollstonecraft), but it would be a mistake to regard him as a protofeminist himself. There are indeed troubling assumptions about gender that structure his theorizing, both on morality and on political economy. See Maureen Harkin, "Adam Smith on Women."

62. See especially Fricker, *Epistemic Injustice*. In the same year that this book came out, Charles Mills raised many of the same issues in a racial context, albeit without using the phrase "epistemic injustice"; see his "White Ignorance."

63. Fricker, *Epistemic Injustice*, 148–50.

64. Ibid., 35–41.

NOTES TO PAGES 71–78

65. Ibid., 10–14, 90.

66. Gaile Pohlhaus, in "Discerning the Primary Epistemic Harm in Cases of Testimonial Injustice," has argued that epistemic injustice depends precisely on its victims being subjects, not objects. The victims play the role of confirming their victimizers' sense of superiority, which they could not do unless they could *testify* to that superiority. But only subjects, not objects, can offer testimony—albeit inferior subjects, semihumans, who thereby allow their victimizers to maintain their hierarchical view of the human world. This seems right to me; but it is, I think, a friendly amendment to Fricker's position.

67. Edward Craig, *Knowledge and the State of Nature*; Bernard Williams, *Truth and Truthfulness*.

68. Williams capitalizes these terms (Accuracy and Sincerity), to indicate that his use of them need not coincide in every respect with ordinary usage, and Fricker follows him by capitalizing Testimonial Justice. I shall omit this wrinkle, since the differences between the coined terms and ordinary usage won't affect us here.

69. Fricker, *Epistemic Injustice*, 169.

70. Jones argues that empathy is crucial to sustaining both our trust in others and our trust in ourselves, and that we need both of these kinds of trust to judge wisely, especially concerning reports of events far outside our usual course of experience.—Karen Jones, "The Politics of Credibility," in *A Mind of One's Own*, 172.

71. See above, section 3.

72. Michael Slote argues that open-mindedness depends on empathy in Slote, *A Sentimentalist Theory of the Mind*, 14–18.

73. This is not to deny that in some places Jews do make up a disproportionately large percentage of landlords who exploit the poor, or that in some places black people do conduct a disproportionately large part of the drug trade. Prejudice does not always consist in making up facts out of whole cloth. Exaggerating germs of truth, misinterpreting their significance, or explaining them in ways that attribute evil to the makeup of a type of person (as opposed to, in these cases, considering the possibility that anti-Semitism and racism, respectively, might be *causes* of the conditions that make for exploitative Jewish landlords and drug-dealing black people) is at least as common a way for it to express itself.

74. It's worth recalling here that on the conception of perspectives I defended in chapter 2 (see section 6, especially), they consist precisely in pre-doxastic attitudes and modes of perception. So entering into a prejudiced person's perspective will be essential to helping her correct for her biases. And entering into our own perspective, with the empathy of the impartial spectator, will be essential to helping ourselves correct for our own biases.

Chapter Four

1. Griswold, "Smith and Rousseau in Dialogue," 70.

2. But see chapter 1, note 4, above.

3. See especially Montesquieu's *Persian Letters*, Hume's "A Dialogue," and Lessing's *Nathan the Wise*. For discussion of the Montesquieu, see Dennis Rasmussen, *The Pragmatic Enlightenment*, and Genevieve Lloyd, *Enlightenment's Shadows*, chapter 1. For discussion of the Hume, see Kate Abramson, "Hume on Cultural Conflicts of Values." For discussion of the Lessing, see Fleischacker, *Ethics of Culture*, chapter 5. For the importance of cultural diversity to the Enlightenment in general, see also Michael Frazer, *The Enlightenment of Sympathy*, and Sankar Muthu, *Enlightenment against Empire*.

186 NOTES TO PAGES 78–82

4. Forster, *Herder's Writings*, 296.

5. Forster, *Herder's Writings*, 188; see also 219–20, 297: "[Nature] put dispositions to manifoldness into the heart, and then a part of the manifoldness in a circle about us, available to us; then she reined in the human view so that after a small period of habituation this circle became horizon for him." Again: "The ideas of every indigenous nation are . . . confined to its own region: if it profess to understand words expressing things utterly foreign to it, we have reason to remain long in doubt of this understanding. . . . [One can] compose a catechism of [the Greenlanders'] theologico-natural philosophy, showing that they can neither answer nor comprehend European questions, otherwise than according to the circle of their own conceptions." Herder, *Reflections on the Philosophy of the History of Mankind*, 41.

6. Forster, *Herder's Writings*, 222–23: "Just as there is a universal *human sensation*, there must also be a universal *human manner of thought* (sensus communis)—but with no term do the moral-philosophical philistines trade in worse contraband than this. . . . To be sure there must be a universal human understanding, . . . but I fear that an individual member of the species . . . could hardly give information about it. . . . As much as we go on about universal reason, just as little have we yet explained what this actually is, and where it resides, . . . where people diverge and where all come together. Universal human reason, as we would like to understand the term, is a cover for our favorite whims, idolatry, blindness, and laziness." See also Frazer, *The Enlightenment of Sympathy*, chapter 6.

7. But again, see chapter 1, note 4.

8. "Horizon," for all its Gadamerian connotations, is Herder's own term: nature "put dispositions of *manifoldness* into the heart," he says, "and then a *part* of the manifoldness [i.e., our cultural and historical context] in a circle about to us . . . ; then she *reined in* the human *view* so that after a small period of habituation this circle became *horizon* for him" (*Herder's Writings*, 297; italics in the original).

9. Wittgenstein, "Remarks on Frazer's *Golden Bough*," in *Philosophical Occasions*, 119.

10. See "Lectures on Religious Belief," in Wittgenstein, *Lectures & Conversations on Aesthetics, Psychology and Religious Belief*, and *On Certainty*. Attending carefully to the passages widely cited from these texts, Gordon Graham argues that too much emphasis has been placed on them, and that Wittgenstein did not necessarily hold the borderline relativistic views about religion that have been attributed to him: Graham, *Wittgenstein and Natural Religion*.

11. Geertz, *The Interpretation of Cultures*, 13.

12. See Julia Penn, *Linguistic Relativity*, 54; Eduard Sapir, "On Herder's 'Ursprung der Sprache"; Levy-Bruhl, "Les idées politique de Herder."

13. For a deep and incisive version of this charge, see Kögler, "Empathy, Dialogical Self, and Reflexive Interpretation," discussed above in chapter 2, section 8.

14. See Jennifer Pitts, *A Turn to Empire*, chapter 2.

15. See Hans Kögler and Karsten Stueber, introduction to *Empathy and Agency*, 27–29; Geertz, *The Interpretation of Cultures*, 80–82; and Taylor, "Interpretation and the Human Sciences," 23–24.

16. Stueber, *Rediscovering Empathy*, especially chapter 4, section 2, and chapter 6.

17. Collingwood, *The Idea of History*, 213.

18. I am thinking here of R. K. Narayan's *The English Teacher* and Rabindranath Tagore's *Gora*.

19. See, for instance, Kögler's assumption of a universal capacity for following along in conversations (discussed above in chapter 2, section 10), and Geertz's argument, in chapter 3 of *The*

NOTES TO PAGES 82–93

Interpretation of Cultures, that the physiology of our brain inclines us to develop differentiated cultures.

Some extreme relativists—taking Herder's anti-universalist polemic further than he did himself—have tried to do away with even this minimal appeal to a universal human nature, saying that the influence of culture is so thoroughgoing that there can be no universalist claims. This, however, is incoherent. If there can be no universalist claims, then we cannot even maintain *that* there can be no universalist claims: the position undermines its own intelligibility.

20. See chapter 2, above.

21. I am grateful to Maria Meija and Atanacio Hernandez for stressing to me the need to make this Kantian point clear.

22. See, for instance, Brian Barry, *Culture and Equality*.

23. See, for instance, Will Kymlicka, *Liberalism, Community and Culture*; Daniel A. Bell, *Communitarianism and Its Critics*; Yael Tamir, *Liberal Nationalism*; or Fleischacker, *The Ethics of Culture*.

24. I defend the value of revealed religion along these lines in *Divine Teaching*.

25. I am indebted to Fania Oz-Salzberger for this objection, and to Joshua Williams for helping me see what was wrong with my initial response to it.

26. Hume, *Enquiry concerning the Principles of Morals*, 275.

27. See my *Ethics of Culture*, chapter 5.

28. This is how Sankar Muthu reads Herder: "Herder . . . treats humans as constitutively cultural agents, whose very humanity is an indication both of sameness and of difference. To some extent, then, the respect for humans as humans will entail some kind of respect for the variety of beliefs, practices, and languages. . . . 'Humanity' is the essential and important, but ultimately also the somewhat amorphous, material that is shaped and moulded *diversely* by free and active human powers. Hence, for Herder, respecting humanity necessarily entails respecting human diversity" (*Enlightenment against Empire*, pp. 232, 238).

Chapter Five

1. See Charles Mills, *The Racial Contract*, for a searing account of the way in which supposedly egalitarian liberals have for centuries actually promoted white racism.

2. On this issue, see Fonna Forman-Barzilai, *Adam Smith and the Circles of Sympathy*.

3. All "sensible" beings, actually: *TMS* VI.ii.1; 235.

4. For a rich account of the relationship between spatial proximity and affection in Smith, see Forman-Barzilai, *Adam Smith and the Circles of Sympathy*, 120–26, 139–50.

5. Again, see Forman-Barzilai, *Adam Smith and the Circles of Sympathy*, especially 85–93, and my "Smith und der Kulturelativismus."

6. Hume, "Of National Characters," 203.

7. Anderson, *Imagined Communities*, chapter 2.

8. Letter to Gilbert Elliot, September 22, 1764, in *The Letters of David Hume*, volume 1, 470.

9. Compare Forman-Barzilai, *Adam Smith and the Circles of Sympathy*, 120–31.

10. Here is a more complete excerpt from the passage: "The love of our own nation often disposes us to view, with the most malignant jealousy and envy, the prosperity and aggrandisement of any other neighboring nation. . . . Each nation foresees, or imagines it foresees, its own subjugation in the increasing power and aggrandisement of any of its neighbours; and the mean principle of national prejudices is often founded upon the noble one of the love of our own

188 NOTES TO PAGES 93–102

country. . . . France and England may each of them have some reason to dread the increase of the naval and military power of the other; but for either of them to envy the internal happiness and prosperity of the other, the cultivation of its lands, the advancement of its manufactures, the increase of its commerce, the security and number of its ports and harbours, its proficiency in all the liberal arts and sciences, is surely beneath the dignity of two such great nations. These are all real improvements of the world we live in. Mankind are benefited, human nature is ennobled by them. In such improvements, each nation ought, not only to endeavour itself to excel, but from the love of mankind, to promote, instead of obstructing the excellence of its neighbours."

11. See, for instance, L. M. Brown, M. Bradley, and P. Lang, "Affective Reactions to Pictures of Ingroup and Outgroup Members"; and Stürmer et al., "Prosocial Emotions."

12. See Yiftah Elazar, "The True Spirit of a Republican," for a beautiful elaboration of the importance for Smith of this pragmatic reason for valuing local ties.

13. For case studies, see Erica Bornstein, "Child Sponsorship, Evangelism, and Belonging in the Work of World Vision Zimbabwe"; Erica Caple James, "Witchcraft, Bureaucraft, and the Social Life of (US) Aid in Haiti"; or the essays in Victoria Bernal and Indrepal Grewal, eds., *Theorizing NGOs*. I am indebted to Noa Fleischacker for introducing me to this literature.

14. Mill, *Utilitarianism*, chapter 3, 33.

15. Sen, *The Idea of Justice*, 123; see also 125, 128, 136, 144, 149, and 151.

16. He did say that in international disputes the only impartial spectators are neutral nations (*TMS* III.3.42, 154). But Sen's concerns are hardly limited to international disputes.

17. Intimacy and *equality*, of course; interacting on a daily basis with people who are below or above us in a racial or class hierarchy breeds contempt and humiliation, not empathy. Smith would probably acknowledge that point. He was in any case a strong believer in human equality, and his account of empathy presupposes an equality of the people empathizing with one another. See Darwall, "Sympathetic Liberalism"; my "Adam Smith on Equality"; and Elizabeth Anderson, "Equality."

18. Nicholas Phillipson characterizes the whole of Adam Smith's moral and political writings as "a discourse on the social and ethical significance of face-to-face relationships between independently-minded individuals." Phillipson, "Adam Smith as Civic Moralist," 198.

19. On the difficulties involved in defining a "people," see my *What Is Peoplehood?*

Chapter Six

1. Prinz, "Against Empathy" (hereafter *AEP*); Bloom, "Against Empathy," *Boston Review*; Bloom, *Against Empathy* (hereafter *AEB*).

2. In arguing that empathy should play an essential but not exhaustive role in moral and political decision making, I agree strongly with Nancy Sherman:

> We are in a position to help others in meaningful ways when we have some feel for their circumstances as they appear to them. . . . [This does not mean that we need] to accede to the wishes of those being helped. . . . Empathy is a form of understanding. It informs our appreciation of others. But how we go on to help another in morally appropriate ways is not simply a matter of *endorsing* another's self-conception or self-conceived means for amelioration, though these may be *acknowledged* within a sensitive intervention. . . . Similar remarks apply in conceiving of the sort of social intelligence involved in constructing social policies. Economic, political, sociological, demographic expertise enter, but so too does a more concrete and less theory-driven grasp of the lives of those

NOTES TO PAGES 102–7

affected by various policies. Here the concrete lives of individuals as opposed to those statistically grasped becomes relevant ("Empathy and Imagination," 110–11).

Chapters 7 and 8, below, may be taken as an attempt to spell out what an approach based on these suggestive remarks might look like in practice.

3. "Against Empathy," *Boston Review*.

4. Bloom, "The Dark Side of Empathy"; *AEB* 191–95.

5. Bloom, "Against Empathy," 3–4.

6. Compare Goldie, who describes imagining, when standing on an ancient road in the Pyrenees, what it might have been like to be a Roman foot soldier climbing up that road: "One can, in such circumstances, empathize with a narrator as a *type*; one can think afterwards of the narrator, perhaps as 'that soldier' or 'him,' whilst acknowledging that one knows nothing particular about him which enables one to individuate him from others of the type" (*The Emotions*, 204).

7. Compare our empathy for fictional characters, discussed above in chapter 3, section 3. Just as the empathy we have for a fictional character can give us a new way of looking at real people, so the empathy we have for a notional future person can lead us to do things for real future people.

8. *TMS* I.i.4.6–7, 21–22; Bloom notes this on *AEB* 68.

9. Bloom relies largely on evidence that cognitive and emotional empathy are carried out by different parts of the brain, in support of his distinction between the two (*AEB* 71). But elsewhere he is wary of how much we can learn about psychological processes based on the part of the brain with which they are associated (59–60). Indeed, he concedes that the very research he cites about the involvement of different parts of the brain in knowing what others feel versus sharing those feelings does not show that the knowing and the feeling are unrelated. "Smell, vision, and taste are separate," he says, "but they come together in the appreciation of a meal" (72). Exactly; one might even say that someone who cannot see, or has lost her sense of smell, cannot fully *understand* what I am appreciating when I delight in a beautifully presented aromatic meal. But if we can say that, then surely we can also say that another may not truly *empathize* with us unless they are capable of the combination of cognitive and emotional skills that go into sharing what I am feeling or am likely to feel. And for moral purposes we may find it helpful or necessary to define empathy in such a way. In any case, the conceptual point about whether empathy should be defined so as to include some kind of emotional identification with others cannot be settled by what goes on in our brains. Brain processes, here and elsewhere, underdetermine psychological concepts.

10. Prinz talks mostly about Hume, but indicates that he sees Hume and Smith as holding more or less the same view: see Prinz, "Is Empathy Necessary for Morality?" 212, 215.

11. Hume writes, in a passage Prinz quotes, that what he calls "sympathy"—his term, remember, for what we call "empathy"—"account[s] for" approbation and esteem. In another passage Hume says that we are pleased with qualities or characters that have "a tendency to the good of mankind" because we share in the pleasures of others by sympathy (T 3.3.1, quoted in *AEP* 215 and 216). But these passages are ambiguous. They may mean just that sympathy is a *means* to moral approval: that I need first to feel other people's pleasures before I can feel that the cause of those pleasures is worthy of approval. This fits better with what Hume says elsewhere, in which moral approval is simply a pleasure taken in "the . . . survey" of intentions and qualities of character that benefit the agent or another person. So there are two kinds of pleasure involved in the evaluative process: first, a pleasure in the pleasures of others, and second, a pleasure in the cause of this pleasure. Empathy gives us the first of these pleasures but not the second. The second, however, is moral approval proper. (Prinz appears to recognize this in another paper, where he

190   NOTES TO PAGES 107–12

describes empathy, for Hume, as a "precursor to moral judgment" rather than a component of it: "Is Empathy . . . ?" 214).

12. Goldie makes a similar point: "Sympathy is partial, and there is no requirement internal to the concept of sympathy to correct this partiality" (216).

13. *AEP* 231, 220; and Prinz, "Is Empathy . . . ?" 217.

14. Bloom agrees that other emotions tend also to be biased (*AEB* 50, 87, 211), though he says that empathy is "the worst" of them all in this respect. This is also baffling, however. Surely anger is worse than empathy, if only because of its tendency to violence, its overpowering nature, and its extreme resistance to correction. If I feel merely *empathetic* to a kinsman who seems to me under threat from a stranger, I'm probably still open to a gentle and careful explanation of why my kinsman is in the wrong and the stranger's behavior is justified; if I am *angry* at the stranger, I am unlikely even to let you give me that explanation.

15. Smith, *Inquiry into the Nature and Causes of the Wealth of Nations*, 97, 99–100. (References to this book will henceforth be incorporated into the text with "*WN*" and page number.) I have argued elsewhere that the *Wealth of Nations* is designed to arouse the empathy of comfortable readers for poor people, see the sources cited in chapter 2, note 58, and chapter 3, note 48.

16. See C. Daniel Batson et al., "Empathy and Attitudes."

17. Prinz, "Against Empathy," 228.

18. See note 15 above.

19. Hannah Arendt describes something like this process under the heading of what she calls "representative thinking": "I form an opinion by considering a given issue from different viewpoints, by making present to my mind the standpoints of those who are absent . . . The more people's standpoints I have present in my mind . . . , and the better I can imagine how I would feel and think if I were in their place, the stronger will be my capacity for representative thinking and the more valid my final conclusions." In an unpublished lecture, she illustrates this process by saying that I might come to an opinion about poverty and misery by looking at a slum dwelling and "representing to myself how I would feel if I had to live there"—by "think[ing] in the place of the slum-dweller" (Arendt, "Truth and Politics," 141, and New School lecture course, 1965, as cited in Arendt, *Lectures on Kant's Political Philosophy*, 107–8). Arendt ties this view of political thinking to the "enlarged mentality" that Kant describes in the *Critique of Judgment*; I think she would have done better to draw on Smith.

20. In the *Wealth of Nations* he seems to have reconciled himself to them: *WN* 872, 891.

21. Writings about the poor, in both Scotland and England, were permeated by the assumption that the poor tend to be people of inherent and ineradicable vices, prime among which is an addiction to alcohol. "The Scottish Poor Law," says T. M. Devine, "was underpinned by a set of values and attitudes which assumed that . . . the poor were poor because of defects of character, idleness and intemperance" (T. M. Devine, "The Urban Crisis," 412–13). Even the radical reformer John Bellers recommended his proposals to help the poor by saying that they may remove "the Profaneness of Swearing, Drunkenness, etc. with the Idleness and Penury of many in the Nation; which evil Qualities of the Poor, are an Objection with some against this Undertaking, though with others a great Reason for it " (Clarke, ed., *John Bellers*, 55; see also 52). For Daniel Defoe, the linked vices of indolence and alcoholism may be a racial trait, something peculiar to the English poor:

> There is a general taint of Slothfulness upon our Poor, there's nothing more frequent, than for an Englishman to Work till he has got his Pocket full of Money, and then go

NOTES TO PAGES 112–17

and be idle, or perhaps drunk, till 'tis all gone, and perhaps himself in Debt; and ask him in his Cups what he intends, he'll tell you honestly, he'll drink as long as it lasts, and then go to work for more. (Defoe, "Giving Alms no Charity," 186–88).

These views continued into the next century. Both when the original act for the protection of Friendly Societies was proposed in 1793, and when it was amended in 1819, the debate turned considerably on whether such societies contributed to or detracted from alleviating the alcoholic tendencies of the poor. (From the Board of Agriculture report against benefit clubs, 1793: "Benefit clubs, holden at public houses, increase the number of those houses, and naturally lead to idleness and intemperance."). See P. H. J. H. Gosden, *The Friendly Societies in England*, especially 3, 117–18, and 122.

22. *WN* 100, from which the rest of the quotations in this paragraph also come.

23. For a nuanced treatment of this problem—more friendly than I am to the idea that there is a problem to be explained here—see Leonidas Montes, *Adam Smith in Context*, chapter 2.

24. See my *On Adam Smith's Wealth of Nations*, chapter 5.

25. We are "non-tuists" in economic transactions, to use Lionel Robbins' term; we are not egoists. See Robbins, *A History of Economic Thought*, 132.

26. Smith makes it even clearer that the point of his comparison with other animals is that we alone understand one another's interests in passages in his *Lectures of Jurisprudence* that anticipate *WN* I.ii.2: see Smith, *Lectures on Jurisprudence*, 352–53, 493–94.

27. There is a similar unity between the two books if, as I argue elsewhere (see sources in note 15 above), Smith uses the techniques for raising empathy that he describes in the *Theory of Moral Sentiments* in order to arouse empathy for the poor in the *Wealth of Nations*.

28. Besides being hard to read for anyone without a sophisticated education (and very long: not something that a worker was likely to have time for), the *Wealth of Nations* was an expensive book. Ian Ross says that it probably sold for one pound, sixteen shillings, which Ross calls "a very modest price" (Ross, *Life of Adam Smith*, 270). But it is hard to understand how he arrives at that judgment. Hume's *Essays* could be bought at the same time for twelve shillings or less, Locke's *Essay Concerning Human Understanding* for five shillings. In any case, workers tended to take home between twelve and twenty shillings a week, and even military officers made less than one pound, nine shillings, per day. So the *Wealth of Nations* cost more than a day's wage for comfortably-off people, and more than a week's wage for a worker. See J. E. Elliott, "The Cost of Reading in Eighteenth-Century Britain," for details on prices and wages.

Chapter Seven

1. Sunstein, "Cognition and Cost-Benefit Analysis." I thank Joe Persky for drawing my attention to this essay.

2. Sunstein takes his point to be a general one, but it is telling that his examples are limited to these areas. He does not even consider tradeoffs between, say, environmental protections and the rights of indigenous peoples—though he does have a nuanced discussion of how we might avoid resting policy purely on cost-benefit calculations when we are faced with a disproportionate health cost to a minority group. The issues I am about to raise about recognizing "harm" are far less likely to come up regarding issues of health and the environment than regarding matters of human dignity; we are in far greater agreement about what harm to the environment or our health looks like than about harm to our dignity.

3. See, for instance, Bernard Williams, "A Critique of Utilitarianism"; James Griffin, *Well-Being*, chapters 1 and 2; Robert Adams, *Finite and Infinite Goods*, 84–93; and Richard Kraut, *What Is Good and Why*, 120–30.

4. Nussbaum, *Political Emotions*, 145. Nussbaum has worked with the notion of flourishing for years, developing her influential "capabilities" theory as an account of what it might mean.

5. See Amartya Sen, *Resources, Values and Development*, 309–10; and Nussbaum, *Women and Human Development*, 139.

6. Forster, *Passage to India*, 58, 78.

7. It is "a critical commonplace," says Suzanne Keen, "that Charles Dickens's condemnation of the New Poor Law's workhouse system in *Oliver Twist* . . . prevented the full implementation of the law." Keen, *Empathy and the Novel*, 52. Despite the hedging implied in the phrase "critical commonplace," Keen seems to endorse this claim; see 38, 118, and 140.

8. George Eliot wrote, of her intentions as a novelist, that "the only effect I ardently long to produce by my writings, is that those who read them should be better able to *imagine* and *feel* the pains and joys of those who differ from themselves in everything but the broad fact of being struggling erring human creatures." Letter to Charles Bray, July 5, 1859, quoted in Keen, 54.

9. Compare this example, from Shirley Williams's novel *Dessa Rose*, of a white woman who suddenly sees, via empathy, what is demeaning about her demand for proof of a runaway slave's suffering:

"The mistress have to see the welts in the darky's hide, eh?"
"Ye—" His tone implied that her desire for proof was mean and petty and she flushed hotly, as the image of herself inspecting the wench's naked loins flashed vividly to life in her mind.

Quoted in Karen Jones, "The Politics of Credibility," 172.

10. The vast literature on "adaptive preferences" brings out well how oppressed people develop preferences that reflect rather than resist their own oppression. See, for instance, Jon Elster, *Sour Grapes*, chapter 3; Martha Nussbaum, "Adaptive Preferences and Women's Options"; and Serene Khader, *Adaptive Preferences and Women's Empowerment*.

11. For a rich elaboration of the implications of this thought, see Darwall, *Welfare and Rational Care*.

12. Chapter 2, section 9; and chapter 3, section 3. We need not suppose that fiction alone achieves this goal, by the way; certain forms of journalism and history may do so as well. But there are some advantages to fiction. As Suzanne Keen points out (see chapter 3, note 12, and text thereto), fiction can release us "from the obligations of self-protection through skepticism and suspicion" by which we normally react to certain groups of people. And the kinds of journalism and history that evoke empathy in any case normally employ some of the imaginative techniques characteristic of fiction.

13. At an event on Holocaust Remembrance Day sponsored by two strongly anti-Zionist organizations, one speaker told of her childhood in Hamburg, Germany, her internment in four Nazi camps, and her arrival, from there, at a kibbutz in British Palestine in 1947. The effect on the audience was striking: "A student wearing a keffiyeh told Ms. Bell that this was the first time she had heard someone capture the feeling of home and belonging in Israel. Until that night, the student said she had only heard of Israel as an oppressor." Nancy Bernstein and Maya Haber, "The Real Edith Bell." Similar stories are told by Palestinian students who went with their professor on a trip to Auschwitz—see Zeina M. Barakat, "A Palestinian Student Defends Her Visit to Auschwitz"—and parallel ones by Jewish participants in trips to the West Bank organized by such groups as Breaking

NOTES TO PAGES 125–29

the Silence and Encounter. The Bereaved Parents Circle, which brings together Israelis and Palestinians who have lost loved ones to the violence of the conflict, is also known for its impact on people with widely ranging political views, and for including in its ranks people who at one point would have been unwilling to sit with anyone on the other side of the conflict.

14. See Jonathan Haidt, *The Righteous Mind*, part 1.

15. See chapter 3, note 8.

16. See above, chapter 6, sections 3 and 6.

17. See note 7 above.

18. See Dancy, *Ethics without Principles*, especially chapter 5.

19. Recall here the particularist structure of Smithian empathy discussed in chapter 1, section 8.

Chapter Eight

1. Rawls, *Theory of Justice*, 27.

2. See Taylor, *Sources of the Self*, part 1; Adams, *Finite and Infinite Goods*, chapters 3 and 10; Thomson, "Goodness and Utilitarianism"; Parfit, *On What Matters*; and Williams, "Critique of Utilitarianism."

3. Greene, *Moral Tribes*, chapters 7–8. Haidt says, "I don't know what the best normative ethical theory is for individuals in their private lives. But when we talk about making laws and implementing public policies in Western democracies that contain some degree of ethnic and moral diversity, then I think there is no compelling alternative to utilitarianism." Haidt, *The Righteous Mind*, 316.

Cathy Gere offers an incisive analysis of the social and political factors making for the current revival of utilitarianism in Gere, *Pain, Pleasure, and the Greater Good*, chapter 6.

4. Judith Jarvis Thomson began her 1992 Presidential Address to the American Philosophical Association with an amusing summary of how irritating the perennial return of utilitarianism is to philosophers who see it as shallow and simplistic:

Many of us who work in moral philosophy spend a lot of time worrying about utilitarianism. Our problem isn't merely that it continues to have its friends, though it does; our problem is deeper, lying in the fact that we haven't found—and its friends are delighted to draw our attention to the fact that we haven't found—a way of positively killing it off. No amount of mowing and tugging seems to work: it keeps on reappearing, every spring, like a weed with a long root (Thomson, "Goodness and Utilitarianism," 7).

That was twenty-seven years ago. Things have not improved since then.

5. Greene, *Moral Tribes*, 15, 188–208.

6. He compares Kant's "pure practical reasoning" to mathematical reasoning (183–84), which assimilates Kant to realists like Samuel Clarke, and entirely misses the force of the word "practical" in the phrase "pure practical reasoning" (on Clarke and Kant, see Korsgaard, *Sources of Normativity*, lecture I). He also tries to lay out Kant's views without mentioning the word "freedom": that for Kant morality is supposed to be an expression of our freedom (the central point of Kant's moral philosophy) seems to have escaped him entirely. But then, Greene is cheerfully dismissive of philosophers who disagree with him. Rather than take up Kant's thought in any depth, he prefers to mock it by repeatedly citing an absurd comment Kant made about masturbation (300, 332); and he knows so little about Kant that he makes the astonishingly false claim that Kant was "very religious" (386, note to 338). In fact, Kant was such a heretic that he was at one point forbidden by the Prussian king from writing anything further on religion.

7. On this subject, see T. H. Irwin, *Aristotle's First Principles* (Oxford: Clarendon, 1988), 334–38; John McDowell, "Some Issues in Aristotle's Moral Psychology" and "Might There Be External Reasons?" in his *Mind, Value and Reality*; Sarah Broadie, *Ethics with Aristotle*, 232–42; and Rosalind Hursthouse, *On Virtue Ethics*, part 1.

8. Stephen Darwall has brought this out clearly. See his *Welfare and Rational Care*, 108, note 25; and *The Second-Person Standpoint*, 314–15.

9. Williams, *Ethics and the Limits of Philosophy*, 108–10. See also Williams, "Critique of Utilitarianism," 138–39.

10. Sidgwick, *The Methods of Ethics*, 490.

11. See my *Third Concept of Liberty*, chapter 5.

12. Let alone gaining the pleasure of the video game by working *against* immigrants' rights, ruining the experiments of other scientists, or giving into temptation.

13. Mill, *Utilitarianism*, 13.

14. But see my *Third Concept of Liberty*, 116–18; and Steven Gerrard, "Desire and Desirability: Bradley, Russell and Moore versus Mill."

15. Nietzsche, *Twilight of the Idols*, section 12.

16. Williams, "Critique of Utilitarianism," 135.

17. See Greene, *Moral Tribes*, chapters 7–8; and my *Good and the Good Book*, chapter 2.

18. See Rawls, *Justice as Fairness*, 1–29.

19. Rawls, *Theory of Justice*, 92.

20. To pursue our own "life-plan" and "comprehensive conception of the good," in Rawls's terminology.

21. Rawls, *Theory of Justice*, pp. 175–83. See also Rawls, *Political Liberalism*, 66–71.

22. On the problems for Rawls arising from the differences in particular individuals' circumstances, see Amartya Sen, "Equality of What?"

23. See John Finnis, *Natural Law and Natural Rights*, chapter 4; James Griffin, *Well-Being*, chapter 7; Sen, "Capability and Well-Being"; and Martha Nussbaum, *Creating Capabilities*.

24. Nussbaum says that her account "is meant to be both tentative and open-ended. We allow explicitly for the possibility that we will learn from our encounters with other human societies to recognize things about ourselves that we had not seen before, or even to change in certain ways, according more importance to something we had thought more peripheral." Later, she describes her list of capabilities as "a working list." "It is put out to generate debate," she says, adding, "It has done so and will continue to do so, and it will be revised accordingly." Nussbaum, "Human Capabilities, Female Human Beings," 74, 80.

25. T. M. Scanlon, *What We Owe to Each Other*; and Gerald Gaus, *The Order of Public Reason*.

26. Compare Stephen Darwall, on the advantages of a conception of each person's welfare that is developed from the standpoint of one caring for that person: "Empathy, Sympathy, Care," 262–63 and 275–79, and Darwall, *Welfare and Rational Care*.

27. Note that in this latter set of cases, the problem is not simply that our target is doing things that are in fact harmful to others; if we are engaging in truly Smithian empathy, the empathy of the impartial spectator, we can see *that* clearly enough by empathizing with those others. The problem is that our target herself fails to recognize this point, and that our attempts to empathize with her therefore lead us to a position in which we need to see what we would otherwise take as a harm in a light that makes it out to be good. This is not an abstract theoretical concern. Attempts to empathize with racists, for instance, will inevitably put us in such a position.

28. For instance, in the remark just quoted about being out of debt, but also in his condemnation of slavery, and in various remarks in the *Wealth of Nations* in praise of "independency" and "the liberty and security of individuals" (e.g., *WN* III.i.3, 378; III.iii.12, 405; III.iv.4, 412).

29. Smith, *Lectures on Jurisprudence*, 378. Food, clothing and lodging also appear as the basic human needs in *TMS* IV.i.11, 186.

30. For a nuanced and thoughtful account of Smith's critique of utilitarianism, see James Otteson, *Adam Smith's Marketplace of Life*, 50–58. Otteson makes Smith out to be a kind of rule-utilitarian *malgré lui*, however, at the end of his book (249–52). For Otteson, the norms of morality on which the impartial spectator operates in each generation evolve so as to enhance individual and communal happiness. I disagree with this. For happiness to serve as a cross-generational "criterion of selection" (Otteson's term) for moral norms, it would have to be definable independent of morality. That is impossible, for Smith: our happiness consists overwhelmingly, for him, in our being virtuous. (See my "Adam Smith's Moral and Political Philosophy.") However, Otteson is right to say that moral norms evolve for Smith, and that Smith needs some criterion of selection in order to judge that they are evolving for the better rather than the worse. That criterion of selection can be an immanent than a transcendent one, however. It could, for instance, make use, in each generation, of impartial-spectator norms that are already accepted in a society, and, to the extent that it does transcend a society's given norms, it could appeal to freedom and dignity as well as happiness. That seems to be Smith's own practice in assessing changes of law over time in his *Lectures on Jurisprudence*.

An account of how a society's impartial spectator procedure can be turned on its own norms that fits this latter description rather than Otteson's can be found in Sayre-McCord, "Sentiments and Spectators: Adam Smith's Theory of Moral Judgment" and "Hume and Smith on Sympathy, Approbation, and Moral Judgment."

31. Indeed, "of all other rational creatures" (III.5.7, 166).

32. See my discussion of Kögler, "Empathy, Dialogical Self, and Reflexive Interpretation," in chapter 2, section 10, and the notes thereto.

33. Recall Jamison, in *The Empathy Exams*: "Empathy isn't just listening, . . . It's asking the questions whose answers need to be listened to. Empathy requires inquiry as much as imagination." Quoted above, text to chapter 1, note 25.

34. Henry Sidgwick maintained that "a man's future good on the whole is what he would now desire and seek on the whole if all the consequences of all the different lines of conduct open to him were accurately foreseen and adequately realized in imagination at the present point of time" (*The Methods of Ethics*, 111–12). We might say that my account of a person's "good on the whole" is what she "would now desire and seek" if, in addition to knowing the consequences of her action, she had "adequately [discussed and] realized in imagination" the perspectives on her desires of every other reasonable being, and had entered into all of their perspectives and the desires they give rise to. Like Sidgwick, I acknowledge that this "elaborate and complex . . . conception" is not what we ordinarily mean by "good"; but I would argue that it "supplies an intelligible and admissible interpretation" of that term that "giv[es] philosophical precision" to it. And the idea that our ordinary use of "good" is a provisional approximation to this more precise meaning has advantages for both the practice and the theory of morality (see below).

35. These parallels should not be surprising. Who we take ourselves to be is intimately bound up with what we consider to be good—what we aim at.

It's worth stressing that all three sides of this triangulating process give it advantages in humility over utilitarianism. Most directly, it requires me to listen to you before deciding what is good for you. At the same time, it reminds me of the peculiarities about *me* that might lead me to read myself into you rather than listen to you. Finally, it calls on me to adapt whatever conception of morality I uphold—utilitarian, Kantian, Christian, Muslim—to what the many different people in the world actually say and think they want out of life: to humanize these general principles. In all these ways, it keeps me from simply imposing the conception of goods and harms I have developed by myself on everyone else, as if my reasoning to that conception is decisive. Indeed, it ensures, by its very complexity as well as the uncertain results that each of its pieces is likely to yield, that I will never achieve a decisive conception of human goods and harms—that every attempt to establish them must be provisional and corrigible.

36. Note that structural features of this approach to the true good implicitly reflect the respect for every human being that is so appealing in the Kantian tradition, even while its content will reflect the emphasis on our emotions, and on what we experience as pleasurable, that is appealing in the sentimentalist and utilitarian traditions. The approach is also hospitable to virtue ethics and religiously based ethical systems, insofar as the perspectives of people participating in the hypothesized conversation endorse ethical views of these kinds. This approach to the good can therefore provide an excellent focus for the eclecticism about ethics that I defend in *Divine Teaching* and *The Good and the Good Book*, and endorse above in chapter 3, section 11.

37. All who *wish* to protect and pursue the ends of others, at least—all who are "reasonable," in the sense that Rawls used that term in his later writings.

Chapter Nine

1. Aristotle, *Politics* I.2, 1253a27–30.

2. *Politics* I.5, 1254a18.

3. See chapter 3, section 5.

4. On self-governance as the defining mark of humanity, see Korsgaard, "Reflections on the Evolution of Morality." Smithian empathy is of course an essential part of self-governance, on the view I have been developing in this book—essential, indeed, to our very conception of our selves.

5. For rich treatments of bestialization, see Nussbaum, *Political Emotions*, 182–91; and Charles Mills, "Kant and Race, Redux." I believe, contra Mills, that Kant's mature moral system does not allow for a category of *Untermenschen*. But there is no question that at least until his Critical period, Kant did regard Africans and Native Americans in that way.

6. I have found it only at "History of Astronomy" III.2, 49; and *TMS* III.ii.2.9, 118. In the latter passage, it is a metaphor for pangs of conscience.

7. "The pride of man makes him love to domineer." *WN* III.2.10; 388.

8. Smith and Kant have a number of striking affinities: see my "Philosophy in Moral Practice" and "Values Behind the Market: Kant's Response to the *Wealth of Nations*."

9. My talk of a "sense of common humanity," here and in what follows, has affinities with what Kant calls "the *sensus communis*" in section 40 of his *Critique of the Power of Judgment*. But Kant insisted that that shared sense could not contribute to morality. For reflections on parallels between Smith's *Theory of Moral Sentiments* and Kant's *Critique of the Power of Judgment*, in part with regard to the *sensus communis*, see my *Third Concept of Liberty*.

10. Kant, *Religion within the Boundaries*, 59 (Ak 6:36). Further references to this work will be incorporated into the text with the prefix "*RWR*."

11. He thus fends off a long tradition that construes our sexuality or instinct for self-preservation as intrinsically evil.

NOTES TO PAGES 154–60

12. "Ideas," for Kant, are rational constructions used for assessing empirical reality, which cannot be instantiated by any empirical particular.

13. To be clear: I don't mean to deny that Kant may himself have thought that we can freely will only good actions. It's just that that view has notorious problems; it seems, above all, to deprive us of any responsibility for wrongdoing. (*RWR* is taken by many as attempting to get around this problem by distinguishing sharply between two faculties of willing—*Wille* and *Willkür*—one of which can make bad choices, and one of which cannot. I don't think this distinction solves the problem.) And there are texts in *RWR* that point in a different direction. I rely on these texts as a basis on which to construct an argument for the "no demons" thesis that Kant himself does not explicitly give. Of course, if it is *true* that we cannot freely will wrongdoing, that will strengthen the case for the "no demons" thesis. I thank Daniel Sutherland and Matt Boyle for pressing me to clarify this point.

14. David Sussman gives a lucid account of this view (a modest version of it, at least) in "For Badness' Sake."

15. See, for instance, the papers collected in Sergio Tenenbaum's *Desire, Practical Reason and the Good*.

16. Manson's horrific early life fits this story perfectly. There are fictional portrayals of criminals who are wholly sane but nevertheless enjoy the death or suffering of others; Hannibal Lecter comes to mind. In real life, however, we would seek psychological or physiological causes for anyone who resembled a Hannibal Lecter. It is an interesting question why certain literary forms avoid such modes of explanation. The thought that there might be demons is perhaps partly attractive to us: it relieves us of responsibility for the evil in the world, and suggests that there could be an easy solution to it (we just need to get rid of the demons). Alternatively, having a demonic villain provides a good excuse for inflicting terrific violence on that villain, which audiences can enjoy without guilt. Mark Alznauer has suggested a third possibility to me: that in fictional demons, we admire or vicariously enjoy the freedom and courage that we imagine might come with throwing off the constraints of morality.

17. Kant, *Groundwork*, 19 (Ak 4:407).

18. Kant seems to echo Hume several times in the transcendental deduction. See Robert Paul Wolff, "Kant's Debt to Hume via Beattie."

19. Kant actually calls this predisposition "humanity," but that is confusing—both because I use that word in a very different way, and because Kant himself uses that word very differently in his other moral writings (see, for instance, *Groundwork* 4:430, or *Metaphysics of Morals* 6:237). The content of the predisposition is very much what Rousseau had called amour propre: an inclination "to gain worth in the opinion of others." (*RWR* 6:27, 51).

20. Kant regards his moral faith as an answer to the third of the four questions he thinks philosophy should address: "For what may we hope?" (The other three are "What can we know?" "What should we do?" and "What is the human being?")

21. Dennett, *The Intentional Stance*.

22. This is implicit throughout his theory of interpretation, but perhaps made clearest in "Belief and the Basis of Meaning," 145–46. For the explicit and somewhat different use of "triangulation" that Davidson employed later in his career, see the essays collected in Davidson, *Subjective, Intersubjective, Objective*; and Peter Pagin, "Semantic Triangulation." For a method of interpretive triangulation exactly parallel to the one I invoke here, see Bernard Williams, "Deciding to Believe," 144.

23. It's worth emphasizing that I want by no means to deny the reality of evil, nor does Kant do that. I am just trying to give an account of evil that shows it to be a possibility for all of us. I

think this sort of account in fact brings out the true horror of human evil more than demonization does.

It's also worth emphasizing that it is not my purpose to rule out the punishment of evildoers. Understanding how people's actions arise from their perspectives by no means leads us to think that they should never be punished for those actions. I am likely to think *I* should be punished for some things I do, after all, even if I would rather shirk that punishment. Punishment can be justified on grounds of deterrence, of removing people from situations in which they can harm others, of restoring the dignity of victims, and in many other ways. The one thing that follows from the "no demons" thesis as regards punishment is that no one should be punished in ways that we think we ourselves would not deserve to be punished. That may mean that there are certain kinds of punishment that should never be inflicted on any human being—torture is probably ruled out thereby, though the death penalty may not be (other considerations may, however, rule it out)—and that no one should be punished to a degree vastly disproportionate to what he or she has done. Perhaps not coincidentally, Kant's own views of punishment have these implications: see my "Kant's Theory of Punishment." I am grateful to Tony Coady for prodding me to comment on this issue.

24. Nagel, "What Is It Like to Be a Bat?"

25. A reader for this book worried that I am begging a question here. The demonizer does not regard the people he refuses to empathize with *as* human beings at all. So his refusal to empathize with them is not, by his lights, a refusal to empathize with a human perspective: he is still willing to empathize with everyone he regards as human. My response is that recognizing others as human precedes our ideological and moral views, on the Smithian account I have been developing here (and, I think, in fact). The recognition of others as human comes with empathy, which we engage in before we develop moralities and ideologies. So a refusal to empathize, on ideological grounds, is in part an effort in bad faith (we know perfectly well, on some level, that the others we are writing out of the human community are in fact human), and in part a deliberate closing off of a capacity to which we are naturally disposed. And closing off that capacity has devastating effects, I believe, on our ability to maintain a humanistic morality—indeed, on our ability to regard our purported moral norms as truly moral at all.

26. On this subject, see Joshua Trachtenberg, *The Devil and the Jews.*

27. See Raya Jalabi, "Who Are the Yazidis and Why Is ISIS Hunting Them?"

28. See chapter 8, section 9, and note 34 thereto.

29. There is a version of this point on the Kantian view as well. For Kant, we perceive the good by way of reason, and in principle we need access to no other rational being's perspective in order to do that. But how do we know that we are rational beings? Presumably, by understanding ourselves as like other rational beings. (For Habermas—a modern Kantian—we need to participate in rational discourse with others to achieve this recognition.) So if we cut ourselves off from being able to recognize ourselves in some set of other rational beings, we threaten our ability to see ourselves as rational.

30. It happens that, a day after I wrote this sentence, the *New York Times* reported that Robert Bowers, who killed eleven Jews at a Saturday morning service in Pittsburgh, had written online, "Jews are the children of Satan" (Keven Roose, "Social Site Let Suspect's Hate Spill Unbridled," *New York Times*, 10/27/2018, p. 14). So that sort of view is by no means dead, and can be very dangerous. But it is no longer common, and—in the United States and Europe, at least—it is rarely part of public discourse.

31. Thanks to Gene Goldstein-Plesser for formulating this distinction between binary and nonbinary forms of demonization.

NOTES TO PAGES 163–65

32. "There's something profoundly sexual to the Zionist pleasure w/#Israel's aggression," he tweeted, on the second day of the Gaza war in 2014; "Sublimation through bloodletting, a common perversion." Whatever one thinks of Israel or its attack on Gaza, there is no reason to reach for a sexual explanation of the solidarity of Israelis behind the Gaza war, especially when far more plausible ones are ready to hand: that Israelis were afraid of the harm that Hamas could do, or were infuriated at the kidnapping and murder of Israeli teenagers that preceded the attack, or were obsessed for religious or nationalist reasons with maintaining control over Palestinian lands. All of these explanations are far more humanistic than one that posits a sexual pleasure in the blood of others (which also, of course, also calls up an old image of Jews as enjoying non-Jewish blood: an image tied to the idea that Jews incarnate the devil). The alternative explanations appeal to motivations that Salaita himself can presumably imagine having in certain circumstances, even if he thinks he might be wrong to have them; the explanation to which he actually appealed makes Jews out to be a kind of creature utterly different from him.

33. See Bruce B. Lawrence, "The Jihad of Pamela Geller." Lawrence says of Geller, "There is no humanity in those whom Geller decries. They are subhuman beasts, worthy of any assault, whether a punitive police or all-out military action" (ibid.). This seems right, except that I think it more accurate to say that Geller portrays Muslims as superhuman demons rather than subhuman beasts. Beasts can be forgiven, for they know not what they do. Demons, by contrast, must be wiped out. And that is what Geller, who advocates a worldwide Jewish-Christian war against Islam, seems to want.

34. Societies are more often demonized than are individuals. It is hard, in the modern day, to persuade people that any single individual could be committed to evil for its own sake, but easy to persuade them that certain groups, and group ideologies, are so committed. I think it is a grave mistake to view any group, even ISIS or the Nazis, in that way. Both the views and the actions of ISIS are certainly evil, but I find it hard to believe that *they* see their actions in that way: they are far more likely to interpret what they are doing under the guise of the good. In any case, demonizing them puts them beyond the reach of naturalistic explanation. This means that we lose our grip on the sort of understanding that could help us to change the minds of their members and potential members, or to prevent groups like them from arising in the first place. We also open ourselves once again to the dangerous temptation to treat them as they treat us: to dehumanize them, and thereby dehumanize ourselves. That serves neither our pragmatic nor our moral interests.

35. Compare Bloom, *ABE* 184–85, on the ways in which morality can inspire cruelty and violence. Bloom's discussion of dehumanization more generally (180–87) is astute and interesting.

36. Compare Christopher Browning, on his methods in writing a history of a Nazi police battalion that committed a series of horrific massacres of Jews in 1942: "Clearly the writing of such a history requires the rejection of demonization. The policemen in the battalion who carried out the massacres and deportations, like the much smaller number who refused or evaded, were human beings. I must recognize that in the same situation, I could have been either a killer or an evader—both were human—if I want to understand and explain the behavior of both as best I can. What I do not accept, however, are the old clichés that to explain is to excuse, to understand is to forgive. Explaining is not excusing; understanding is not forgiving." Browning, *Ordinary Men*, xx.

Bibliography

Abramson, Kate. "Hume on Cultural Conflicts of Values." *Philosophical Studies* 94 (1999).

Adams, Robert. *Finite and Infinite Goods*. Oxford, UK: Oxford University Press, 1999.

Ainslie, Donald. "Skepticism about Persons in Book II of Hume's *Treatise*." *Journal of the History of Philosophy* 37, no. 3 (1999).

———. "Sympathy and the Unity of Hume's Idea of Self." In *Persons and Passions: Essays in Honor of Annette Baier*, ed. J. Jenkins, J. Whiting, and C. Williams. Notre Dame, IN: University of Notre Dame Press, 2005.

Allison, Henry. *Lessing and the Enlightenment*. Ann Arbor: University of Michigan Press, 1966.

Anderson, Benedict. *Imagined Communities*. London: Verso, 1983.

Anderson, Elizabeth. "Equality." In *Adam Smith: His Life, Thought and Legacy*, ed. R. Hanley. Princeton, NJ: Princeton University Press, 2016.

Arendt, Hannah. *Lectures on Kant's Political Philosophy*, ed. R. Beiner. Chicago: University of Chicago Press, 1982.

———. "Truth and Politics." In *Between Past and Future*. New York: Viking, 1968.

Aristotle. *Politics*. In *The Complete Works of Aristotle*, ed. J. Barnes. Princeton, NJ: Princeton University Press, 1984.

Bailey, Olivia. "Empathy, Concern, and Understanding in *The Theory of Moral Sentiments*." *Adam Smith Review* 9.

———. "The Ethics and Epistemology of Empathy." PhD dissertation, Harvard University, 2018.

Barakat, Zeina M. "A Palestinian Student Defends Her Visit to Auschwitz." *Atlantic*, April 28, 2014.

Barry, Brian. *Culture and Equality*. Cambridge: Polity Press, 2001.

Batson, C. D. *Altruism in Humans*. Oxford: Oxford University Press, 2011.

Batson, C. Daniel, et al. "Empathy and Attitudes: Can Feeling for a Member of a Stigmatized Group Improve Feelings toward the Group?" *Journal of Personality and Social Psychology* 72, no. 1 (1997).

Batson, C. Daniel, J. Chang, R. Orr, and J. Rowland. "Empathy, Attitudes, and Action: Can Feeling for a Member of a Stigmatized Group Motivate One to Help the Group?" *Personality and Social Psychology Bulletin* 28, no. 12 (2002).

Bell, Daniel A. *Communitarianism and Its Critics*. Oxford, UK: Clarendon Press, 1993.

Bellers, John. *John Bellers: His Life, Times, and Writings*, ed. G. Clarke. London: Routledge and Kegan Paul, 1987.

Bernal, Victoria, and Indrepal Grewal, eds. *Theorizing NGOs: States, Feminisms, and Neoliberalism*. Durham, NC: Duke University Press, 2014.

Bernstein, Nancy, and Maya Haber. "The Real Edith Bell." *Pittsburgh Post-Gazette*, April 21, 2015.

Bloom, Paul. "Against Empathy." *Boston Review*, September 10, 2014.

——. *Against Empathy*. London: Bodley Head, 2016.

——. "The Dark Side of Empathy." *Atlantic Monthly* (online), September 25, 2015.

Booth, Wayne. *The Company We Keep*. Berkeley: University of California Press, 1988.

Bornstein, Erica. "Child Sponsorship, Evangelism, and Belonging in the Work of World Vision Zimbabwe." *American Ethnologist* 28, no. 3 (2001).

Broadie, Sarah. *Ethics with Aristotle*. New York: Oxford University Press, 1991.

Brown, L. M., M. Bradley, and P. Lang. "Affective Reactions to Pictures of Ingroup and Outgroup Members." *Biological Psychology* 71 (2006): 301–11.

Brown, Vivienne, and Samuel Fleischacker, eds. *The Philosophy of Adam Smith*. Abingdon, UK: Routledge, 2010.

Browning, Christopher. *Ordinary Men*. New York: HarperPerennial, 1998.

Canetti, Elias. *Crowds and Power*, trans. C. Stewart. New York: Farrar, Straus & Giroux, 1984.

Carrasco, Maria Alejandra. "Adam Smith: Self-Command, Practical Reason, and Deontological Insights." *British Journal for the History of Philosophy* 20, no. 2 (2012).

——. "Adam Smith's Reconstruction of Practical Reason." *Review of Metaphysics* 58, no. 1 (2004).

Cavell, Stanley. *Must We Mean What We Say?* Cambridge: Cambridge University Press, 1976.

Collingwood, R. G. *The Idea of History*. Oxford, UK: Clarendon, 1946.

Coplan, Amy, and Peter Goldie, eds. *Emotions: Philosophical and Psychological Perspectives*. Oxford, UK: Oxford University Press, 2011.

Craig, Edward. *Knowledge and the State of Nature*. Oxford, UK: Clarendon, 1990.

Cropsey, Joseph. *Polity and Society*. South Bend, IN: St. Augustine Press, 2001.

Currie, Gregory. "Empathy for Objects." In *Empathy: Philosophical and Psychological Perspectives*, ed. A. Coplan and P. Goldie. Oxford, UK: Oxford University Press, 2011.

Dancy, Jonathan. *Ethics without Principles*. Oxford, UK: Oxford University Press, 2004.

Darwall, Stephen. "Empathy, Sympathy, Care." *Philosophical Studies* 89 (1998).

——. *The Second-Person Standpoint*. Cambridge, MA: Harvard University Press, 2006.

——. "Sympathetic Liberalism." *Philosophy and Public Affairs* 28, no. 2 (1999).

——. *Welfare and Rational Care*. Princeton, NJ: Princeton University Press, 2002.

Davidson, Donald. "Belief and the Basis of Meaning." In Davidson, *Inquiries into Truth and Interpretation*. Oxford: Clarendon Press, 1984.

——. *Subjective, Intersubjective, Objective*. Oxford: Clarendon Press, 2001.

——. "Thought and Talk." In *Inquiries into Truth and Interpretation*. Oxford, UK: Clarendon Press, 1982.

Davies, Martin. "The Mental Simulation Debate." *Philosophical Issues* 5 (1994).

Debes, Remy. "The Authority of Empathy." In *Ethical Sentimentalism: New Perspectives*, ed. R. Debes and K. Stueber. Cambridge: Cambridge University Press, 2017.

——. "From *Einfühlung* to Empathy: Sympathy in Early Phenomenology and Psychology." In *Sympathy: A History*, ed. E. Schliesser. Oxford, UK: Oxford University Press, 2015.

——. "Which Empathy? Limitations in the Mirrored 'Understanding' of Emotion." *Synthese* (2010).

BIBLIOGRAPHY

Defoe, Daniel. "Giving Alms No Charity." In *The Shortest Way with the Dissenters and Other Pamphlets*. Oxford, UK: Oxford University Press, 1927.

Dennett, Daniel. *The Intentional Stance*. Cambridge, MA: MIT Press, 1989.

De Sousa, Ronald. *The Rationality of Emotion*. Cambridge, MA: MIT Press, 1987.

Devine, T. M. "The Urban Crisis." In *Glasgow*, vol. 1, ed. T. M. Devine and G. Jackson. Manchester, UK: Manchester University Press, 1995.

De Waal, Frans. *The Age of Empathy*. New York: Random House, 2009.

Diamond, Cora. "Eating Meat and Eating People." *Philosophy* 53 (1978).

Dovidio, John, Judith Allen, and David Schroeder. "Specificity of Empathy-Induced Helping." *Journal of Personality and Social Psychology* 59, no. 2 (1990).

Elazar, Yiftah. "The True Spirit of a Republican: Adam Smith's Ideal of Impartial Patriotism." Unpublished manuscript.

Elliott, J. E. "The Cost of Reading in Eighteenth-Century Britain." *ELH* 77, no. 2 (2010).

Elster, Jon. *Sour Grapes*. Cambridge, UK: Cambridge University Press, 1983.

Finnis, John, *Natural Law and Natural Rights*. Oxford, UK: Clarendon, 1980.

Fleischacker, Samuel. "Adam Smith on Equality." In *The Oxford Handbook of Adam Smith*, ed. C. Berry, M. Paganelli, and C. Smith. Oxford, UK: Oxford University Press, 2013.

———. "Adam Smith's Moral and Political Philosophy." In *Stanford Encyclopedia of Philosophy*, 2013.

———. "Bringing Home the Case of the Poor: The Rhetorical Achievement of Adam Smith's *Wealth of Nations*." In *The Oxford Handbook of Rhetoric and Political Theory*, ed. Dilip Gaonkar and Keith Topper. Oxford, UK: Oxford University Press, forthcoming.

———. *Divine Teaching and the Way of the World*. Oxford, UK: Oxford University Press, 2011.

———. *The Ethics of Culture*. Ithaca, NY: Cornell University Press, 1994.

———. *The Good and the Good Book*. Oxford, UK: Oxford University Press, 2015.

———. "Kant's Theory of Punishment." *Kant-Studien* 79, no. 4 (1988).

———. *On Adam Smith's "Wealth of Nations": A Philosophical Companion*. Princeton, NJ: Princeton University Press, 2004.

———. "Philosophy in Moral Practice: Kant and Adam Smith." *Kant-Studien* 82, no. 3 (1991).

———. *A Short History of Distributive Justice*. Cambridge, MA: Harvard University Press, 2004.

———. "Smith und der Kulturelativismus." In *Adam Smith als Moral Philosoph*, ed. C. Fricke and H. Schütt. Berlin: De Gruyter, 2005. Published in English as "Adam Smith and Cultural Relativism" in the online *Erasmus Journal for Philosophy and Economics* 4, issue 2 (Autumn 2011).

———. "Sympathy in Hume and Smith: A Comparison, Contrast, and Reconstruction." *Intersubjectivity and Objectivity in Adam Smith and Edmund Husserl*, eds. C. Fricke and D. Føllesdal. Frankfurt: Ontos Verlag, 2012.

———. *A Third Concept of Liberty*. Princeton, NJ: Princeton University Press, 1999.

———. "Values behind the Market: Kant's Response to the *Wealth of Nations*." *History of Political Thought*, Fall 1996.

———. "What Is Peoplehood?" Unpublished manuscript.

Forman-Barzilai, Fonna. *Adam Smith and the Circles of Sympathy*. Cambridge: Cambridge University Press, 2010.

Forster, E. M. *Passage to India*. New York: Harcourt Brace Jovanovich, 1924.

Forster, Michael. *After Herder*. Oxford, UK: Oxford University Press, 2010.

———. Introduction to *Philosophical Writings* by Johann Gottfried von Herder, trans. and ed. M. Forster. Cambridge: Cambridge University Press, 2002.

Foucault, Michel. "Truth and Power." In *Power/Knowledge*. New York: Pantheon Books, 1980.

Frazer, Michael. *The Enlightenment of Sympathy*. Oxford, UK: Oxford University Press, 2010.

Fricker, Miranda. *Epistemic Injustice*. Oxford, UK: Oxford University Press, 2007.

Gadamer, Hans-Georg. *Truth and Method*. New York: Crossroad, 1975.

Gaus, Gerald. *The Order of Public Reason*. Cambridge: Cambridge University Press, 2011.

Geertz, Clifford. *The Interpretation of Cultures*. New York: Basic Books, 1973.

Gere, Cathy. *Pain, Pleasure, and the Greater Good*. Chicago: University of Chicago Press, 2017.

Gerrard, Steven. "Desire and Desirability: Bradley, Russell and Moore versus Mill." In *Early Analytic Philosophy*, ed. W. W. Tait. Chicago: Open Court, 1997.

Gibbard, Allan. *Wise Feelings, Apt Choices*. Cambridge, MA: Harvard University Press, 1992.

Gill, Michael. *The British Moralists on Human Nature and the Birth of Secular Ethics*. Cambridge: Cambridge University Press, 2006.

Gilligan, Carol. *In a Different Voice*. Cambridge, MA: Harvard University Press, 1982.

Glover, Jonathan. *Humanity*. New Haven: Yale University Press, 1999.

Goldie, Peter. *The Emotions: A Philosophical Exploration*. Oxford, UK: Oxford University Press, 2000.

Goldman, Alvin. *Simulating Minds*. Oxford, UK: Oxford University Press, 2006.

Gosden, P. H. J. H. *The Friendly Societies in England, 1815–1875*. Manchester, UK: Manchester University Press, 1961.

Graham, Gordon. *Wittgenstein and Natural Religion*. Oxford, UK: Oxford University Press, 2014.

Greene, Joshua. *Moral Tribes*. New York: Penguin, 2013.

Greiner, Rae. "1909: The Introduction of the Word 'Empathy' into English." http://www.branch collective.org/?ps_articles=rae-greiner-1909-the-introduction-of-the-word-empathy-into -english.

Griffin, James. *Well-Being*. Oxford, UK: Clarendon Press, 1986.

Griswold, Charles. *Adam Smith and the Virtues of Enlightenment*. Cambridge: Cambridge University Press, 1999.

———. "Smith and Rousseau in Dialogue." In *The Philosophy of Adam Smith.*, ed. Vivienne Brown and Samuel Fleischacker. Abingdon, UK: Routledge, 2010.

Gruen, Lori. *Entangled Empathy*. New York: Lantern Books, 2014.

Haidt, Jonathan. *The Righteous Mind*. New York: Vintage Books, 2012.

Hanne, Michael. *The Power of the Story: Fiction and Political Change*. New York: Berghahn, 2000.

Harkin, Maureen. "Adam Smith on Women." In *The Oxford Handbook of Adam Smith*, ed. C. Berry, M. Paganelli, and C. Smith. Oxford, UK: Oxford University Press, 2013.

Harries, Karsten. *Infinity and Perspective*. Cambridge, MA: MIT Press, 2001.

Held, Virginia. *The Ethics of Care*. Oxford, UK: Oxford University Press, 2006.

Herder, Johann Gottfried von. *Johann Gottfried Herder Werke*, ed. U. Gaier et al. Frankfurt am Main, 1985–.

———. *Philosophical Writings*, trans. and ed. M. Forster. Cambridge: Cambridge University Press, 2002.

———. *Reflections on the Philosophy of the History of Mankind*. Abridged and introduced by Frank E. Manuel. Chicago: University of Chicago Press, 1968.

Hoffman, Martin. *Empathy and Moral Development*. Cambridge: Cambridge University Press, 2000.

Hollis Martin, and Steven Lukes, eds. *Rationality and Relativism*, Cambridge, MA: MIT Press, 1982.

BIBLIOGRAPHY

Horkheimer, Max, and Theodor Adorno. *Dialectic of Enlightenment*. Stanford, CA: Stanford University Press, 2002. Originally published in 1944.

Hume, David. *Enquiry Concerning the Principles of Morals, in Enquiries Concerning Human Understanding and Concerning the Principles of Morals*, third edition, ed. P. H. Nidditch. Oxford, UK: Clarendon Press, 1975.

———. *Essays Moral Political and Literary*, ed. E. Miller. Indianapolis: Liberty Fund, 1987.

———. Letter to Gilbert Elliot, September 22, 1764. In *The Letters of David Hume*, vol. 1, ed. J. Y. T. Greig. Oxford, UK: Oxford University Press, 1932.

———. *Treatise of Human Nature*, second edition, ed. L. A. Selby-Bigge and P. H. Nidditch. Oxford, UK: Clarendon Press, 1978.

Hunt, Lynn. *Inventing Human Rights*. New York: W. W. Norton, 2007.

Hursthouse, Rosalind. *On Virtue Ethics*. Oxford, UK: Oxford University Press, 1999.

Irwin, T. H. *Aristotle's First Principles*. Oxford, UK: Clarendon, 1988.

Jalabi, Raya. "Who Are the Yazidis and Why Is ISIS Hunting Them?" *Guardian*, August 11, 2014.

James, Erica Caple. "Witchcraft, Bureaucraft, and the Social Life of (US) Aid in Haiti." *Cultural Anthropology* 27, no. 1 (2012).

Jamison, Leslie. *The Empathy Exams*. Minneapolis: Graywolf Press, 2014.

Jones, Karen. "The Politics of Credibility." In *A Mind of One's Own*, second edition, ed. L. Antony and C. Witt. Cambridge, MA: Westview Press, 2002.

Kahneman, Daniel, and Amos Tversky. "The Simulation Heuristic." In *Judgment under Uncertainty*, ed. D. Kahneman, P. Slovic, and A. Tversky. Cambridge: Cambridge University Press, 1982.

Kant, Immanuel. *Critique of the Power of Judgment*, ed. P. Guyer, trans. P, Guyer and E. Matthews. Cambridge: Cambridge University Press, 2000.

———. *Groundwork for the Metaphysics of Morals*, ed. M. Gregor. Cambridge: Cambridge University Press, 1997.

———. *The Metaphysics of Morals*. In Kant, *Practical Philosophy*, trans. and ed. M. Gregor. Cambridge: Cambridge University Press, 1996.

———. *Religion within the Boundaries of Mere Reason*, ed. A. Wood and G. Giovanni. Cambridge: Cambridge University Press, 1998.

Keen, Suzanne. *Empathy and the Novel*. Oxford, UK: Oxford University Press, 2007.

Khader, Serene. *Adaptive Preferences and Women's Empowerment*. Oxford, UK: Oxford University Press, 2011.

Klein, Daniel, ed. "My Understanding of Adam Smith's Impartial Spectator." *Econ Journal Watch* 13, no. 2 (2016).

Kögler, Hans, and Karsten Stuebner, eds. *Empathy and Agency*. Boulder, CO: Westview Press, 2000.

———. "Empathy, Dialogical Self, and Reflexive Interpretation." In *Empathy and Agency*, ed. H. Kögler and K. Stuebner. Boulder, CO: Westview Press, 2000.

Korsgaard, Christine. *Fellow Creatures*. Oxford: Oxford University Press, 2018.

———. "Reflections on the Evolution of Morality." Amherst Lecture in Philosophy. Accessed at http://www.amherstlecture.org/korsgaard2010/.

———. *Self-Constitution*. Oxford, UK: Oxford University Press, 2009.

———. *The Sources of Normativity*. Cambridge: Cambridge University Press, 1996.

Kraut, Richard. *What Is Good and Why*. Cambridge, MA: Harvard University Press, 2007.

Kymlicka, Will. *Liberalism, Community and Culture*. Oxford, UK: Clarendon Press, 1989.

Laqueur, Thomas. "Bodies, Details, and the Humanitarian Narrative." In *The New Cultural History*. ed. Lynn Hunt. Berkeley: University of California Press, 1989.

Lawrence, Bruce B. "The Jihad of Pamela Geller." *Religion News Service*, May 6, 2015.

Lévy-Bruhl, Lucien. "Les idées politique de Herder." *La Revue des deux mondes* 80 (April 15, 1887).

Lewis, Karyn, and Sara Hodges. "Empathy Is Not Always as Personal as You May Think." In *Empathy: From Bench to Bedside*, ed. J. Decety. Cambridge, MA: MIT Press, 2012.

Lloyd, Genevieve. *Enlightenment's Shadows*. Oxford, UK: Oxford University Press, 2013.

MacIntyre, Alasdair. *After Virtue*. Notre Dame, IN: Notre Dame University Press, 1984.

McDowell, John. *Mind, Value and Reality*. Cambridge, MA: Harvard University Press, 1998.

———. "Virtue and Reason." *Monist* 62 (1979).

McHugh, John. "Ways of Desiring Mutual Sympathy in Adam Smith's Moral Philosophy." *British Journal for the History of Philosophy* 24, no. 4 (2016).

Mencius. *The Book of Mencius*. As translated at http://nothingistic.org/library/mencius/mencius12.html.

Miller, David. *Friends and Other Strangers*. New York: Columbia University Press, 2016.

Mill, John Stuart. *Utilitarianism*, second edition, ed. G. Sher. Indianapolis: Hackett, 2001.

Mills, Charles. "Kant and Race, Redux." *Graduate Faculty Philosophy Journal* 35 (2014).

———. *The Racial Contract*. Ithaca, NY: Cornell University Press, 1997.

———. "White Ignorance." In S. Sullivan and N. Tuana, *Race and Epistemologies*. Albany: SUNY Press, 2007.

Montes, Leon. *Adam Smith in Context*. New York: Palgrave Macmillan, 2004.

Muthu, Sankar. *Enlightenment against Empire*. Princeton, NJ: Princeton University Press, 2003.

Nagel, Thomas. "What Is It Like To Be a Bat?" In *Mortal Questions*. Cambridge: Cambridge University Press, 1979.

Nanay, Bence. "Adam Smith's Concept of Sympathy and Its Contemporary Interpretations." In Vivienne Brown and Samuel Fleischacker, eds., *The Philosophy of Adam Smith*. Abingdon, UK: Routledge, 2010.

Narayan, R. K. *The English Teacher*. London: William Heinemann, 1945.

Nietzsche, Friedrich. *Twilight of the Idols*, ed. M. Tanner, trans. R. J. Hollingdale. London: Penguin, 1990.

Noddings, Nel. *Caring: A Relational Approach to Ethics and Education*. Berkeley: University of California Press, 1984. Updated edition, 2013.

Norman, Richard. "Ethics and the Sacred." *Analyse & Kritik* 39, no. 1 (2017).

Nussbaum, Martha. "Adaptive Preferences and Women's Options." *Economics and Philosophy* 17 (2001).

———. *Creating Capabilities*. Cambridge, MA: Belknap, 2011.

———. *The Fragility of Goodness*. Cambridge: Cambridge University Press, 1986.

———. "Human Capabilities, Female Human Beings." In *Women, Culture and Development*, ed. M. Nussbaum and J. Glover. Oxford, UK: Oxford University Press, 1995.

———. *Love's Knowledge*. Oxford, UK: Oxford University Press, 1990.

———. *Political Emotions*. Cambridge, MA: Harvard University Press, 2015.

———. *Women and Human Development*. Cambridge: Cambridge University Press, 2000.

Otteson, James. *Adam Smith's Marketplace of Life*. Cambridge: Cambridge University Press, 2002.

Pagin, Peter. "Semantic Triangulation." In *Interpreting Davidson*, ed. P. Kotatko, P. Pagin, and G. Segal. Stanford, CA: Center for the Study of Language and Information, 2001.

BIBLIOGRAPHY

Parfit, Darek. *On What Matters*. Oxford, UK: Oxford University Press, 2011.

Penn, Julia. *Linguistic Relativity versus Innate Ideas*. Berlin: De Gruyter Mouton, 1972.

Phillipson, Nicholas. "Adam Smith as Civic Moralist." In *Wealth and Virtue*, ed. I. Hont and M. Ignatieff. Cambridge: Cambridge University Press, 1983.

Pitts, Jennifer. *A Turn to Empire: The Rise of Imperial Liberalism in Britain and France*. Princeton, NJ: Princeton University Press, 2005.

Plimpton, George, ed. *Writers at Work: The Paris Review Interviews*, Fourth Series. New York: Viking, 1976.

Pohlhaus, Gaile. "Discerning the Primary Epistemic Harm in Cases of Testimonial Injustice." *Social Epistemology* 28, no. 2 (2014).

Preston, Stephanie, and Frans de Waal, "Empathy: Its Ultimate and Proximate Causes." *Behavioral and Brain Sciences* 25 (2002).

Prinz, Jesse. "Against Empathy." *Southern Journal of Philosophy* 49 (2011).

———. "Is Empathy Necessary for Morality?" In *Emotions: Philosophical and Psychological Perspectives*, ed. Amy Coplan and Peter Goldie. Oxford, UK: Oxford University Press, 2011.

Quine, Willard van Orman. *Word and Object*. Cambridge, MA: MIT Press, 1960.

Rasmussen, Dennis. *The Pragmatic Enlightenment*. Cambridge: Cambridge University Press, 2014.

Rawls, John. *Political Liberalism*, expanded edition. New York: Columbia University Press, 2005.

———. *Theory of Justice*. Cambridge, MA: Harvard University Press, 1971.

Raynor, David. "Adam Smith and the Virtues." *Adam Smith Review* 2 (2006).

Robbins, Lionel. *A History of Economic Thought*, eds. S. G. Medema and W. Samuels. Princeton, NJ: Princeton University Press, 1998.

Rothman, Aviva. *The Pursuit of Harmony: Kepler on Cosmos, Confession and Community*. Chicago: University of Chicago Press, 2017.

Salaita, Steven. Twitter post at https://twitter.com/stevesalaita/status/486703517751869440?lang=en. 2014.

Sapir, Eduard. "On Herder's 'Ursprung der Sprache.'" *Modern Philology* 5 (1907).

Sayre-McCord, Geoffrey. "Hume and Smith on Sympathy, Approbation, and Moral Judgment." *Social Philosophy and Policy* 30 (2013).

———. "Sentiments and Spectators: Adam Smith's Theory of Moral Judgment." In *The Philosophy of Adam Smith*, ed. Vivienne Brown and Samuel Fleischacker. Abingdon, UK: Routledge, 2010.

Scanlon, T. M. *What We Owe to Each Other*. Cambridge, MA: Belknap, 1998.

Sen, Amartya. "Capability and Well-Being." In *The Quality of Life*, ed. Martha Nussbaum and Amartya Sen. Oxford, UK: Clarendon, 1993.

———. "Equality of What?" In *Choice, Welfare and Measurement*. Oxford, UK: Blackwell, 1982.

———. *The Idea of Justice*. Cambridge, MA: Harvard University Press, 2009.

———. *Resources, Values and Development*. Cambridge, MA: Harvard University Press, 1984.

Sherman, Nancy. "Empathy and Imagination." *Midwest Studies in Philosophy* 22 (1998).

Sidgwick, Henry, *The Methods of Ethics*, seventh edition (1874). Indianapolis: Hackett, 1981.

Slote, Michael. *The Ethics of Care and Empathy*. Abingdon, UK: Routledge, 2007.

———. "Saucers of Mud: Why Sympathy and Altruism Require Empathy." *Etica & Politica* 17, no. 2 (2015).

———. *A Sentimentalist Theory of the Mind*. Oxford, UK: Oxford University Press, 2014.

Smith, Adam. *Correspondence of Adam Smith*, ed. E. Mossner and I. Ross. Oxford, UK: Oxford University Press, 1987.

———. "History of Astronomy." In *Essays on Philosophical Subjects*, ed. W. P. D. Wightman and J. C. Bryce. Oxford, UK: Oxford University Press, 1980.

———. *An Inquiry into the Nature and Causes of the Wealth of Nations*, ed. R. H. Campbell, A. S. Skinner, and W. B. Todd. Oxford, UK: Oxford University Press, 1976.

———. *Lectures on Jurisprudence*, ed. R. L. Meek, D. D. Raphael, and P. G. Stein. Oxford, UK: Oxford University Press, 1978.

———. *Theory of Moral Sentiments*, ed. D. D. Raphael and A. L. Macfie. Oxford, UK: Oxford University Press, 1976.

Stone, Tony, and Martin Davies. "The Mental Simulation Debate: A Progress Report." In *Theories of Theories of Mind*, ed. P. Carruthers and P. K. Smith. Cambridge: Cambridge University Press, 1996.

Stueber, Karsten. *Rediscovering Empathy*. Cambridge: MIT Press, 2006.

Stürmer, S., M. Snyder, and A. Omoto. "Prosocial Emotions and Helping: The Moderating Role of Group Membership." *Journal of Personality and Social Psychology* 88, no. 3 (2005).

Sunstein, Cass. "Cognition and Cost-Benefit Analysis." *Journal of Legal Studies* 29 (2000).

Sussman, David. "For Badness' Sake." *Journal of Philosophy* 106, no. 11 (2009).

Tagore, Rabindranath. New Delhi: Rupa Publications, 2002.

Tamir, Yael. *Liberal Nationalism*. Princeton, NJ: Princeton University Press, 1993.

Taylor, Charles. "Interpretation and the Sciences of Man." In *Philosophy and the Human Sciences*. Cambridge: Cambridge University Press, 1985.

———. *Sources of the Self*. Cambridge, MA: Harvard University Press, 1989.

Tenenbaum, Sergio. *Desire, Practical Reason and the Good*. Oxford, UK: Oxford University Press, 2010.

Thiel, Udo. *The Early Modern Subject*. Oxford, UK: Oxford University Press, 2011.

Thomson, Judith Jarvis. "Goodness and Utilitarianism." *Proceedings and Addresses of the APA* 67, no. 4 (1992).

Tolstoy, Leo. "The Kreutzer Sonata." In *Collected Shorter Fiction*, vol. 2, trans. L. and A. Maude and N. J. Cooper. New York: Alfred A. Knopf, 2001.

Trachtenberg, Joshua. *The Devil and the Jews*. New Haven: Yale University Press, 1943.

Tugendhat, Ernst. "Universally Approved Intersubjective Attitudes: Adam Smith." *Adam Smith Review* 1 (2004).

Vedantam, Shankar. "Does Reading Harry Potter Have an Effect on Your Behavior?" *Morning Edition*, National Public Radio, May 1, 2015.

Williams, Bernard. "A Critique of Utilitarianism." In J. J. C. Smart and Bernard Williams, *Utilitarianism: For and Against*. Cambridge: Cambridge University Press, 1973.

———. *Ethics and the Limits of Philosophy*. Cambridge, MA: Harvard University Press, 1985.

———. *Problems of the Self*. Cambridge: Cambridge University Press, 1973.

———. *Truth and Truthfulness*. Princeton, NJ: Princeton University Press, 2002.

Wittgenstein, Ludwig. *Lectures and Conversations on Aesthetics, Psychology and Religious Belief*, ed. C. Barrett. Berkeley: University of California Press, 1967.

———. *On Certainty*. Oxford, UK: Basil Blackwell, 1969.

———. *Philosophical Investigations*, trans. G. E. M. Anscombe. New York: Macmillan, 1958.

———. "Remarks on Frazer's *Golden Bough*." In *Philosophical Occasions*, ed. J. Klagge and A. Nordmann. Indianapolis: Hackett, 1993.

Wolff, Robert Paul. "Kant's Debt to Hume via Beattie." *Journal of the History of Ideas* 21, no. 1 (1960).

Index

Abramson, Kate, 185n3
accuracy, 40, 72, 170n19, 185n68
Achebe, Chinua, 99
Adams, Robert, 128, 192n3, 193n2
Adorno, Theodor, 181n5
aesthetics, 2, 32, 33
affections, affectional ties, xi, 10, 33, 58, 69, 84, 89, 90, 91, 92, 94, 96, 98, 99, 101, 114, 171n28, 175n26, 187n4
Agee, James, 170n17
agency, agents, 15, 51, 56, 71, 80, 83, 101, 112, 113, 128, 129, 153, 156, 158, 174n20, 178n45, 184n56, 187n28, 189n11
Ainslie, Donald, 178n42
akrasia, 65
Alceste (fictional character), 174n17
Allen, Judith, 183n37
All-India Institute of Hygiene and Public Health, 118
Allison, Henry, 175n26
Al Pacino, 29
altruism: empathy and, x, 49, 61, 62, 63, 66, 73, 75, 178n45, 182n20, 183nn40–41; Smithian empathy and, 62, 63–65
Alznauer, Mark, 197n16
Amazon.com, 51
Anderson, Benedict, 92, 98, 180n62, 187n7
Anderson, Elizabeth, 188n17
Andrei, Prince (fictional character), 176n34
animals, x, 10, 20–21, 31, 49, 56–59, 75, 112, 114, 133, 149, 150, 154–55, 156, 158, 159, 173n14, 182n20, 182n26, 182nn28–29, 191n26, 196n5
anthropology, 180n63
anti-Semitism, 74
approbation, 26, 27, 32, 107, 151, 173n10, 183n49, 189n11, 195n30

approval, 20, 28, 32, 54, 107, 122, 189n11
a priori, 158, 164, 174n18
Arabs, 65, 125, 164
Arendt, Hannah, 190n19
Aristotle, 149, 150, 194n7, 196nn1–2
Arthur, T. S., 181n8
attention, 9, 38, 52, 58, 61, 65, 66, 69, 99, 103, 110–13, 116, 119, 120, 130, 137, 174n14, 176n33, 181n8
Augustine, 46
Auschwitz, 125, 192n13

Baha'i, 96
Bailey, Olivia, 64, 167, 177n39, 183nn41–42
Barak, Ehud, 52
Barakat, Zeina M., 192n13
Barry, Brian, 187n22
Batson, C. Daniel, 3, 61–63, 169n6, 176n33, 181n9, 182nn33–34, 183nn35–37, 190n16
being-in-the-world, 32
Bell, Daniel A., 187n23
Bell, Edith, 192n13
Bellers, John, 190n21
Bencomo, Susan, 167
Benedict, Ruth, 79
Bentham, Jeremy, 129, 131–33
Bereaved Parents' Circle, 125
Bernal, Victoria, 188n13
Bernstein, Nancy, 192n13
bestialization, 150, 196n5
Bezuhov, Pierre (fictional character), 46
biology, 10, 30, 91, 94, 171n21
Bloom, Paul, ix, xi, xii, xiii, 1, 2, 9, 102–10, 115, 116, 126, 128, 130, 145, 169n5, 170n15, 182n30, 183n42, 188n1, 189nn3–5, 189nn8–9, 190n14, 199n35
Bloor, David, 79
Boas, Franz, 79

Boeker, Ruth, 167, 178n41
Booth, Wayne, 181n8
Bornstein, Erica, 188n13
Boyle, Matthew, 197n13
Bradley, Margaret, 188n11
Brahmo, 82
Breaking the Silence, 125
Britain, 52, 67, 112, 118–20, 151, 184n58, 191n28; British Empire, 118–20, 129, 136, 137
Broadie, Sarah, 194n7
Brothers Karamazov (Dostoevsky), 125
Brown, Lisa, 188n11
Browning, Christopher, 199n36
Buddenbrooks (Mann), 46
Buddha, 6

Cabrini-Green Homes, 130
Camp David negotiations, 52
Canetti, Elias, 170n10
capitalism, xii, 119, 151, 164
care: caring about/caring for distinction, 1–3, 60, 62, 63, 65, 101; caring for, 5–7, 47, 55, 62, 65, 94, 142, 150; duty-based care, 7, 8; empathetic care, xi, 5, 6, 7, 65, 66, 70, 90, 112; ethics of care, 66, 69–70, 183n46, 184nn59–60, 192n11; habitual care, 5, 6; ideological care, 7; instinctual care, 6; non-empathetic care, 4, 6; rational care, 183n46, 192n11, 194n26; religious care, 8
Carrasco, Maria Alejandra, 183n53
categorical imperative, 66, 67, 84
Catholics, 100, 164
Cavell, Stanley, 33, 175n23
Centre for the History of the Emotions, 167
certainty/uncertainty, 122, 157, 158, 196n35
charity, 62, 135, 145, 181n8, 190n21
Cherry, Myisha, 167
Cho, Kyoung Min, 167
Christ, 6, 7, 153, 154
Christianity, 6, 40, 67, 93, 123, 124, 131, 134, 150, 153–55, 157, 158, 162–64, 196n25, 199n33
Chrysippus, 171n28
Cicero, 184n58
circle of conceptions, 78–82, 84, 180n63, 186n5, 186n8
circles of sympathy, xi, 7, 90–101, 108, 187n2, 187nn4–5, 187n9
Clarissa (Richardson), 45
Clarke, Samuel, 193n6
Coady, Tony, 198n23
cognition, 58, 71–74, 82, 96, 116, 108, 130, 176n33, 191, 198
cognitive abilities, 71, 170n19
cognitive empathy, x, 9, 61, 63, 105, 183n40, 189n9
Collingwood, R. G., 81, 82, 186n17
colonialism, xii, 126
communism, 81, 134

communitarianism, 84, 187n23
compassion, 182n20
conformism, 40, 66, 80, 174n14
Conrad, Joseph, 119
consciousness, 25, 44, 53, 110, 140, 162, 171n23, 175n21, 176n33, 178n41, 178n43
contagion, x, 3–13, 16, 19–21, 23, 27, 57, 65, 105, 170n11, 170n17, 171n23, 171n31, 172nn4–5, 173n5, 179n55
conventionalism, 46, 67
Coplan, Amy, 3, 34, 37, 41, 169n5, 169n7, 171n23, 175n30, 176n33
Cornish, 123
cost-benefit analysis, 102, 116, 119, 130, 191nn1–2
cosmopolitanism, xi, xii, 1, 6, 81, 93–97, 100, 101, 130
Craig, Edward, 71, 72, 185n67
Cropsey, Joseph, 170n13
Currie, Gregory, 169n4

Dahmer, Jeffrey, 156
Dalton, Allen, 167
Dana, Richard Henry, 181n8
Dancy, Jonathan, 68, 126, 183n52, 193n18
Darwall, Stephen, 24, 25, 34, 37, 41, 169n5, 172n34, 173nn7–8, 177n36, 182n30, 183n36, 183n46, 188n17, 192n11, 194n8, 194n26
Davidson, Donald, 158, 182n25, 197n22
Davies, Martin, 181nn1–2
Death and the King's Horseman (Soyinka), 82
death penalty, 198n23
Debes, Remy, 167, 169n3, 174n20, 182n15
Defoe, Daniel, 190–91n21
de Grouchy, Sophie, 184n61
demonization, xii, 100, 149–65, 197n13, 197n16, 198n23, 198n25, 198n31, 199nn33–34, 199n36
Dennett, Daniel, 158, 197n21
de Palma, Brian, 28
Desai, Anita, 99
desire, xi, 24, 54, 93, 112, 119, 123, 124, 129, 133, 150, 155, 156, 158, 163, 174n14, 182n30, 195n34
de Sousa, Ronald, 171n33
devil, 150, 151, 154, 162, 198n26, 199n32
Devine, T. M., 190n21
de Waal, Frans, 21, 57, 172nn35–36, 182nn16–17, 182n19, 182n21
Dewey, John, 96
Diamond, Cora, 182n28
Dickens, Charles, 46, 53, 119, 126, 192n7
dignity, 118–22, 124, 125, 136, 141, 143, 144, 150, 163, 174n20, 188n10, 191n2, 195n30, 198n23
Dilthey, Wilhelm, 44, 79
diversity, 86, 141, 185n3, 187n28, 193n3
Dostoevsky, Fyodor, 46, 125
Dovidio, John, 183n37
Dr. Aziz (fictional character), 118

INDEX

Ecclesiastes, 27
effeminacy, 184n61
Einfühlung, 2, 169nn4–5
Elazar, Yiftah, 167, 188n12
Elliot, Gilbert, 187n8
Elliott, J. E., 191n28
Elster, Jon, 192n10
emotions, x, xi, xii, 3, 5, 6, 8–11, 14, 15, 17, 20, 21,
    26, 28, 31–33, 35, 37, 41–42, 45, 53, 54, 61, 66, 77,
    81, 84, 92, 103, 105, 108, 117, 124, 125, 128, 161,
    170n19, 170n21, 171n23, 171n31, 171n33, 174n14,
    175n21, 179n47, 182n32, 183n40, 190n14, 196n36;
    emotional identification, 105, 176n33, 189n9
empathetic horizon, 120, 164
empathic concern, 61, 62
empathy: cognitive, 63, 105, 164n15, 183; conta-
    gious, 4, 8, 9–12, 16, 21, 57, 171n31, 179n55; dan-
    gers of, ix, xi, 1, 69, 93, 102–4, 107–11, 190n14;
    emotional, 189n9, 189n11; empathic abilities,
    170n19, 189n9; and humanity, x, xii, 1, 15, 21, 28,
    30–31, 41, 45, 47, 48, 56, 83–85, 89, 91–92, 96, 114,
    138, 148, 152–53, 160–65, 174nn14–15, 174nn18–19,
    196n4, 196n9, 198n25; and inquiry, 195n33; with
    oneself, 15, 39, 54, 75, 107; perspectival, 25–47,
    51–52, 57, 58–60; phenomenology of, 25, 40, 41,
    42; projective, 4, 6, 8–10, 12, 13, 16, 21, 23–47, 57,
    170n17, 171n23, 172n5, 172n34, 177n36, 182n26,
    189n6, 189n7, 192n9; in *Wealth of Nations*,
    190n15, 191n27. *See also* contagion; Smithian
    empathy
English Teacher, The (Narayan), 125, 186n18
Enlightenment, 77, 79, 151, 175n26, 185n3
Epictetus, 171n28
equality, 15, 41, 60, 69, 71, 75, 83, 85, 86, 90, 95, 98,
    103, 124, 125, 130, 135, 143, 188n17, 194n22
ethics, 1, 6, 21, 22, 50, 51, 53, 59, 60, 61, 75, 84, 85,
    96, 124, 127, 129, 136, 150, 157, 175n26, 182n29,
    184nn58–60, 188n18, 193n3, 196n36
ethnicity, 95, 171n21, 193n3
ethnocentrism, ix, 1
evil, 74, 135, 149, 150, 151, 153–65, 185n73, 190n21,
    196n11, 197n16, 197n23, 199n32, 199n34
explanation, 10–12, 15, 18–19, 24, 29, 33, 40, 44, 50,
    57, 74, 78, 81, 84, 91, 118, 146, 151–22, 156–58, 163–
    65, 170n19, 172n5, 185n73, 186n6, 190n14, 191n23,
    197n16, 199n32, 199n34, 199n36

facial expression, 8, 170n19
fairness, 1, 15, 66, 68, 83, 98, 103, 112, 124, 137, 144,
    146
faith, 6, 67, 85, 86, 151, 153, 158, 175n25, 197n20
feeling-language, 18, 19
feminism, 66, 70, 184n61
fiction, 15, 39–40, 54, 61, 72, 87, 109, 125, 155,
    176n33, 181n9, 189n7, 192n12, 197n16
Fielding (fictional character), 118–20

Finnis, John, 194n23
Flanders, Moll (fictional character), 46
Fleischacker, Noa, 188n13
Fleischacker, Sam, 170n13, 171n31, 172n2, 173n5,
    173n11, 174nn18–19, 175nn25–26, 178n41, 179n48,
    180n58, 180n63, 183n48, 184nn57–58, 187n5,
    187n27, 188n17, 188n19, 191n24, 194n11, 194n14,
    194n17, 195n30, 196nn8–9, 198n23
Forman-Barzilai, Fonna, 187n2, 187n4, 187n5,
    187n9
Forster, E. M., 82, 118–20, 192n6
Forster, Michael, 169n4
Foucault, Michel, 71, 181n5
Frazer, James, 79
Frazer, Michael, 185n3, 186n6
freedom, 12, 16, 83, 135, 136, 140, 141, 144, 145, 146,
    195n30, 197n16; free will, 21, 59, 153, 155, 157,
    187n28, 193n6, 197n13
Freud, Sigmund, 55
Fricker, Miranda, 70–75, 175n23, 184nn62–63,
    185n66, 185nn68–69
Fugard, Athol, 125

Gadamer, Hans Georg, 44, 79, 180n56, 181n4,
    186n8
Gandhi, Mohandas, 100, 101
Gaus, Gerald, 137, 194n25
Geertz, Clifford, 79, 82, 186n11, 186n15, 186n19
Geller, Pamela, 163, 199n33
gender, 118, 126, 130, 136, 137, 184nn60–61. *See also*
    transgender
Gere, Cathy, 193n3
Gerrard, Steven, 194n14
Gettier, Edmund, 71
Gibbard, Allan, 172n34
Gill, Michael, 172n5
Gilligan, Carol, 183n46, 184n59
Glied, Sherry, 167, 168
Glover, Jonathan, 63, 183n39
Goldie, Peter, 34, 37, 41, 51, 54, 66, 170n11, 173n7,
    175n28, 176nn32–34, 177n34, 179n47, 181n6,
    182n13, 182n30, 182n32, 183n45, 189n6, 190n12
Goldman, Alvin, 170n13
Goldstein-Plesser, Gene, 198n31
Gosden, P. H. J. H., 191n21
Graham, Gordon, 186n10
Great Expectations (Dickens), 46
Greece, ancient, 78
Greene, Graham, 82
Greene, Joshua, xi, 102, 128–32, 134, 135, 137, 141,
    193n3, 193nn5–6, 194n17
Greiner, Rae, 169n3
Grewal, Indrepal, 188n13
Griffin, James, 192n3, 194n23
Griswold, Charles, 41–43, 77, 175n29, 177n40,
    178n45, 179n49, 185n1

212 INDEX

Gruen, Lori, 57, 63, 170n8, 176n33, 182n18, 182n20, 183n40, 184n60
"guise of the good" thesis, 155, 157, 164, 199n34

Haber, Maya, 192n13
Habermas, Jürgen, 137, 138, 144, 198n29
habit, 5–7, 21, 32, 36, 62, 118, 186n5, 186n8; habitual sympathy, 89–94, 98, 99, 101, 114
Haidt, Jonathan, xi, 102, 128, 132, 145, 193n3, 193n14
Hamas, 199n32
Hamlet (Shakespeare), 46
Hanne, Michael, 181n8
Hannibal Lecter (fictional character), 197n16
happiness, xii, 18, 32, 60, 65, 68–69, 78, 90, 91, 94, 118, 123–24, 127, 128, 129, 131–35, 136, 145, 175n27, 184n56, 188n10, 195n30; thin theory of, 140–44, 146–47. *See also* utilitarianism
Hard Times (Dickens), 119
Harkin, Maureen, 184n61
harm, xii, 15, 16, 60, 64, 74, 95, 108, 111, 116–24, 126, 130, 131, 135–39, 141, 143–48, 150, 156, 159, 183n54, 191n2, 194n27, 196n35, 198n23, 199n32
Harmon, Zac, 167
Harries, Karsten, 175n26
Harry Potter (fictional character), 53, 181n10
Heidegger, Martin, 32, 180n56
Held, Virginia, 183
Herder, Johann Gottfried von, 186, 187
Herderian empathy, xi, 77, 79, 83–85, 87, 88, 123
hermeneutic circle, 44, 179n47
Hernandez, Tony, 167, 187n21
Highsmith, Patricia, 70
Hinduism, 125
Hitler, Adolf, 156, 160
Hodges, Sara, 10, 170n19
Hoffman, Martin, 10, 170n18
Holocaust, 192n13
horizon, 79, 120, 164, 186n5, 186n8
Horkheimer, Max, 181n5
Horton, Robin, 181n4
Hübner, Karolina, 167
humanism, 59, 83–85, 97, 101, 148, 150–51, 160, 162, 165, 198n25, 199n32
humanitarian, 6, 45, 95, 100
humanity, ix–xii, 1, 6–7, 15, 20–21, 28, 30, 31, 37, 41, 45–48, 50, 56, 59, 82–97, 100, 101, 109, 112–15, 125, 138, 140, 142, 149–54, 159–65, 174nn14–15, 174nn18–19, 186n6, 187n28, 196n4, 196n9, 196n35, 197n19, 198n23, 198n25, 199nn32–36
human nature, 78, 80, 106, 145, 158, 187n19, 188n10
Hume, David, x, xii, xiii, 3, 4, 9–11, 15–17, 23–27, 32, 38–40, 78, 79, 86, 92, 93, 104, 110, 169n2, 169n5, 170n13, 170n20, 170n21, 171n21–22, 171nn30–31, 172nn1–5, 173n9, 175nn21–22, 178n42, 185n3, 187n6, 187n8, 187n26, 189nn10–11, 190n28, 197n18; Humean, 4, 31, 47, 65, 107, 179n55

Hunt, Lynn, 45, 46, 180nn59–61
Hursthouse, Rosalind, 128, 194n7
Hutcheson, Frances, 113, 142

Iago (fictional character), 46
identification, emotional, 5, 10, 12, 45–46, 59, 105, 118, 138, 176n33, 180n62, 189n9
identity, 7, 21, 33, 39–41, 50, 55, 57, 67, 106, 136, 147, 176n33; and cognition, 71, 176n33; cultural, 84, 88; group, 100, 101, 111; personal identity, 39, 157, 178n43
Idiot, The (Dostoevsky), 125
imagination, x, 3, 12, 20, 52, 58, 59, 72–73, 74, 79, 88, 94, 98, 99, 161, 192n8, 192n12, 195n34, 199n32; and empathy, 8–9, 11–13, 15, 17, 20–21, 23–27, 34–43, 50–51, 53–54, 61–64, 67, 72, 78–82, 104–6, 108–11, 114, 118, 120, 124–26, 138, 139, 147, 150, 163–65, 170n12, 173n7, 175nn28–29, 175n31, 176n32, 176n34, 177n39, 178n45, 182n30, 189n6, 190n19, 195n33
immigrants, 53, 96, 97, 101, 132, 194n12
impartial spectator, xi, 15, 36, 37, 39–42, 54, 55, 65–69, 87, 88, 107, 108, 110, 111, 140, 142, 145, 171n27, 177n37, 178n45, 179n46, 183n49, 185n74, 188n16, 194n27, 195n30
imperialism, 80, 82
individualism, 174n19
individuality, x, 6, 32, 59
in-his-shoes imagining, 34, 37
injustice, 85, 129, 152, 159; epistemic injustice, 70–75, 184n62, 185n66; hermeneutical injustice, 71–73, 75; testimonial injustice, 70, 72, 74, 75
instinct, 4, 6–8, 12, 21, 62, 75, 90, 91, 117, 196n11
intentional stance, 158
interpretation, 39–44, 66, 67, 79, 82, 87, 88, 106, 121, 139, 142–44, 149, 155, 157–58, 163, 174n15, 178n45, 179n47, 180n54, 195n34, 197n22
intersubjectivity, 44, 177n38
intimacy, 51, 74, 92, 98–101, 188n17
Irwin, T. H., 194n7
ISIS, 162, 164, 199n34
Islam, 96, 122, 123, 125, 199n33
Islam, Ahmadi, 96

Jalabi, Raya, 198n27
James, Erica Caple, 188n13
Jamison, Leslie, 5, 9, 12, 15, 170n17, 171n25, 195n33
Jesus, 134
Jews, xii, 7, 33, 40, 65, 73, 74, 75, 101, 150, 151, 154, 156, 162–64, 185n73, 192n13, 198n30, 199nn32–33, 199n36
Jones, Karen, 72, 74, 185n70, 192n9
journalism, 192n12
Julie (Rousseau), 45, 46
justice, x, xii, 16, 50, 59, 66, 68, 69–75, 85, 93, 111, 136, 162, 184n60. *See also* injustice

INDEX

Kaczynski, Ted, 30
Kahneman, Daniel, 24, 25, 173n6
Kant, Immanuel, x, 7, 30, 38, 39, 47, 48, 78, 83, 84,
 86, 101, 124, 151–58, 160, 162, 164, 170n9, 174n18,
 179n48, 180n64, 183n53, 187n21, 190n19, 193,
 196n5, 196nn8–11, 197nn12–13, 197nn17–19,
 197n23, 198n29; Kantian moral faith, 153, 158,
 175n25, 197n20; Kantian morality, 66–68,
 70, 125, 128–29, 138, 184n58, 193n6, 196n9,
 196nn35–36, 197n19
Kashua, Sayed, 125
Keen, Suzanne, 53, 81
Kepler, Johannes, 175n26
Khader, Serene, 192n10
Khamenei, Ayatollah, 163
Khmer Rouge, 156
Kim, Jun Young, 167
Klein, Daniel, 183n47
knowledge, 17–21, 42, 44, 71, 72, 78, 79, 99, 113–14,
 117, 137, 139, 142, 145, 158, 161, 172n3, 173n10,
 175n26, 189n9, 197n20, 198n29
Kögler, Hans, 44, 45, 179n55, 180n56, 182n24,
 186n13, 186n15, 186n19, 195n32
Kohut, Heinz, 54
Korsgaard, Christine, 41, 57, 179n48, 182n22, 193n6,
 196n4
Kraut, Richard, 192n3
Krishna, 6, 7
Kuni (name of a bonobo), 57, 59
Kymlicka, Will, 187n23

Lang, Peter, 188n11
Laqueur, Thomas, 45, 46, 180n57
Lawrence, Bruce B., 199n33
Leibniz, Gottfried Wilhelm, 88, 175n26, 178n41,
 180n63
Lessing, Gotthold, 78, 175, 185n3
Lewis, Karyn, 10, 170n19
Lévy-Bruhl, Lucien, 79
liberalism, 33, 84, 129, 135, 137, 138, 145, 151, 164,
 174n19, 187n1, 195n28
Lipps, Walter, 2
Lloyd, Genevieve, 185n3
Lubavitcher Rebbe, 6
Lukes, Steven, 181n4

Macbeth (Shakespeare), 28, 29
MacIntyre, Alasdair, 116, 128, 181n5
Mahfouz, Naguib, 99
man of system, 181n7
Manson, Charles, 156, 160, 197n16
Marx, Karl, 96
Marxism, 96, 124, 125
Master Harold . . . and the Boys (Fugard), 125
Maugham, Somerset, 119
Maurivaux, Pierre, 171n28

Mauthausen, 63
Maxi experiment, 44, 180n55
McDowell, John, 116, 128, 183n52, 194n7
McHugh, John, 174n14, 179n46
Mead, Margaret, 79
Meija, Maria, 167, 187n21
Mencius, 2, 4, 62, 169n1
Mill, John Stuart, 69, 94, 96, 119, 129, 129, 132, 133,
 184n58, 188n14, 194n13
Miller, Richard, 9, 170n14
Mills, Charles, 183n50, 184n62, 187n1, 196n15
mirroring emotions, 10, 27, 38, 54, 104, 105, 177n36,
 177n40
mirror neurons, 10, 57, 182n15
Molière, 174n17
monadology, monads, 88, 175n26, 180n63
Montes, Leonidas, 167, 183n53, 191n23
Montesquieu, 78, 98, 185n3
moral currency, 128–29, 132, 133–37, 145
moral development, 15, 16, 113
moral eclecticism, 69–70, 184n58, 196n36
moral emotions, xi, 60, 69, 93, 110, 124
morality, 39, 53, 83, 86, 87, 95, 96, 106, 108, 110,
 137, 148, 162, 164, 195–96n35, 197n16, 199n35;
 and empathy, ix, xi, xii, 1, 4, 10, 14–17, 35, 39,
 64–65, 67–70, 83–84, 86, 89, 98, 103, 106–8,
 115, 124, 176n33, 182n26, 188n2, 189n9, 189n11,
 198n25; humanistic, 87–88, 148, 150, 160, 162,
 196n4, 198n25. *See also* ethics; Kant, Immanuel;
 utilitarianism
moral judgment, xii, 14–16, 36, 38, 54, 59, 68,
 69, 78, 96, 97, 99, 126, 129, 171n21, 183n49,
 189–90n11
moral language, 171n21
moral norms, 68, 69, 86, 100, 11, 160, 162, 195n30,
 198n25
moral particularism. *See* particularism
moral philosophy, moral theory, x, xii, 5, 13, 15,
 39, 45, 49–50, 62, 66–70, 98, 102, 110, 111, 113,
 116, 127, 131, 134, 141, 142, 148, 157, 193nn3–4,
 193n6
Morvarid, Hashem, 167
Moshe, Nir Ben, 167
Mother Theresa, 103, 176n32
Mr. Crane (fictional character), 24, 25
Mr. Tees (fictional character), 24, 25
Muhammad, 122, 124
Muslims, xii, 67, 73, 100, 101, 122, 125, 154, 163, 164,
 196n35, 199n33
Muthu, Sankar, 185n3, 187n28

Nagel, Thomas, 161, 198n28
Nanay, Bence, 175n29, 175n31, 181n3
Narayan, R. K., 125, 186n18
nationalism, 84, 100, 123, 131, 134, 147, 148, 151,
 180n62, 199n32

Nazis, xii, 151, 156, 162, 164, 165, 192n13, 199n34, 199n36
Netanyahu, Bibi, 163
Newton, Sasha, 167
Nicholas of Cusa, 175n26
Nietzsche, Friedrich, 133, 194n15
Noddings, Nel, 183n46, 184n59
Norman, Richard, 182n27
normativity, 20, 49, 69, 75, 172n34, 193n3
Notes from Underground (Dostoevsky), 46
novelists, 46, 60–63, 109, 119, 123, 192n8
novels, x, 15, 28, 45, 46, 49, 53, 54, 56, 70, 73, 75, 82, 92, 98, 99, 119, 120, 126, 161, 176n34, 179n55, 181n8, 192n9
Nussbaum, Martha, 117, 136, 137, 182n20, 182n28, 182n30–31, 183n52, 192nn4–5, 192n10, 194nn23–24, 196n5

Oliver Twist (Dickens), 53, 119, 192n7
oppression, 71, 75, 97, 118, 119, 124, 125, 192n10, 192n13
organism, whirl of, 33
original sin, 153
Orwell, George, 119
Otteson, James, 195n30
Oz-Salzberger, Fania, 167, 187n25

Pagin, Peter, 197n22
Pamela (Richardson), 45, 46
Parfit, Derek, 128, 193n2
particularism, 14–15, 22, 66, 68–69, 118, 123, 126, 171n27, 183n51, 193n19
Passage to India, A (Forster), 53, 120, 126
paternalism, 80, 129, 130
Paul (apostle), 46
Penn, Julia, 186n12
Persky, Joe, 191n1
perspectival/empathetic approach to the good, 138–40, 144, 146, 148
perspectivalism, 34, 45, 47–48, 58, 59, 138–40, 144, 146, 148, 175n26, 180n63
perspectives, x, xii, 1, 9, 15, 21, 25, 30–47, 51, 52, 58–60, 63, 65, 72–76, 80, 82–84, 87–88, 99, 112, 121, 123–25, 136–48, 153, 161, 162, 174n20, 176n34, 178n45, 179n46, 179n55, 180n63, 182n26, 185n74, 195n34, 196n36, 198n23, 198n25, 198n29; perspective-taking, 9, 15, 21, 34, 57, 61, 114, 180n55, 183n35
Phillipson, Nicholas, 188n18
philosophy of mind, x, 49
Pitts, Jennifer, 186n14
Plato, 30, 155
Plimpton, George, 173n14
Plizga, Robert, 167
Palestine Liberation Organization (PLO), 52
pluralism, 78, 19, 160, 180n63

Pohlhaus, Gaile, 185n66
political economy, 113, 184n61
politics, xii, 33, 45, 47, 52, 70, 78, 96, 97, 110, 115, 116, 117, 130, 131, 135, 136, 139, 145, 146, 151, 152, 164, 165, 174n19, 188n2, 188n18, 190n15, 193n3, 193n13
Polito, Bertin, 167
Pol Pot, 156
poor laws, 190n21, 192n7
power, 71, 120, 130, 156, 181n5, 187n10
Pòzdnyshev (fictional character), 177n35
prejudice, ix, xi, 53, 67, 70, 72–75, 93, 96, 98, 110, 111, 122, 124, 125, 139, 142, 143, 175n24, 185n73, 185n74, 187n10
Preston, Stephanie, 57, 182n17
Prinz, Jesse, ix, xi, xii, 9, 102, 104, 107–10, 115–17, 126, 128, 130, 145, 169n5, 170n16, 188n1, 189nn10–11, 190n13, 190n17
projection, 3–7, 9, 10, 13, 17, 19, 20, 26, 35, 52, 62, 64, 79, 82, 104, 105, 110, 144, 145, 170n17, 172n2, 172nn4–5. *See also* empathy: projective
Protestants, 100, 164
Psalms, 46
psychology, ix, 1, 35, 40, 41, 44, 49, 50, 52, 61, 94, 109, 163–64, 175n31, 189n9, 197n16; psycho-analysis, 54–56, 171n29
punishment, 59, 103, 111–12, 131, 198n23

Qiang, Li, 167
Quiet American, The (Greene), 82
Quine, Willard van Orman, 50, 181n2

Racine, 171n28
racism, xii, 14, 66, 73, 74, 85, 86, 103, 124, 125, 131, 175n24, 185n73, 187n1, 194n27
Rand, Ayn, 181n8
Rasmussen, Dennis, 185n3
rationalism, 66, 69, 126, 174n18, 175n26
rationality, x, xi, 21, 30–33, 53, 59, 84, 94, 133, 135, 137, 138, 142, 144–46, 153–58, 160–61, 195n31, 198n29. *See also* reason
Rawls, John, 48, 116, 128, 135, 136, 144, 180n66, 193n1, 194nn18–22, 196n37
Raynor, David, 170n13, 173n11
reason, xii, 30, 31, 46, 47, 54, 68, 69, 70, 81, 82, 83, 103, 112, 125, 126, 128, 135, 148, 153, 180n63, 186n6, 198n29; reasonable, 137, 147, 171n21, 195n34, 196n37; reasoning, 30, 47, 124–26, 129, 144, 157, 193n6, 196n35
Reichert, Amy, 168
relativism, 67, 71, 87, 186n10, 187n19
religion, ix, 6, 7, 8, 30, 73, 80, 84, 85, 86, 89, 93, 95, 96, 97, 107, 110, 111, 113, 122, 124, 125, 130, 135, 136, 139, 151–54, 158, 162, 163, 165, 186n10, 187n24, 193n6, 196n36, 199n32; religious belief, 33, 78–79, 139, 175n25, 186n10; religious experience, 46, 176n33

INDEX

Riccoboni, Marie Jeanne, 171n28
Richardson, Samuel, 45, 46, 171n28
rights, 40, 45–46, 59, 83–85, 100, 109, 125, 132, 136, 148, 160, 191n2, 194n12
Robbins, Lionel, 191n25
Robert Taylor Homes, 130
Rogers, Carl, 54
Ronny Heaslop (fictional character), 119
Ross, Ian, 191n28
Rothman, Aviva, 175n26
Rousseau, Jean-Jacques, 45, 46, 197n19
Rushdie, Salman, 125

Salaita, Steven, 163, 199n32
Sapir, Eduard, 186n12
Sapir-Whorf hypothesis, 79
Satan, 154, 155, 163, 198n30
Satanic Verses, The (Rushdie), 125
Sayre-McCord, Geoffrey, 183n49, 195n30
Scanlon, T. M., 137, 194n25
Scarface (de Palma), 28, 29
Scheler, Max, 176n33
Schlesinger, Hanan, 167
Schön Graben, battle of, 176n34
Schroeder, David, 183n37
science fiction, 176n33
Second Person Singular (Kashua), 125
self, 14, 16, 23, 36, 37, 44, 71, 88, 118, 157, 174n18, 177n41, 188n2; and other, 5, 35, 171n23, 176n33; Smith's account of, 37–43, 44, 47, 82, 106, 177nn40–41, 178n44
self-command/self-governance, 36, 37, 78, 149, 150, 196n4
self-consciousness, 44, 58
self-deception, 65, 68, 122, 143, 178n41
self-empathy, 15, 54, 75, 107–8
self-interest/self-love, 2, 64–65, 113–14, 153, 154, 156, 157, 158, 160, 164, 174n19
self-respect, 35, 40, 119, 135–36, 144
Sen, Amartya, 98, 188nn15–16, 192n5, 194nn22–23
sensations, 17–18, 27, 132, 173n10, 186n6
sensus communis, 174n18, 186n6, 196n9
sentiments, 26–27, 30–33, 38, 46, 60, 69, 70, 93, 110, 138, 171n27, 174n18, 175n21, 180nn62–63, 181n8, 184n56, 196n36
sexism, 66, 73, 122, 124, 125, 184n61
sexuality, 21, 111, 137, 160, 162, 163, 176n33, 196n11, 199n32
Sherman, Nancy, 54–56, 171n29, 177n39, 182n14, 188n2
Sherwood, Marge (fictional character), 70, 72
Sidgwick, Henry, 129, 136, 194n10, 195n34
Simmel, Georg, 79
simulation, 50, 172n2, 181n1
sincerity, 72, 174n17, 185n68
Singer, Peter, 128

skepticism, 54, 72, 73, 142, 163, 192n12
slavery, 45, 66, 67, 78, 80, 109, 126, 139, 140, 142–44, 150, 152, 162, 192n9, 195n28
Slote, Michael, 63, 183n38, 183n46, 185n72
Smith, Adam: conception of agency, 83; moral judgment, xii, 14–16, 36, 54, 59, 68, 69, 78, 96, 97, 126, 129, 190n19, 195n30; moral theory, x, xii, 13, 39, 49, 50, 62, 66–68, 111, 127, 131, 134, 141, 148, 157, 171n27, 188n18; *Lectures on Jurisprudence*, 111–12, 140, 151, 191n26, 195nn29–30; *Theory of Moral Sentiments*, xii, 13–17, 23–26, 32, 34, 36, 38, 41–43, 52, 60, 65–69, 77–78, 89–95, 98, 110–11, 113–14, 126, 140, 142, 151–52, 170n12, 171nn27–28, 172n3, 173n10, 173n13, 175n27, 175n29, 178n45, 179n46, 179n52, 179nn54–55, 181n7, 183nn43–44, 183n54, 184n56, 184n61, 187n3, 188n16, 189n8, 191n27, 195n29, 196n6, 196n9; *Wealth of Nations*, xii, 34, 45, 52, 69, 98, 109–15, 126, 141, 152, 183n48, 190n15, 190n20, 191n22, 191nn26–28, 195n28, 196n7
Smithian empathy, 1, 2, 31, 60, 88, 89, 90, 92, 93, 98–99, 102, 104–11, 113, 114, 118–19, 123, 126, 136, 150, 151, 169n2, 169n5, 170n15, 170n17, 171n26, 172n5, 173n7, 173n10, 172n13, 174nn14–15, 174n18, 175n29, 175n31, 177n34, 177n37, 177n41, 178n45, 179n46, 179n55, 182n26, 183n36, 183n54, 187n4, 188n17, 191n27, 193n19, 194n27, 196n4, 198n25
social science, x, 88, 123, 152
society, 38, 52, 56, 66, 69, 70, 73, 75, 91, 98, 111, 120, 130, 133, 135, 136, 139, 141, 142, 147, 149, 150, 156, 160, 163, 178n43, 181n7, 184n56, 194n24, 195n30, 199n34
solidarity, 6, 28, 41, 65, 85, 96, 105, 121, 124, 173n10, 174n14, 199n32
Soyinka, Wole, 82
Stanislavski school, 176n34
Steinbeck, John, 126, 173n14
stoicism, 20, 24, 40, 52, 55, 93, 96, 133
Stone, Tony, 181n1
Stueber, Karsten, 81, 177n38, 186nn15–16
Stürmer, Stefan, 188n11
suffering, 2, 5, 9, 12, 14, 20, 23, 25, 27, 42, 45, 53, 73, 90, 96, 103, 104, 107, 117, 121, 143, 150, 123, 133, 155, 156, 159, 164, 178n45, 182n30, 183n42, 183n44, 192n9, 197n16
Sunstein, Cass, 116, 117, 191nn1–2
Sussman, David, 197n14
Sutherland, Daniel, 197n13
Suzuki, Shinichi, 96
sympathy, xi, 4, 5, 57, 89–101, 114, 190n12; and empathy, 2–5, 63, 66, 89, 98, 182n30; "empathy" in Hume and Smith, 3, 24, 26, 27, 32, 89–90, 169n2, 169n5, 170n21, 172n3, 172n5, 173n10, 173n13, 174n14, 175n22, 175n31, 177n40, 178n45, 179n46, 183n44, 184n56, 189n11. *See also* empathy
Szustak, Bailey, 167

INDEX

Tagore, Rabindranath, 186n18
Talented Mr. Ripley, The (Highsmith), 71, 74
Tamil, 123, 134, 147
Tamir, Yael, 187n23
Tanizaki, Janichiro, 99
Taylor, Charles, 116, 128, 181nn4–5, 186n15, 193n2
Tenenbaum, Sergio, 197n15
Thiel, Udo, 178n41
Thomson, Judith Jarvis, 128, 193n2, 193n4
Titchener, Edward, 2
To Kill a Mockingbird (Lee), 71, 74
Tom Robinson (fictional character), 71, 72, 74
torture, 60–64, 150, 156, 159, 164, 198n23
Trachtenberg, Joshua, 198n26
transgender, 118, 121, 122, 124, 126, 136, 137, 144
transvestites, 7
triangulation, 40, 50, 67, 76, 145, 158, 195n35, 197n22
truth, 71–74, 185n73
Tugendhat, Ernst, 183n53
Tversky, Amos, 24, 25, 173n6

Uncle Tom's Cabin (Stowe), 53, 126, 181n8
utilitarianism, xi, xii, 66, 67, 69, 84, 102, 107, 111, 114, 116, 119, 126–38, 140, 142, 145–48, 184n55, 184n58, 193nn3–4, 195n30, 195n35, 196n36

Vedantam, Shankar, 53, 181n10
Verstehen method, 79
video game, 20, 132, 194n12
violence, 85, 95, 97, 100, 104, 118, 124, 146, 164, 190n14, 193n13, 197n16, 199n35

virtue, 2, 14, 15, 41, 52, 59, 69, 78, 110, 130, 141, 142, 149, 155, 171n21, 175n27, 177n37, 183n55, 195n30; epistemic virtues, 71–72; virtue ethics, 128, 129, 196n36
Vischer, Robert, 2
Voltaire, 78, 171n28

Waal, Frans de, 21, 57, 172nn35–36, 182nn16–17, 182n19, 182n21
War and Peace (Tolstoy), 54
Warrier, Niranjana, 167
Weber, Max, 79
welfare, 3, 61, 62, 100, 108, 130, 183, 192, 194
well-being, 60, 61, 62, 64, 65, 93, 118, 123, 124, 130, 192, 194
Williams, Bernard, 69, 71, 72, 116, 128, 129, 131, 134, 184n58, 185nn67–68, 192n3, 193n2, 194n9, 194n16, 197n22
Williams, Joshua, 167, 187n25
Williams, Shirley, 192n9
Winch, Peter, 79
Wittgenstein, Ludwig, 17–19, 33, 79, 171n32, 186nn9–10
Wolff, Robert Paul, 197n18
Wollstonecraft, Mary, 184n61

Zeno, 171n28
Ziliak, Steve, 167
Zion, Noam, 167
Zionism, 163, 192n13, 199n32
Zola, Émile, 126
Zuckert, Rachel, 167

Printed in Great Britain
by Amazon

13203962R00131